8/05

D0074934

Food Culture in
Great Britain

0 50 100 150 km

0 50 100 150 mi

The Island of Rockall
not shown.

North
Atlantic
Ocean

Voe Shetland
Islands

Orkney
Islands

Hebrides

Scotland

Aberdeen

Dundee

North
Sea

Grangemouth

Edinburgh

Glasgow

Newcastle
upon Tyne

Londonderry

Northern
Ireland

Middlesbrough

Belfast

Isle
of Man
(U.K.)

Kingston
upon Hull

Irish
Sea

Manchester

IRELAND

Liverpool

England

Wales

Birmingham

Cardiff

LONDON

Bristol

Dover

Portsmouth

Southhampton

Channel
Tunnel

Celtic
Sea

English Channel

Guernsey (U.K.)

Jersey (U.K.)

FRANCE

Cartography by Bookcomp, Inc.

Food Culture in
Great Britain

LAURA MASON

Food Culture around the World

Ken Albala, Series Editor

GREENWOOD PRESS

Westport, Connecticut · London

Library of Congress Cataloging-in-Publication Data

Mason, Laura, 1957–
  Food culture in Great Britain / Laura Mason.
      p. cm.—(Food culture around the world, ISSN: 1545–2638)
  ISBN: 0–313–32798–X
  Includes bibliographical references and index.
    1. Cookery, English. 2. Cookery—Great Britain. 3. Food habits—Great Britain.
I. Title. II. Series.
  TX717.M387   2004
  394.1'0941—dc22   2004014056

British Library Cataloguing in Publication Data is available.

Library of Congress Catalog Card Number: 2004014056
ISBN: 0–313–32798–X
ISSN: 1545–2638

First published in 2004

Greenwood Press, 88 Post Road West, Westport, CT 06881
An imprint of Greenwood Publishing Group, Inc.
www.greenwood.com

Printed in the United States of America

The paper used in this book complies with the
Permanent Paper Standard issued by the National
Information Standards Organization (Z39.48–1984).

10 9 8 7 6 5 4 3 2 1

Illustrations by J. Susan Cole Stone.

The publisher has done its best to make sure the instructions and/or recipes in this book
are correct. However, users should apply judgment and experience when preparing recipes,
especially parents and teachers working with young people. The publisher accepts no responsibility for the outcome of any recipe included in this volume.

Contents

Series Foreword

The appearance of the Food Culture around the World series marks a definitive stage in the maturation of Food Studies as a discipline to reach a wider audience of students, general readers, and foodies alike. In comprehensive interdisciplinary reference volumes, each on the food culture of a country or region for which information is most in demand, a remarkable team of experts from around the world offers a deeper understanding and appreciation of the role of food in shaping human culture for a whole new generation. I am honored to have been associated with this project as series editor.

Each volume follows a series format, with a chronology of food-related dates and narrative chapters entitled Introduction, Historical Overview, Major Foods and Ingredients, Cooking, Typical Meals, Eating Out, Special Occasions, and Diet and Health. Each also includes a glossary, bibliography, resource guide, and illustrations.

Finding or growing food has of course been the major preoccupation of our species throughout history, but how various peoples around the world learn to exploit their natural resources, come to esteem or shun specific foods and develop unique cuisines reveals much more about what it is to be human. There is perhaps no better way to understand a culture, its values, preoccupations and fears, than by examining its attitudes toward food. Food provides the daily sustenance around which families and communities bond. It provides the material basis for rituals through which people celebrate the passage of life stages and their connection to divinity. Food preferences also serve to separate individuals and groups from each other, and as one of the most powerful factors in the construction of identity, we physically, emotionally and spiritually become what we eat.

By studying the foodways of people different from ourselves we also grow to understand and tolerate the rich diversity of practices around the world. What seems strange or frightening among other people becomes perfectly rational when set in context. It is my hope that readers will gain from these volumes not only an aesthetic appreciation for the glories of the many culinary traditions described, but also ultimately a more profound respect for the peoples who devised them. Whether it is eating New Year's dumplings in China, folding tamales with friends in Mexico or going out to a famous Michelin-starred restaurant in France, understanding these food traditions helps us to understand the people themselves.

As globalization proceeds apace in the twenty-first century it is also more important than ever to preserve unique local and regional traditions. In many cases these books describe ways of eating that have already begun to disappear or have been seriously transformed by modernity. To know how and why these losses occur today also enables us to decide what traditions, whether from our own heritage or that of others, we wish to keep alive. These books are thus not only about the food and culture of peoples around the world, but also about ourselves and who we hope to be.

Ken Albala
University of the Pacific

Introduction

The reaction of many people to the idea of a food culture of Great Britain is to question whether such a thing exists. For most of the twentieth century, the idea would have been greeted with ridicule by the minority who cared about food quality and with incomprehension by the rest of the population. But everyone has to eat, and inevitably a food culture does exist. It is the perception of it that is missing.

British food is heavily industrialized and dependent on imports, both of raw ingredients and ideas. It is urban and metropolitan, dominated by London as a source of new ideas. Food habits in Britain over the past 150 years have shown a strong tendency to be national. They can be discerned, in a liking for "meat and two veg" (meat served with potatoes and other vegetables), for white wheat bread, and in the adoption of curries and other "foreign" foods as popular dishes. Elements of food culture that are highly valued in southern Europe, such as regional attachments, have either never existed or almost vanished under the onslaught of industrialization. For much of the twentieth century, favorite items such as roast beef, lamb with mint sauce, fruit cake, and mince pies were invoked under the banner of "tradition," but little attention was paid to the idea of a canon of recipes and foods. British food lacks the subtlety of French cuisine and the robustness of Italian cooking but has developed a heavy emphasis on perceptions of food in relation to fashion, publishing, eating out, and health and safety. Despite this, a holistic approach to the subject is generally lacking.

Food has not, on the whole, been valued as an aspect of wider British culture in recent times. Attitudes toward it sometimes suggested it was considered a painful necessity. Well into the 1950s, plainness in food was seen as a virtue. English domestic cookery had gained a reputation for being heavy and monotonous, prepared without any particular skill or enjoyment in food. The uniformity and blandness characteristic of much early twentieth-century cooking, as well as a perception that food should be cheap, may, in part, have been an inheritance from the extreme poverty of the nineteenth century, when few people could afford more than the most basic foods. Conservatism in food was possibly more apparent than real, since in earlier centuries, the British absorbed and reinterpreted many dishes from other cultures.

Although food is of fundamental importance to any society, it was only considered a subject worthy of study or discussion in Britain in the late twentieth century. Economic and political importance have long been acknowledged in official statistics, and the development of nutrition as a science led to theories about better diets in the twentieth century. But as a craft and an art, a source of pleasure and creativity, food was largely unconsidered until after the Second World War. Since the 1960s, it has gained a much higher profile, as influential writers and chefs had an impact on postwar eating habits, and both cooking and eating out have become leisure pursuits.

Since the 1970s, interest in the history of food has grown in the United Kingdom. Books on the subject include *Food and Drink in Britain* (C. Anne Wilson), which remains the most comprehensive in terms of timescale, and the information given here draws heavily on this. Shorter periods are covered in *British Food* (Colin Spencer), *The Englishman's Food* (J. C. Drummond and Anne Wilbraham), and *Plenty and Want* (John Burnett). *From Plain Fare to Fusion Food* (Derek J. Oddy) complements these, bringing the information up to the millennium. Much information can also be found in *The Oxford Companion to Food* (Alan Davidson). Numerous smaller books and articles deal with specific periods, foods, or social and economic aspects of food, and many reprints of early cookery books are available. (See Resource Guide.)

A growth in advertising, in food and cookery as a subject for printed and electronic media, and the expansion in the number and range of places to eat out have played a part in increasing interest in food. Foreign travel became a possibility for many British people in the 1970s and 1980s, introducing them to the eating habits of Mediterranean countries. Migrants into the United Kingdom also brought new ideas. New products, such as an increasing range of fresh produce sourced from all over the world and sold through a handful of highly competitive retail chains, have also helped to stimulate interest. Increasing affluence played a part as well. Kitchens and their equipment, food and its cooking have become a means of expressing cultural capital, and food, through choices such as vegetarianism, a form of self-expression.

Eating habits generally have also changed. Women work more outside the home and have less time to cook; supermarkets have become the main source of food and many more pre-prepared foods are available. An un-spoken consensus about meal patterns, timings, and ideas about the struc-ture of meals appears to have existed into the 1970s, but subsequently eating habits have become less formal and more people eat out. Food and health have become more of a concern, but alongside this, insecurities about its quality and safety, and a concentration on body shape rather than overall good health have become apparent.

In the final three decades of the twentieth century, observers became united in stating that British ideas about food are changing, but the na-ture, depth, and direction of changes are unclear. The last 30 years have seen many new ideas superimposed on historic patterns of eating. Eating habits have become individualized to an extent that would have been ex-traordinary 50 years ago. Many people still alive can recall constraints im-posed by lack of money and stronger social conventions in the first two-thirds of that century; and also by lack of access to food, particularly severe in rationing during and after the Second World War. Since the 1950s, the variety of ingredients available, recipes for using them, and the combinations considered appropriate for meals have shown much change. What is undeniable is that the closer one got to the end of the twentieth century, the faster the process appeared to become.

FOOD IN THE TWENTY-FIRST CENTURY

Diversity appears to be the only adjective to describe British food cul-ture at the present time. That diversity includes some who adhere to the conservative eating habits of earlier decades, and many who may not sub-scribe to them, but remember them. Anyone born before 1960 will have clear memories of a plain, semiformal regime of eating. Those who can remember back before the Second World War recall a world in which some households still had servants, and cooking was carried out on cast-iron kitchen ranges. Nowadays, a trip to the supermarket provides a dazzling array of fruit, vegetables, and dry goods sourced from all over the world and a range of pre-prepared and packaged foods to make up a fortnight's menu for any family wealthy enough to shop in this way. It does not necessarily provide the knowledge, attention, and freshness of produce that were available from the best of the more traditional shops.

If there is a single theme in late twentieth-century food habits in Britain, it is lack of cohesion. This applies to cooking techniques and meal composition as well as to food choices. The social and economic factors which allowed this change in eating habits reach back, in some cases to the late nineteenth century, and include developments in retailing, cooking technology, and the start of commercial advertising and mass media. Others are twentieth-century phenomena and include the increase in married women working outside the home (especially since the war), rising personal disposable income, and the presence of substantial ethnic minorities in some areas. Since the 1970s, household structure has changed toward more single-person or one-parent households. Supermarkets have developed an increasing control of the food chain; the introduction of the microwave oven and the development of cook-chill convenience meals have perhaps both encouraged individuality in eating and enabled it. The pattern of meals has changed, and notions of regionality have been further eroded. Issues relating to food tend to focus on health and environmental aspects, and enormous amounts of attention are given to cookery books and television programs but much less to developing practical cookery skills in the population. It remains to be seen whether the changes of the postwar period are a matter of evolution in the long history of British eating habits, or another example of the dislocation that has been apparent since the increase in urbanization, which began in the late eighteenth century.

Change is a major theme, but traces of a deeper pattern remain—disjointed and mutable, but echoing the food eaten centuries ago; and much of the highly valued British landscape is a by-product of millennia of food production.

GEOGRAPHICAL AND POLITICAL BACKGROUND

The eating habits of any country start with topography and climate. Great Britain comprises one large island and numerous smaller islands situated on the northwestern continental shelf of Europe. Ireland lies to the west. The political unit of United Kingdom of Great Britain and Northern Ireland contains four semiautonomous regions: England, Wales, Scotland, and Northern Ireland. The Straits of Dover, the narrowest sea lane between Britain and the continent, is about 25 miles wide. The island is much longer than it is wide, with a heavily indented coastline so that no point is further than 70 miles from tidal waters. The southeastern part is a mixture of flat or rolling plains and ridges of hills, few of which rise above 1,000 feet. To the west and north the land rises with several areas of low mountains between 2,000 and 3,000 feet high. The highest hills, in Scotland, are just over 4,000 feet. A complex geology underlies the island, from the chalk of the south coast through rich fenland alluvium, heavy clays, and thin acidic moorland soils to the blanket peat of northern Scotland, providing a variety of habitats.

Britain has a temperate climate, moderated by the relatively warm waters of the Gulf Stream and prevailing southwesterly winds. The summer climate tends to be warmer and drier in the southeast. Areas of lowest rainfall in the east part of the country receive around 600 mm (23.6 in.) a year; highest rainfall is in the north and west, at about 1700 mm (66.9 in.) in parts of Scotland. Maximum summer temperatures are generally in the low 20s Celsius (high 60s and low 70s Fahrenheit); winter temperatures rarely drop more than two or three degrees below freezing, although they may hover around it for several days. Within these parameters, the major characteristic of the climate is unpredictability. About 25 percent of agricultural land in Great Britain is arable, principally in southern and eastern England, and northward up the east coast into Scotland. In the west and north, the emphasis is on cattle and sheep.

The early history of Britain is one of migration with waves of settlers arriving from continental Europe: Celtic tribes, Roman armies, Saxon settlers, trading Norsemen. They must all have contributed to national tastes in food, but their influence is impossible to define. In 1066 the Norman French conquered southern England, bringing a new language and a new aristocracy to rule the country and extending their territorial ambitions to the rest of the islands. The political units of England, Wales, Scotland, and Ireland were fixed in terms of basic geography by the late Middle Ages and have had a changing and complex political relationship. During the Middle Ages, the English crown also owned a considerable portion of western France, but this had been lost by the sixteenth century. Ireland was invaded by the Anglo-Normans in 1169 and was ruled from England until 1921. After this, only the northeasternmost part was retained in the United Kingdom, as the Province of Northern Ireland. Wales has been ruled from England since 1284, and Scotland since 1707. Although regional nuances are detectable in the food traditions of each country, many underlying tastes are shared. Smaller administrative divisions are recognized as counties, the names of which are sometimes attached to foods (for instance, Yorkshire pudding, Cornish pasty).

For much of recorded history, trade has been important to Britain. The sea which moderates the climate also provided a means of transporting bulky goods, including many foodstuffs. Luxuries such as dried fruit, wine, and sugar were imported in the Middle Ages. By the nineteenth century, many necessities were imported as well. And refugees and migrants arrived from the continent—Huguenots, East European Jews, Italians in search of work. A combination of politics and trading ambitions led to the growth of colonial possessions during the seventeenth and eighteenth centuries. By the late nineteenth century, the English crown claimed sovereignty over a huge global empire on which "the sun never set." Although this had disintegrated by the 1960s, it has had a far-reaching effect on food habits in Britain. Emigrants from Britain took their food habits with them to influence those of North America, South Africa, Australia, and New Zealand, and absorbed elements of those from countries they ruled, notably the Indian subcontinent. In the twentieth century, migrants from former colonies in the West Indies, the Indian subcontinent, and Hong Kong brought their ideas about food with them when they settled in Britain.

A dramatic increase in population and increasing urbanization mean that the ability of the country to produce food was long ago outstripped, and Britain is now heavily dependent on imported foodstuffs. The current U.K. population is about 59,778,000 people. Migration is still important; at present, just under 3 percent of the population originate from former colonies in the West Indies or the Indian subcontinent. Other significant ethnic minorities include Italians, Chinese, and Cypriot Greeks and Turks. London has numerous enclaves, including people of Middle Eastern, African, Japanese, and Hispanic origin, bringing foods and ideas that enrich British eating habits.

Administrative centralization in London, good communications developed from the late eighteenth century onward, and a complex retailing system have all contributed to British eating habits and perceptions of food. In 1973, the United Kingdom joined the European Economic Community (now the European Union, or EU), subordinating national policies relating to food and agricultural production to those of the Common Agricultural Policy (CAP). Agriculture in Britain is now intensive and efficient, fulfilling about 60 percent of the county's food needs but employing only 1 percent of the labor force (about 297,000 people). However, processing and selling food are both important employers: food and drink manufacturing employs another 500,000 people, and retailing about 900,000.

Timeline

c. 10,000 B.C.E.	End of last ice age.
c. 6000 B.C.E.	Britain becomes a series of islands as the sea level rises.
c. 3500 B.C.E.	Neolithic migrants introduce domesticated cattle, sheep, and pigs, primitive wheat and barley, and pottery.
c. 1800 B.C.E.	Bronze age; introduction of metal implements.
c. 700 B.C.E.	Apparent decline in consumption of horsemeat as food, perhaps associated with the start of breaking horses to harness.
c. 600 B.C.E.	Celtic migrations; use of iron cooking utensils; evidence for salt-winning in British Isles; oats and rye introduced, also possibly the clay dome oven.
c. 100 B.C.E.	Introduction of rotary quern (ancient handmill).
43 C.E.	Roman invasion introduces many new foods, the fixed domed oven, and viticulture. Domestic fowl become common. Cheesemaking with rennet (enzyme from calves) first described in written sources.
410	Withdrawal of Roman troops from Britain, increased settlement by Germanic tribes; the herring fishery begins sometime around this date.
691	Salt workings (*salinae*) recorded as active in Droitwich.

762	Water mills had reached Britain.
800–900	Records of stockfish imports from Norway.
1066	The Norman Conquest.
1080	Guild of Butchers first recorded.
1086	The Domesday Book, a survey of land and other resources, commissioned by William the Conqueror, compiled.
1180	Guild of Pepperers first recorded.
1191	Crusaders from Britain are exposed to foods such as sugar in the Levant (Israel, etc.).
1266	The Assize of Bread and The Assize of Ale (early regulatory bodies for food quality) first fully recorded.
1289	Records of imported citrus fruit being purchased for Queen Eleanor.
late 1200s	Development of herring smoking.
c. 1307	The companies of the white bakers and the brown bakers are incorporated.
1316	Pepperers issue series of ordinances relating to quality of spices.
1348–50	Black Death; about one-third of the population perish.
1378	Records exist for prices in London cook-shops.
late 1300s	Written recipes become available in the Forme of Cury and other medieval cookery manuscripts.
1418	Evidence for hopped beer being made in England.
1420	Record of *sitrenade* (probably a sweet preserve of lemons) being imported to London on an Italian galley.
c. 1450	John Russell's *Boke of Nurture* gives information on food habits including composition of meals.
1500	The first known printed cookery book in English, *A Noble Boke of Cokery* is published.
1505	Attempts made to control distilling of usquebaugh (whiskey) in the Scottish highlands.
1527	First English translation of continental manual for distillers.
1541	First written record of turkeys in England.

1544	First sugar refinery in England.
1548	Raspberries recorded as garden fruits in England.
late 1500s	The fricassee starts to evolve. Potting as a preservation method is first mentioned. Potatoes and sweet potatoes are introduced. Sweet potatoes fall out of use, but ordinary potatoes are gradually accepted.
1600	The East India Company established.
1615	Gervase Markham publishes *The English Hus-wife*.
1637	Legislation controlling brewing introduced.
1643	Duty imposed on salt, beer.
1640s	English sugar plantations established in the West Indies, especially Barbados.
1642	The Virginian strawberry recorded as being cultivated in Europe.
1650	First English coffeehouse is established at The Angel in Oxford. Chocolate and tea are also introduced sometime in this decade. Potatoes become a major crop in Ireland.
1651	Import duty imposed on sugar.
1652	The first coffeehouse recorded in London.
1653	*The French Cook*, an English edition of La Varenne's *Cuisinier François*, is published.
1660	Robert May publishes *The Accomplisht Cook*.
1664	The East India Company starts importing tea to England.
1670	Rock salt discovered in Cheshire, eventually becoming a major industry.
1670s	Invention of glass bottles strong enough to hold fermenting drinks.
1680s	Lime juice imported in barrels from Jamaica.
1701	*The Court and Country Cook* (translated from French), introduces confections such as meringues and new ideas about dessert.
1718	The first published recipe for ice cream in English appears in Mrs Mary Eales' *Receipts*.

1726	First record of Stilton cheese.
1736	The Gin Act (unsuccessfully) prohibits sale of gin in small quantities and increases duty.
c. 1750	Developments in agriculture lead to "improved" breeds of sheep and cattle.
1757	*Poison Detected*, drawing attention to adulteration of bread, tea, beer, and wine, is published anonymously in London.
1764–75	Sequence of poor harvests leads to high grain and bread prices.
1773	First known recipe for sandwiches (actually thought to have been invented about 1760).
1780	The kitchen range invented. Sometime in this decade, the thermometer comes into use for some processes.
1784	Duty on tea is reduced. It is now a drink for all classes.
1790	Soda water first made commercially in England.
1794	Bread prices rise dramatically after a poor harvest.
late 1700s	Market gardening expands. Canal building eases problems of transporting food to growing towns. The idea of food requirements for energy becomes established. The Admiralty adopts lemon juice as protection against scurvy on ships.
1806	Modern strawberry varieties develop from a hybrid between old and new world species. Nicolas Appert cans fruit and other food successfully.
1812	Commercial canning of food in Britain begins. After series of poor harvests, England comes near to real famine.
1815	The Corn Laws are passed, fixing an artificially high price for wheat.
1816–17	Antonin Carême, the most famous nineteenth-century French chef, works in London for the Prince Regent (later George IV).
1819	Riots over food prices after a sequence of poor harvests.
1820	Frederick Accum publishes *A Treatise on the Adulterations of Food*.
1830s	Railway-building begins, revolutionizing transport of food. Growth of the temperance movement occurs. Commercial cultivation of tea starts in India. Industrialization changes the making of ship's biscuits.

1831	Cadbury's, chocolate makers, established as a factory-based firm.
1841	Huntley and Palmer biscuit-making partnership begins.
1844	Establishment of the Rochdale Co-operative Society.
1845	Friedrich Engels publishes *The Condition of the Working Class in England*. Wages are at their lowest level for a century, there is a poor corn harvest, and blight leads to the Irish potato famine.
1846	Repeal of the Corn Laws; abolition of sugar tax.
1847–49	Cholera epidemic draws attention to water purity. A canning factory opens in Australia.
1855	Domestic gas ovens offered for sale. Rail transport increasingly used for milk.
1859–61	Isabella Beeton's articles, which later become *Beeton's Book of Household Management*, published in magazine installments.
1860	Food and Drugs Act passed. In France, Ferdinand Carre develops an efficient ice making machine.
1865–67	Disease kills a large proportion of cattle. Town dairies decline.
1866	Canned meat imported from Australia to the United Kingdom on a large scale. U.S. corn belt opens up.
1867	First patent baby food introduced by Justus Leibig.
1870s	Margarine invented. Commercial cultivation of tea begins in Ceylon (now Sri Lanka).
1871	Future tea purveyor Thomas Lipton opens grocer's shop in Glasgow.
1872	First roller mill in operation.
1875	Sale of Food and Drugs Act.
1876	Fry's Chocolate Cream, the first branded confectionery bar introduced.
1880	The United States begins exporting tinned vegetables, especially tomatoes, to Britain. Refrigerated Australian meat is first successfully exported to Britain.
1885	Hovis formula for flour with high wheat germ content patented.
1887	Margarine Act clearly defines the difference between margarine and butter.
1889	Medical Congress report finds many children suffer from rickets.

1890s	Pasteurization of milk becomes common practice. French chef Auguste Escoffier and hotelier César Ritz set new standards in hotels, managing the Savoy Hotel in London (1890–97), then moving to the Ritz Carlton Hotel.
1894	The first Lyons teashop opens in Piccadilly.
1899–1902	Boer War.
1900	*Poverty: A Study in Town Life* published by Seebholm Rowntree. Work on rice establishes foundations for discovery of vitamins.
1904	Report of the Inter-departmental Committee on Physical Deterioration shows that malnutrition is a major problem among the poor.
1906	Education (Provision of Meals) Act allows education authorities to provide meals for undernourished schoolchildren.
1912	Importance of vitamins established.
1914	First World War starts.
1916	"War bread" with a higher extraction rate (retaining more germ and bran than white bread) is introduced. A Ministry of Food is created to deal with the emergency.
1918	Rationing is introduced on a limited scale. It lingers into the 1920s.
1919	Departments of State for Health for England and Wales and for Scotland created.
1921	First Ministry of Food disbanded.
1920s	U.S. style breakfast cereals fully introduced.
1928	Heinz baked beans first sold in the United Kingdom.
1930s	National marketing boards created for some agricultural produce, notably milk.
1933	Lyons Corner Houses open.
1934	Subsidized milk introduced in schools.
1937	First Report of the Advisory Commission on Nutrition.
1938	Effective meat inspection introduced.
1939	Second World War starts. New Ministry of Food is formed. Food is rationed.

1940	National Food Survey begins.
1944	Education Act introduces free school milk, widens school meal provision, and introduces nutritional standards for these.
1945	End of Second World War.
1946–48	Severe world shortage of cereals; bread rationed.
1947	Food Standards Committee formed.
1948	Establishment of Welfare State, including various benefits aimed at improving nutrition.
1950s	Introduction of supermarkets; spread of Chinese restaurants.
1950	Raymond Postgate founds the Good Food Club. Elizabeth David publishes *A Book of Mediterranean Food*.
1951	First edition of *The Good Food Guide*.
1954	End of rationing; Ministry of Food merged with Ministry of Agriculture; first Family Expenditure Survey.
1955	Food and Drugs Act, Food Hygiene Regulations.
1957	Consumer's Association founded.
1961	Vesta packet curry, the first convenience meal, introduced.
1964	Abolition of retail price maintenance on food, which allowed producers to set prices.
1967	First Japanese restaurant in London opens. A fashion for tandoori cooking spreads. Derek Cooper publishes *The Bad Food Guide*.
1970	Campaign for Real Ale (CAMRA) founded.
1973	The United Kingdom joins the European Economic Community.
1974	Dispossessed Greek Cypriots move to London, building on an already established cafe trade. Michelin publishes its first Red Guide to Britain and Ireland.
1980	Education Act frees Local Education Authorities from obligation of nutritional standards and price restraints.
1983	Food Advisory Committee replaced 1947 and 1964 committees.
1983	National Advisory Committee on Nutrition Education (NACNE) report makes recommendations about fat, sugar, and salt intakes.

1986   Bovine Spongiform encephalopathy (BSE) first fully diagnosed.

1988   Salmonella in egg production becomes a matter of public concern.

1996   BSE becomes a point of public concern.

1999   Debate over genetically-modified (GM) food begins in the United Kingdom.

2000   Producer and consumer interests are divided by the dismantling of the Ministry of Agriculture, Fisheries and Food, and the creation of the Department for Environment, Food and Rural Affairs and the Food Standards Agency in their place.

2001   Epidemic of foot-and-mouth disease among livestock contributes to growing public concern about food production methods.

2004   Major public health concerns include rising obesity levels and low intakes of polyunsaturated fatty acids.

1

Historical Overview

Two generalizations can be made about food from the earliest human occupation of Britain up until about the 1850s. One is that food supplies were largely seasonal, influenced by the breeding cycles of animals and the growing and ripening of crops. The other is that they were frequently insecure because of fluctuations in climate or social and economic factors. Finding or producing enough to eat was a major preoccupation. Historically, a wide range of animals, fish, and plants were eaten. There was no standardization in terms of quality, and measures varied according to time and place, until the Imperial system of standardized weights and measures was introduced in the nineteenth century. In particular, a pint was 16 fl oz for much of the early modern period (as it still is in the United States); the Imperial pint, introduced in 1878, is 20 fl oz.

THE PREHISTORIC PERIOD

The prehistoric epoch, long in time but short in evidence, covers from about 300,000 years ago, when the first evidence of hominid hunter-gatherers becomes available, up to the Roman invasion. It encompasses numerous changes in climate, culture, and technology. At times, the sea level was lower and the British Isles formed part of the continental landmass. During ice ages, the maximum extent of glaciation reached as far south as the Thames valley, the site of modern London. Humans, animals, and plants were distributed across the area according to environmental factors. During warmer interglacials, lush vegetation covered the area. Animals present included now-extinct species of elephant, rhinoceros, and various big cats. Humans relied entirely on animal and plant life around them, and stone tools were used for hunting and dismembering animals. At the end of the last ice age, about 10,000 years ago, the sea level began to rise, and first Ireland and then Great Britain became the islands as they are known today. Isolation restricted movement of animal and plant species. From this time, any new ones were deliberate or accidental introductions by humans.

As the climate warmed, vegetation changed from tundra with herds of large mammals such as reindeer, to birch and pine forest, and then to deciduous woodland inhabited by red and roe deer, wild pigs, and wild oxen. Mesolithic sites at Starr Carr (c. 8700 B.C.E.) in north Yorkshire have yielded evidence of hunters visiting the shore of a postglacial lake, hunting deer, wild oxen, elk, and wild boar over a period of two or three centuries.[1] Small game, wild fowl, and fish were available, as were plant foods, including berries, nuts, tubers, and green plants. The human population must have exploited all these, although little evidence remains.

Information about food at this time comes from two sources. First, the archeological record provides physical remains such as bones, hearths, and stone, pottery or metal objects. Waterlogging preserves fragile remains such as wood, which normally rots. Seed impressions on pottery (introduced c. 3500 B.C.E.), pollen analyses, and carbonized plant material give clues about plant use. Second, tentative extrapolations can be made either from Roman texts about related continental populations or from records of isolated communities on the outer fringes of the British Isles, whose inhabitants preserved old customs into the nineteenth century. These suggest ways in which people may have prepared food millennia ago.

Theories about prehistoric cooking are speculative. Meat and fish could have been cooked in small pieces on flat stones next to a fire, spitted on pieces of green wood and roasted, or possibly grilled, barbecue style. Another possibility is that meat was cooked using the raw hide of the animal as a container, either with potboilers or by suspending it over a fire; the hide would not burn as it cooked with the food. Drying and smoking could also have been used to preserve both meat and fish. Evidence for plant use and perishable materials that might have formed containers (wood, bark, leather, plant or animal fibers) is too scanty to make any assessment about how much these were used at this date.

About 3500 B.C.E., Neolithic migrants from continental Europe introduced agriculture. They brought domesticated cattle, sheep, goats, and pigs. Bone analysis shows that these were small compared with modern livestock. Primitive varieties of wheat and barley were introduced as cultivated crops. They also brought the craft of pottery, providing, for the first time, fireproof vessels in which liquid could be heated. Toward the end of the Neolithic, a particular domestic structure evolved; this was the roundhouse with a central hearth for heat and cooking. Such houses continued to be built until about 200 C.E.

Early farmers must have had considerable impact on the landscape. Cattle and sheep appear to have been gathered in large herds from time to time; some of the earthwork sites scattered across Britain are thought to have been centers for this. Analysis of bones found at the Windmill Hill site (c. 3400 B.C.E.) in southern England shows a high proportion of young cattle, suggesting that veal may have been used by the people here. This opens the possibility that cattle were exploited for milk (sheep and goats were also possible providers of this), but the date at which dairying began in Britain is not clear.

Game animals were still exploited. Some, such as the wild ox, were hunted to extinction in Britain by the end of the Neolithic. It is likely that edible portions of any animal were exploited, including brains, blood, and bone marrow. Entrails and stomach bags could be used as containers for offal, meat, and fat, making primitive sausages or haggis-type products. Other sources of protein included wild fowl and their eggs, and fish. Some birds, such as gannets and solan geese, could be caught by hand in the colonies they formed on cliffs. These, until recently, were important food on islands off the Scottish coast, used fresh or preserved by smoking. Rivers and lakes provided an ample supply of fresh fish, to be caught by spear or trap. Saltwater fish and shellfish were also available to coastal communities. Use of fish roes and livers in remote communities in modern times suggests that these were also valued in the past. Sea mammals such as whales stranded on the shore also provided windfalls of meat, blubber, and hide.

Whether bread was made is not clear. Wheat could have been crushed using a saddle quern or mortar and pestle, kneaded with liquid, and allowed to ferment with a natural sourdough-type leaven (yeast and chemical leavening agents were unknown at the time). The resulting mass could be shaped into small cakes and baked on flat stones beside the fire. Alternatively, whole or crushed grain could be cooked in a pot with water and other ingredients until the grain softened and burst. This would make a *pottage*, the later English name for such semiliquid cereal mixtures. The seeds of weeds growing among the crops were probably crushed with the rest of the grain. Many wild plants native to Britain are edible, and it is fair to assume that they were used from an early date. Several have distinctive flavors—ramsoms or wild garlic (*Allium ursinum*) are oniony, jack-by-the-hedge (*Allieria petiola*) is mustardlike, and wallpepper (*Sedum acre*), as its name suggests, is peppery. Such flavorings were probably valued. Other plants possibly exploited for food include dandelions, chickweed, cresses, nettles, and pignuts (*Conopodium majus*). Seashore plants such as marsh samphire (*Salicornia europaea*), seakale (*Crambe maritima*), laver (*Porphyra umbilicalis*, a relative of nori), and Irish moss (*Chondrus crispus*) may also have been used (as they still are). Wild fruit was abundant in late summer and evidence has been found for the use of blackberries, sloes (wild plums, the fruit of the blackthorn, *Prunus spinosa*), crab apples, and hazelnuts.

The only sweetener available was honey robbed from wild bees. Honey readily diluted with water ferments to make mead. The juices of berries or crab apples might also have been fermented for drinking. By the end of the Neolithic, it is probable that barley was used for malt for brewing beer. Fermented drinks probably appeared as soon as suitable containers for holding liquid were available. Fine late Neolithic pottery includes large vessels which were probably drinking cups.

One Neolithic site which suggests an elaborate domestic life is Skara Brae (Orkney islands).[2] It consists of eight hut circles with interior furnishings constructed of stone. Each layout includes a central hearth and a stone dresser, plus querns, tanks, and drains sunk into the floor. Exactly how these were used, and by whom, remains a matter for conjecture, but they show that considerable attention was paid to food preparation. The buildings were sunk in a mound of domestic waste material (midden).

Introductions of new materials and culture continued. About 2000 B.C.E., a wave of migrants brought metal in the form of copper, bronze, and gold. By the late Bronze Age (early first millennium B.C.E.), bronze was used for large metal cauldrons, much more durable than pottery. High-status items included cups made of gold, amber, or shale. Bronze Age culture was pastoral, with status based on ownership of cattle, and the landscape appears to have been reshaped, establishing field systems that in some areas (for instance Dartmoor, southwest England), have survived until the present day. "Burnt mound" features, found all over the British Isles, are typical of this era and seem to have been cooking sites. They consist of mounds of ash and burnt stones usually associated with hearths, and sunken tanks, often lined with stone to make them watertight. Archeologists think that these were used for cooking large joints of meat, either by roasting or in the tank; the water in this was warmed by heating stones in the fire and dropping them in. "A boiling and a roasting," recorded in ancient Irish tales, is thought to refer to the use of such sites. Modern experiments demonstrate that meat can be cooked successfully, yielding palatable results. Another change that took place in the late Bronze Age was the introduction of horse breaking and an apparent decline in the use of horsemeat as food.

Iron implements were introduced about 600 B.C.E. by further waves of migrants. Blades, fire dogs for supporting spits, and large cauldrons with chains and tripods for suspending them are found on sites from this period. Other introductions included spelt (another wheat variety), oats, rye, and a pulse, the small Celtic bean. Wheat was grown extensively in southern Britain. Sometime during this period ovens appeared, movable clay domes that protected food from hot ash heaped around the sides. About 100 B.C.E. the rotary quern was introduced. An upper stone with a central funnel held corn while the stone was turned with a handle. The corn fell through a hole at the bottom of the funnel onto the lower, fixed stone and was crushed into flour between the two. The Iron Age, too, provides the first evidence of salt-winning in the British Isles, and domesticated chickens had been introduced, although possibly for fighting, not for food.

Classical scholars describe some habits of Celtic tribes on the continent, such as brewing beer, recorded in the third century B.C.E. (*curmi*, the name for this beer, became the Welsh word *cwrw* and the Irish *cuirm*). A description of mealtimes among Celts in Gaul during the second century B.C.E. tells how they sat on straw or hides, with joints cooked on spits or in cauldrons, from which they took mouthfuls "in a cleanly but leonine fashion." Choice pieces went to the best warriors. The related British tribes may have followed similar habits. The extent to which the expanding Roman Empire influenced Britain is difficult to assess, although wine, imported in amphorae, shows that there was contact with continental Europe.

THE ROMAN PERIOD

The Roman invasion in 43 C.E. changed many things, including much to do with food. However, progress was not constant. Northern Scotland and Ireland were never occupied. The main demarcation between the Romanized south and the barbarian north eventually became Hadrian's Wall (between Newcastle upon Tyne and Carlisle). Estimates for the population of Britain during the Roman period suggest that the island supported about 4 million people. Evidence for Roman food habits comes from pottery, metalware, and kitchen debris. Written evidence comes from recipes known under the name *De Re Coquinaria,* attributed to Apicius and thought to date from the late fourth or early fifth century. They show the elaborate, highly flavored food eaten by those who could afford it. Other literature, including descriptions of feasts and books on agriculture, gives clues about food, as do paintings and sculptures from continental sites. In addition, documents written on wooden tablets were discovered at Vindolanda on Hadrian's Wall. They date from 85–130 C.E., and make many references to food.[3]

In Britain the Romans found a fully exploited landscape, but brought new agricultural and land reclamation techniques. Spelt became an important wheat variety, and in the fourth century C.E., Britain exported wheat to the Rhineland. The Romans are also credited with introducing many new foods. New sources of meat included pheasants, peacocks, guinea fowl, and fallow deer. They brought vines, figs, walnuts, medlars, mulberries, and sweet chestnuts, and they are credited with introducing many herbs, vegetables, and salad plants—parsley, alexanders, borage, chervil, coriander, dill, fennel, mint, mustard, thyme, garlic, leek, onion, shallot, hyssop, rosemary, rue, sage, savory, sweet marjoram, radish, cabbage cultivars, celery, lettuce, endive, turnip, mallow, orache, corn salad, and fat hen. In addition, the Romans imported luxuries from the Mediterranean and further east, including dates, almonds, olives, wine, olive oil, pine kernels, pepper, ginger, cinnamon, and *garum,* a sauce made of fermented fish (possibly similar to nam pla made in modern Thailand). They built fixed domed ovens, and Roman sources give the earliest full description of cheesemaking. Roman tableware included elaborate sets of fine pottery, glass and silver, used in well-appointed dining rooms in villas built on an entirely different plan to the British roundhouse. Kitchen facilities were also more elaborate. Excavations indicate that the wealthier and higher status members of the native population adopted villas in preference to roundhouses.

The description of Trimalchio's Feast in Petronius's *Satyricon* (first century C.E.) and *De Re Coquinaria* are cited as evidence for the complexity of Roman food habits. The former illustrates the extravagance and spectacle associated with grand dinners: dormice dipped in honey and sprinkled with poppy seed, a wooden hen over a nest of large "eggs" made from flour fried in oil, containing spiced egg yolk and little birds, a whole pig stuffed with sausages and black puddings, quinces stuck with thorns to resemble sea urchins, and much more served in opulence and luxury. *De Re Coquinaria* reveals a cuisine of complex dishes based on poultry, game, and meat from domestic animals, stuffed, half stewed, and then finished in sauce. It also shows the use of flavorings: herbs, especially the bitter flavors of lovage and rue, and oriental spices—pepper, cinnamon, ginger, nutmeg, and cloves. Sweet dishes and bakery items, although undocumented by Apicius, were also important. The extent to which such sophistication was expressed in Britain is unclear, but given the international nature and excellent organizational skills of Roman life generally, the wealthy and powerful probably indulged such tastes. The late Roman silver dishes found at Mildenhall in Suffolk (now in the British Museum) show they certainly had the tableware available.

These give insights into what people aspired to and sometimes achieved, but are unlikely to be representative of the food habits of ordinary people. They probably relied on cereal foods such as bread (either lower-grade wheat bread, barley bannocks, or mixed grain loaves), and *puls*, a sort of cereal pottage, supplemented by vegetables, beans, cheese, and a little meat or fish from time to time. Soldiers were well fed with imported wine and olive oil, wheat for bread, *puls* (perhaps also based on wheat), meat from domestic and game animals, bacon and ham, fruit, and vegetables. The documents inscribed on wooden tablets from Vindolanda mention venison, spices including pepper, fish sauce, olives, oil, oysters, ham, and chicken, clothes appropriate for dining, tableware, and social invitations. They refer to the household of a high-ranking official, and perhaps mention a better diet than average, or special treats. Analyses of bone from the site show sheep and cattle to predominate, but these foods are not mentioned in the tablets. Bone analyses from other sites suggest some complex food processing: possibilities include preserving meat from cattle shoulders in York, bone-marrow extraction (although not necessarily for food) at several other sites, and garum production in London. Preserved pork, such as ham, was also an important food. Fish of all types were much liked, and shellfish remains are found even at inland sites; British oysters were famous and exported even to Rome itself.

Containers and artifacts associated with food during the Roman period include amphorae for wine and oil imported from the Mediterranean, skillets, strainers, and wide shallow mortars for grinding food. Food was cooked over charcoal stoves; a reconstructed example can be seen in the Roman kitchen at the Museum of London. Romanized Britons followed the custom of reclining on couches to dine at tables spread with fine pottery. This included wares imported from Gaul (France) and native products. Glass, bronze, and services of silver were also utilized. Fingers, knives, and spoons were used for eating. The food enjoyed in Roman Britain reached a level of sophistication that was probably not seen again until the late Middle Ages.

THE DARK AGES/EARLY MEDIEVAL PERIOD

This covers the period after the withdrawal of the Roman army in 410 until the thirteenth century. (Cookery manuscripts survive from the four-teenth and fifteenth centuries, and these years are considered separately.) The food described in *De Re Coquinaria* is unlikely to have survived for long. Also, the trade routes that brought spices west to Europe were dis-rupted during the dark ages. The population probably fell (figures are un-known and estimates range from half a million to two or three million), leading to some land going out of cultivation, and the economy became one of subsistence in which only the wealthy could afford to indulge their tastes. Saxon migrants had settled the eastern and southern shores of Britain before the Roman occupation ended. Over the next 500 years, more groups from Germany, Denmark, and Scandinavia arrived. During this time, Britain was a patchwork of smaller kingdoms, sometimes at peace, sometimes at war. Goods including food were traded with conti-nental Europe, as were ideas, notably Christianity, which became well es-tablished and influential. The Norman Conquest of 1066 was a defining moment in the history of England, unifying the country and introducing a French influenced ruling class. However, the extent to which the change of overlord led to changes in food production or consumption is unclear.

During this time, records are nonexistent or patchy. Close studies of documentary and archeological evidence have yielded some information about food production and consumption in Anglo-Saxon England,[4] and a little for Wales (which remained strongly Celtic). Evidence for cooking methods is limited, although clues can be gleaned from medicinal manu-scripts whose formulae include foodstuffs (leechdoms). The survey of land and other assets recorded in the Domesday Book of 1086 showed the ex-tent of arable land, the number of people available to work it, and assets such as watermills. More documents become available later in the period.

Cattle were important: there was a small black breed, larger white cat-tle (highly prized in Wales), and a red breed probably introduced by the Saxons. Bone analyses from several sites indicate that cattle were a major food resource. Oxen were used for plowing, possibly as early as the seventh century, only becoming beef at the ends of their working lives. High-status Anglo-Saxon households probably indulged a preference for younger, tender beef. Welsh laws state that certain court officials were entitled to particular parts of cattle slaughtered in the palace—the smith got the feet and heads, except for tongues, which went to the judge. By the tenth century pastoral agriculture based on cattle appears to have become important in the western part of Britain, and large tributes of oxen were expected from the rulers of the north Welsh.

Sheep were common and mutton was a lower status meat than beef. It was accessible to most people, as a sheep or two may have been kept even by poor households. They were also valued for wool and milk. The extent to which goats were kept is less clear, and their popularity seems to have declined after the Norman conquest. There is documentary evidence for them, but in smaller numbers than sheep. They provided milk and meat, and the kids were probably a delicacy. Pigs were the other essential domestic animal; quick to breed, and economical to feed, they provided a useful resource of meat. In autumn, herds belonging to large estates were fed on pannage (acorns and beechnuts) in woodland. They were also associated with poorer households, urban and rural, fattened on household scraps. Interpreting bone evidence for pigs is difficult: the bones do not survive well and may be absent if a household relied on salt pork or bacon, which leave no bones at the point of consumption. Pork fat was important for cooking, and sucking pigs were a luxury. Poultry are mentioned in food rents in a context that suggests chickens, too, were luxuries. According to the leechdoms, hens were used to make broth with worts (a general An-

Herdwick sheep.

glian term for plants) and butter for invalids. Geese and ducks were also eaten, and peacocks and swans were kept on large estates. Fallow deer, known to have been present during the Roman period, seem to have vanished, only to be reintroduced by the Normans. Hunting with hawks was a pursuit of the wealthy; birds caught this way had high status on the table.

Meat became identified with physical strength, and by the late thirteenth century the aristocratic diet was based firmly upon it. Game and game birds, as signifiers of land ownership, had the highest status. In Anglo-Saxon leechdoms, the meat from steers stewed in vinegar and oil with herbs and leeks was recommended for a "laboring maw" (stomach of a laborer), foreshadowing, perhaps, the Anglo-Norman attitude to beef as a "grosse" meat fit for the lower classes (despite the probability that the poor had little access to it, and the possibility that the nobility ate it quite a lot).

Fish must have been important in the diet of people living on rivers and coasts, but archeological evidence is patchy (fish bones are difficult to retrieve, and sometimes disappear completely). Finds at York contain more evidence of freshwater and estuarine species before the eleventh century and more marine ones in the later Middle Ages; water pollution is suggested as the reason for this. Stockfish (dried cod) was an important food for the Vikings and was being imported to Britain by the ninth century. Shellfish were plentiful. These included oysters from the Thames estuary, first recorded in Roman times (and still important in the nineteenth century). The herring fishery, using nets, appears to have been established in around the end of the Roman period. By the eleventh century, it was of great economic importance, and herrings were preserved by salting (smoking them did not develop until the thirteenth century).

Fish became more important with the growth of Christianity. By the seventh century, monasteries and nunneries were being established, and fish took the place of meat during fasts. Eventually Wednesdays, Fridays, and the whole of Lent were fast days. (Lent occurs during a season in which food resources would naturally be under stress in Britain, so there may have been an element of making a virtue out of a necessity involved in the timing.) This meant no meat, poultry, animal fats, eggs, or dairy products could be consumed on these days, a rule developed in Mediterranean regions in which oil was easily available. For northern Europeans, including the British, oil was an expensive import. The poor had limited means, and fasts must have meant monotonous food, principally stockfish and herrings. Food saved through fasting was to be given in charity to the destitute. Christianity also affected consumption of horsemeat, which had been eaten in the earlier part of the Anglo-Saxon occupation, but became considered as pagan and disappeared from the diet by the seventh century.

For monks, fish took the place of meat entirely. Numerous ways of using it were devised. In 1180 the monk Giraldus Cambrensis, staying at the Benedictine abbey of St. Augustine in Canterbury, recorded a multitude of dishes on the table, including many kinds of fish, roasted and boiled, stuffed and fried. The lavish food evidently flouted the pious ideal of frugality, and although conversation was forbidden, the meal was accompanied by much communication through gestures as dishes were sent as gifts to lower tables.

Cereals included wheat, barley, rye, and oats. In early Anglo-Saxon settlements, land may have been cultivated by hand, but ox power was used by the seventh century, and a system of strips of land grouped in open fields developed between the ninth and twelfth centuries. It involved a rotation of wheat or rye, followed the next year by oats, barley, peas, or beans, with fallow in the third year. This became common over much of England, especially in the midlands, where it survived until the eighteenth century. Rye is susceptible to the toxic fungus ergot in the damp conditions typical of England, and was probably less important in Britain than on the continent. Wheat became the favored bread grain, probably because it produces light textured, palatable bread. Special festive breads, spiced, sprinkled with seeds, or enriched with fat, eggs, or honey may also have been produced, and pancake-type confections, perhaps ancestors of the modern English crumpets (made from thick, yeast-leavened batter), although the name is thought to derive from a Welsh word, *crempog*. Bread was a staple, eaten with some stronger-tasting, often oily relish— salted butter, fatty meat, cheese, preserved fish. There is also evidence for maslin—mixed crops of wheat and rye—which acted as a fail-safe—one crop might flourish while the other failed. Barley is most likely to have been grown for malting and ale production, but barley bread is mentioned in eleventh and twelfth centuries. Oats were grown, although how much for human and how much for animal food is unknown (one chronicler, Giraldus Cambrensis, claimed the inhabitants of Wales lived almost entirely on oats).[5]

Pulses—dried peas or beans—were also important. They kept well, added protein to one-pot stews, and in times of dearth, pulses, acorns, and beechnuts were ground and added to bread. Watermills for grinding corn appeared in the eighth century, although hand querns survived in the north. The extent to which grains were used in pottages is unclear. These were probably of great importance to the poor. Little information on their food survives, but they probably relied on a monotonous diet of beans or cereals cooked with vegetables in a single pot on the fire.

Numerous edible plants were used in both culinary and medicinal contexts, and some were cultivated. Greenstuff was eaten raw as salad and used in broth and other dishes. There is evidence for garden plots in both England and Wales by the tenth century. Cabbages, leeks, and various *Allium* species were grown; salads seem to have relied heavily on members of the onion family. Carrots, possibly parsnips, and cresses were also grown. Spinach and leafy plants, such as orache, mallow, and fat hen, were cooked and eaten, and seaweed probably continued to be used in coastal areas. Herbs were used as flavorings, as were some flowers.

The idea of the orchard for cultivating fruit trees, probably mostly apples, had emerged by the end of the Anglo-Saxon period in Britain. Pears, plums, cherries, sloes, and berries of various descriptions were also exploited, as were grapes, which were grown in parts of England late in the period. Hazelnuts were common, and walnuts may have been imported from France or cultivated by monastic houses by the tenth century.

Milk came from cows, sheep, and goats. It was utilized efficiently, either by making butter and then cheese from the buttermilk, or by making cheese and using residual fat from the whey to make butter. The liquid residues were used as drinks; the shepherd received a daily bowl of buttermilk and a bowl of whey from the making of ewe's milk cheese in the summer. Butter was an important cooking fat. Sheep's milk was used for butter and cheese in eastern England, and that from cows in the Celtic-influenced north and west.

A few imported spices reached England, probably at great cost, and they must have been used sparingly. Peppered broth was considered a delicacy by one writer. Other imported items included oil and wine, the latter having high status. Some wine may also have been produced in England, as grapes were grown in places, and the climate was slightly more favorable to them at times. Beekeepers were important workers on Anglo-Saxon estates, and honey remained the only sweetener. Drinks included mead, which was of great importance; the lower status ale, brewed from malted barley; and *beor*, which was probably cider or some other fermented fruit juice.

Feasting was an important ritual and a means of displaying status for the Anglo-Saxons. A household giving a feast for a king had its supplies inspected beforehand, as it was a mark of shame for food and drink, and especially mead, to run out. Fish, fat meat (especially roast), hams, poultry, cheese, white bread, ale, and mead were prized for feasts. Consumption, especially of alcoholic drink, appears to have been a primarily male activity, while production of food and serving of drink seem to have been stereotypically female. Feasting had several functions—it reinforced important bonds, especially those of a retainer to a lord, celebrated times of plenty in an uncertain world, and provided an element of escapism. The only eating implements used at table appear to have been knives; plates and wine jugs were used communally. Generosity with food was also important.

After the Norman invasion, the increasingly hierarchical nature of society was expressed through eating.[6] Soon afterward, the rectangular table became the norm, and honored diners were increasingly separated from the mass onto a separate "top" table, perhaps raised on a dais. A knife, a cup, and a piece of bread were placed in front of each diner.

In the tenth century, ideas about Roman dietary traditions began to filter through the Arab world back to European Christendom. Soldiers on the Crusades, the first of which took place in 1099, were also exposed directly to the food of the Near East, including novelties such as sugar (cultivation of this was brought to the countries of the eastern Mediterranean by the Muslims), pomegranates, rice, dates, rosewater, and also brightly colored food—yellow, red, green. Gold was considered to have special virtues, and by extension came the notion that foods made gold or yellow with egg yolk or saffron also had special value. Saffron was grown in England, as was mustard, but most other spices reached Britain via the Mediterranean at inflated prices. Pepper, cinnamon, cloves, mace, nutmegs, and galingale all arrived this way. Ginger also traveled the same route, or came from sources nearer at hand, such as the Arabian peninsula or North Africa. Sugar was imported from the Levant and Egypt, and was considered a medicine. Expensive and exotic, these products demonstrated wealth and status, and were used by all those who could afford them. Other imports from southern Europe in the twelfth and thirteenth centuries included oil, wine, raisins, currants, prunes, almonds, and citrus fruits such as lemons and bitter oranges, fresh in season or preserved in sugar as *succade*. Influences and dishes from this so-called Saracen cookery were incorporated into food in western Europe.[7]

LATE MEDIEVAL FOOD

The late fourteenth century brought the first substantial collections of written recipes in English. *The Forme of Cury* (c. 1390, thought to be a

record of the cooks of King Richard II)[8] is the best-known and most extensive compilation. Several collections are also known from the late
fourteenth century on the continent. They were compiled for aristocratic
households, and probably reflect decades, even centuries, of culinary practice, as medieval food slowly evolved. Together they show that the Anglo-
Norman aristocracy in England shared with much of western Europe a
courtly style of cookery, which displayed many similarities: the use of
spices and almonds, a delight in color, and sweet-sour combinations from
sugar, honey, dried fruit, and grape products (wine, vinegar, and verjuice)
in sauces. The beginnings of a taste for sweetness, alone or in combination
with meat, can also be discerned in English recipes. This international
feel came from a mobile aristocracy, moving between courts as they inter-
married, pursued pilgrimages, or directed wars. Regional variations
showed in choice of oils and fats and tastes for certain spices, but many
dishes were common to western Europe. The households could be enormous: Richard II employed 300 kitchen staff to feed 1,000 people a day.
Medieval records show that professional cooks were often male. Although
they were incorporated as a guild, this took place relatively late in England, during the fifteenth century. In noble households, they were people
of importance, although many more must have made a much humbler living in cookshops, in monastery kitchens, or as lower kitchen servants generally. Kitchen work was heavy, involving much physical strength and
stamina, and workers' bad tempers were frequently remarked upon.

Underpinning ideas about food was the theory of four humours—sanguine, choleric, melancholic, and phlegmatic, composed in different
measures of hot, cold, wet, and dry. This was inherited from the classical
Greek physician Galen. Different foods were considered to share these
qualities in different degrees. (The idea did not relate to actual physical
qualities, but to the balancing effect they were supposed to have on the
body. Beef was considered hot and dry and sugar moderately hot, in a system not dissimilar to that found in traditional Chinese medicine.) One
task of the medieval doctor was to ensure his patron ate a diet in which
the proportions of these qualities balanced his temperament, bringing it
as close as possible to the ideal of sanguine. The cook also had to bear in
mind the seasonal availability of food, and the fast days decreed by the
church calendar.

The spiciness of medieval food is a matter for debate. A myth has grown
up around medieval food, that meat became unacceptably high and the
flavor had to be disguised with spices. There is little to support this, and
considerable evidence to the contrary. Status appears to have been the

main driver for the use of spices. Manuscripts do not usually indicate quantities. Imponderables include freshness or otherwise of spices after their long voyage to Europe, the extent to which desire for status demanded they should be apparent in food, and tastes of individuals. Modern experiments with medieval recipes have tended toward modest spicing. Sugar was classed as both a medicine and a spice. It was often added to meat dishes; again, it is impossible to know how much was added. Another unknown is the texture of food. Many recipes demand that the ingredients be pounded in a mortar before serving (large mortars and pestles were standard kitchen utensils), probably resulting in a thick, unevenly textured purée. Most food was eaten with fingers and a knife, although spoons were available, and bread could be used to sop up broth and runny sauce.

Bread

Bread remained a staple food, baked in domed stone ovens. The aristocratic diner could expect to find a small roll of wastel or pandemain, bread made from the best wheat flour, sieved until almost white, set at his place at the dining table, along with a square slice of coarser, stale trencher bread. The trencher acted as a plate, each diner selecting from communal dishes and putting individual portions on his or her trencher. After the meal, trenchers were collected and given to the poor. Breadcrumbs were used to thicken sauces, and sops—pieces of bread or toast—were served under thin pottages. Small, rich breads kneaded with eggs and butter were also made. A special type of bread was baked for seafarers: unleavened, it was baked, sliced, and returned to the oven to dry completely. This became known as ships' biscuits (from *panis biscoctus*, twice-cooked bread).

Cooking

Meat of all sorts appeared on the aristocratic table. Game animals and birds (pheasant, partridge, and many species no longer considered food, such as heron, curlew, bustard, and crane) were highly prized. Venison was served with frumenty (husked whole wheat grains soaked and cooked gently to make pottage), or peverade, a pepper sauce. Chawdron sauce was made for swan, thickened with the entrails and blood of the bird cooked in spiced broth. Uncooked sauces thickened with soaked and strained bread included camelyn (flavored with cinnamon), and a ginger-flavored sauce, both served with roast meat. A green sauce of chopped herbs and vinegar was served with fish, or vinegar or verjuice alone; and mustard accompanied brawn, which at this date meant large pieces of boar or pork. Although meat from domestic animals was considered low status (beef was thought grosse, or fit for the lower orders), it too must have been served on most occasions, at least to the lower tables. Meat was elaborately prepared, often by a combination of techniques such as boiling followed by roasting. For dishes requiring gentle heat, a chafing dish with a compartment for hot coals below was sometimes used. Smaller pieces of meat such as steaks were simply grilled. Records show that birds could be purchased, ready-roasted from cookshops in the city of London in the late fourteenth century. The great set pieces for feasts included such items as peacocks that had been skinned, roasted, and then redressed in their plumage, and swans with gilded beaks and feet, but these were not everyday food.

The frequency of fasting days meant that fish cookery was highly developed and provided analogues of many meat dishes. There was a much greater reliance on freshwater fish than in later centuries, and many large households maintained fish ponds to provide ready supplies. Whale, porpoise, and other sea mammals were regarded as fish at this date, and made their appearance in menus for the clergy, and for fast days generally. Fish was also to be cooked simply by methods that still seem logical, such as frying in oil. Almond milk was used as a substitute for cow's milk on fast days.

Typical dishes included mortrews, a bland dish of meat or fish that had been reduced to a pulp in the mortar from which the dish took its name; browets of meat, poultry, or fish in spiced and thickened sauce; blancmanger, a dish that included almonds, capon, chicken meat, sugar, and rosewater, regarded as excellent food for invalids; and civets, dishes that had fried onions added during cooking. Also popular were jellied dishes or galantines: the jelly was made with stock from boiling calf's or pig's feet, or fish bones on fast days, and was poured over meat or fish. Jelly seems to have been regarded as a preservative.

Vegetables and salads were rarely mentioned in feast menus, perhaps because they were commonplace and low status, but recipe collections and gardening treatises indicate that they were used. Basic dishes such as pottages of vegetables and dishes of dried beans must have been known at all levels. Fruit was eaten alone, often at the start of the meal to "open" the stomach and prepare it for digestion. It was also cooked: pears in a spiced, sweetened wine syrup, apples made into *appulmos*—a pureed dish—or roasted. Fruit was also preserved with honey or sugar, either whole as *suckets* or in pastes, and almonds were ground with sugar to make marzipan. Dried fruit—currants, raisins, figs, dates—were enjoyed for their sweetness and used in many dishes. Flowers were used for garnish, flavor, and color; sambocade was a dish of fresh cheese baked with elder flowers, and spinée was almond milk thickened with eggs and amidon (starch), flavored with hawthorn flowers.

Pies filled with spiced meat mixtures also featured on the table. The pastry was not necessarily edible, being there principally to protect and hold the contents during cooking. A *crustade* meant a tart with a crust (pie shell); in time the name transferred to the filling of eggs and milk or cream to give English the word *custard*. Meat, spices, and dried fruit were added to these early custards. Animal guts provided containers for sausages made of chopped lean meat and puddings—spiced mixtures of onions, fat, and blood. By the end of the Middle Ages they had developed other forms—forcemeat mixtures used as stuffings, and pale-colored *frawnchemyle*, made of fat and breadcrumbs tinted with saffron.

Other delicacies included gingerbread, a stiff confection of bread-crumbs with sugar or honey, wine, and spices (not necessarily ginger). Thin pancakes, known as *cryspes* were popular, as were fritters of various kinds, and wafers, made between two heated plates similar to a modern waffle iron. *Leach* (which literally meant a slice) was a word applied to various sweet dishes of almonds or fruit and spices, served cold and cut in slices.

Dairy Products

Cows and ewes remained providers of milk, but goats became less important in eastern England. The main types of cheese were hard, long-keeping types made from skimmed milk; a softer type, from whole or semi-skimmed milk; and new or so-called green cheese, fresh, soft, some-times flavored with herbs, and with a short shelflife. In medieval York-shire, cheese was made in large quantities on the great monastic estates in the area. Dairying also seems to have developed as a specialty of the southwest of England toward the end of the Middle Ages. Milk and milk products, known collectively with eggs as "white meats" were food for the poor, although they were used as ingredients in dishes for the wealthy, such as custards and darioles (small cup-shaped pastry cases with dairy-based fillings such as curds). Milk or cream heated with ale made a drink called a posset.

Wine and Other Drinks

Wine was an important beverage and a signifier of status. Red wines from Aquitaine (which belonged to the English crown for part of the period) seems to have been favored, but wines from many other parts of Europe are mentioned, including ones from the Rhine. Red wine was made into a spiced, sweetened drink known as hippocras. Poor quality acid wines and ale were the drinks of poorer people; the latter was brewed by every household of any size. Ale was also soured to make alegar, as wine was to make vinegar. The juice of apples and pears were fermented to make cider and perry respectively, and honey gave mead. Distilling first appeared in Britain in the fourteenth century, to make medicinal drinks. Milk, buttermilk, and whey provided drinks for poorer people and invalids. Water must have been drunk, but is rarely mentioned and must have been of dubious quality at times.

Dining

By the fourteenth century, a system of two meals a day had evolved, with dinner in the late morning or around noon, and a lighter meal known as "supper" (originally based on sops, bread soaking up brothlike soup) at dusk or mid-evening. Breakfast was bread with cold meat or fish if available, and a drink of ale or wine. Dinner, the principal meal of the day, consisted of up to three courses, in each of which a number of dishes were placed on the table together. They were served in portions known as "messes," for two or four people, and diners helped themselves from the dishes nearest to them. The lists of food served at great feasts gives the impression of lavish variety for huge numbers of people, but in practice, only the most important diners were served high status items such as peacock. Honored guests got more and better food, and the top table might get three courses, but only one might have been served to the lower status diners. Servants in the lower hall were given beef and salt meat. Surviving menus show that special treats tended to be served toward the end of the meal.

Elaborate visual conceits were part of late medieval feasts. They were produced at the end of each course and in England became known as sotleties or subtleties (in French, *entremets*). Sometimes they were built of edible materials such as sugar, marzipan, or pastry, and carried religious or political messages—heraldic beasts, items with religious significance, such as the pelican or a patron saint, or tableaux flattering the guest of honor.

One description of a wedding feast mentions a figure of a "wife lying in childbed," presumably intended to focus the bride's attention on her role in life. Descriptions give little clue as to the size of subtleties, and they were not always edible—they might be composed of wax or be tableaux acted out by people. Their function appears to have been to flatter and entertain.

Dining furniture was temporary, the tables being trestles set up as required, and draped with layers of linen tablecloths; one layer, long enough to hang down and cover the guest's knees, was used for wiping fingers. Contemporary books of manners show that high standards were demanded; hands were washed both before and after eating, and it was considered discourteous to spit, talk with one's mouth full, or to fish around for the best morsels in a dish. Tableware included chargers and ewers of earthenware or in wealthy households, silver or gold. Dining plates in the modern sense were unknown, their place taken by the trencher bread set before each diner. Guests generally provided their own knives and food was eaten with the fingers, or possibly with a spoon if very runny. Forks, except as large implements for kitchen use, were virtually unknown. Status was indicated by the proximity to the great salt set in front of the host. At the end of the meal, the tables were dismantled and the final drink of hippocras and some comfits (sugarcoated spices) and wafers formed the *voidee*, signaling the close of the meal. Working with sugar was part of the knowledge of the apothecary, because it was considered medicinal.

The Poor

Few records exist to show what the poor ate. The fourteenth century poem *Piers Plowman* by William Langland gives some clues as to what they might expect in late spring, when the previous year's grain and salted meat was virtually exhausted, but the new season had not yet progressed enough to offer much:

> *I haue no peny . . . poletes forto bigge,*
>
> *Ne neyther gees ne grys but teo grene cheses,*
>
> *A fewe cruddes and creem and an hauer cake,*
>
> *And two loues of benes and bran ybake for my fauntis.*
>
> *And yet I sey, by my soule I haue no salt bacoun,*
>
> *Ne no kokeney, by cryst, coloppes forto maken.*

Ac I haue percil and porettes and many kole-plantes,

And eke a cow and calf. . . .

And bi þis lyflode we mot lyue til lammasse tyme;

And bi þat, i hope to haue heurest in my croft;

And panne may I digte þi dyner as me dere liketh.

I have no money to buy pullets, no geese nor pigs, only two fresh cheeses, a few curds and cream and an oatcake and two loaves of beans and bran baked for my children. I have no bacon or eggs by Christ, but I have parsley and leeks and many cabbages and also a cow and a calf … and I must sustain myself on this fare till Lammas when I hope to have harvest in my barn, and then I can have the kind of meal I like.

Loaves of beans and bran must have been typical of the coarse, dark bread eaten by the poor for whom fine wheat bread was probably a rare treat. Wholemeal bread, using maslin flour, ground beans, or, in extremis, acorns, was their daily bread. Cereals were also made into pottages such as frumenty. The white meats—milk, curds, cheese, butter, whey, and buttermilk, from either sheep or cows, were important in their diet. Chaucer mentions bread and milk, bacon, the occasional egg, and pottage made of whatever wild greens were available as food for poor women.

It is unlikely that the poor ate much meat, and of that, mutton, pork, and salted pork are likely to have been most common. In the mid-fourteenth century, one meal of fleshmeat in a day was considered appropriate for artisans and servants, the other meals involving butter or cheese. Every edible part of the slaughtered animal was used, including heads, feet, and internal organs. Hens provided eggs, and to a lesser extent, meat. Vegetables included potherbs such as onions, leeks, garlic, and cabbages. For fast days, the poor relied heavily on the cheaper types of preserved fish such as red herrings (heavily salted and smoked) and stockfish. It is probable that much use was made of wild foods, including bird's eggs and plants that would now be considered weeds. The quality and quantity of food eaten by the poor was heavily dependent on climate, and if crops failed, then they ate badly.

There is a little evidence for the eating habits of the more remote parts of the British Isles. The Scots, except for the very poorest, appear to have had access to meat and dairy products such as butter, cheese, and milk. Scottish soldiers are recorded eating meat and oatcakes, and craftsmen working on Cupar abbey received meat or fish daily, with ale and "short white cakes" (it is not clear what these were, but the fact that they were white suggests a relatively luxurious food).[9] In Ireland, animal products, especially milk and various products made from it, were important up until about 1600.[10]

EARLY MODERN PERIOD

The Middle Ages closed with two events that had far-reaching effects on food habits. In the wider world, new trade routes opened up and new foods were being introduced, particularly from the Americas. In England, major political changes were underway, as the power of the church was broken in the 1530s. Religious influence on food gradually waned and the idea of fasting had more or less disappeared by the seventeenth century. There were further religious and political upheavals, including the Civil War during the 1640s. Trade became increasingly important; the East India Company was established in 1600.

Another factor in eating habits from this time on is an increase in population, gradual at first, but increasingly rapid by the close of the eighteenth century. Estimates suggest a population of about five million in 1650 and just over six million in 1750; in 1801 the first census revealed nine million inhabitants. London, with a population of well over 500,000 in 1750, was by far the largest town and drew on the whole country for provisions. Most other towns were small. The picture is complicated by the emergence of a middle class that wished to follow aristocratic fashions, and increasing emphasis on London as a center of social life. By the mid-eighteenth century, anyone with pretensions to fashion spent part of the year in London. Food habits became increasingly national, as ideas were slowly disseminated from London to the provinces. During the eighteenth century, social and economic change gathered momentum. In Britain, excellent cuisine was centered in country houses, especially those belonging to the Whig aristocracy. Enclosures and improved agricultural methods allowed a greater volume of food to be produced from the land, often at the expense of the rural poor.

Foods from the new world were adopted with caution. One that was widely accepted by the mid-sixteenth century was turkey, which took its place as a novelty among the other large birds that graced the tables of the nobility. Tomatoes and potatoes were regarded with suspicion, as they were recognized as belonging to the nightshade family, of which several European species are poisonous. Potatoes were accepted first, although it is difficult to tell if some recipes for potatoes mean sweet potatoes, as these were used in Britain during the late sixteenth and early seventeenth centuries; they could be categorized alongside several sweet-tasting roots such as parsnips and skirrets popular at this time but fell out of favor. Ordinary potatoes gradually found acceptance. Spices from the new world included cayenne, or chili pepper, vanilla, and allspice, which gradually became more common in British cookery during the eighteenth century. Chocolate, mostly consumed as a drink at first, was recorded in Britain in the mid-seventeenth century, together with two other drinks of exotic origin, coffee and tea.

Publishing

The sixteenth century was also notable for the first published books of cookery receipts in English. A Boke of Cokery was published in 1500. It was followed mid-century by A Proper Newe Boke of Cookerye, and books of advice on diet, such as Thomas Elyot's Castel of Helth (1539) and Andrew Boorde's Dyetary of Helth (c. 1542). The cookery books were probably based on texts dating back to the mid-fifteenth century, which in turn contained elements of much older traditions. A handful more cookery books were published in the last decade of the century. The trend toward publishing accelerated during the seventeenth century. Gervase Markham's The English Hus-wife (1615) tells much about the management of modestly wealthy rural households. Robert May's Accomplisht Cook (1660) is laden with nostalgia for the golden age the author recalled before the Civil War. Receipt books were often divided into sections, covering cookery, medicine, cosmetics, distilling, and confectionery: The Queens Closet Opened (1655), which claimed to be transcribed from the receipt books of Queen Henrietta Maria is a good example of these.

At first the books were published under the names of men (although most were based on manuscripts kept by women), but by the end of the seventeenth century, women's names began to appear on the title page, the first one being Hannah Woolley in 1661. The Compleat Housewife by E. Smith (1727; "E" is often said to stand for Eliza, although there is no evidence for this) became the first cookery book to be published in North America. The first receipt book published in Scotland, Mrs. McLintock's Receipts for Cookery and Pastry-Work, appeared in 1736. The contents of books with female authors reflected the food of middle-class households; they became more accessible in price as the century wore on. Men also continued to publish cookery books. Several of these, such as Patrick Lamb's Royal Cookery; or, the Complete Court-Cook (1710) reflected the high status of men as cooks in royal or aristocratic households. French publications, such as those by La Varenne and Massialot were translated into English (1653 and 1702, respectively). The extravagance and elaboration of French cookery was often mocked, but ideas contained in such books were absorbed, interpreted, reduced in scope, and published by eighteenth-century women authors writing for a female audience.[11] The main trend by the mid-eighteenth century was toward books for women who managed middle-class households or wished to better themselves socially by copying the habits and food of households with slightly higher status. From the mid-eighteenth century, Hannah Glasse (*The Art of Cookery Made Plain and Easy*, 1747) and Elizabeth Raffald (*The Experienced English Housekeeper*, 1769) have been the subjects of much modern scrutiny. In the late eighteenth century, several books purporting to be by the male tavern cooks of London appeared, although these were simple plagiarisms of earlier works. Only William Verral's *Complete System of Cookery* (1759) seems rooted in the author's experience, from working with a French master cook and then keeping an inn on the south coast. Books ranged from manuals of household management to specialist volumes on confectionery to small cheap books aimed at the relatively poor. By the late eighteenth century, a national culinary style had developed.

Cookery books generally contained much material plagiarized from earlier authors, and there is also a time lag between practice in cookery and publication of receipts. The seventeenth and eighteenth centuries provide other documentary evidence about food habits in increasing quantities, including diaries, such as those of Samuel Pepys and Parson Woodforde; traveler's accounts, of which Celia Fiennes and Daniel Defoe provide the best known ones; and novels, for instance the work of Tobias Smollett.

Attitudes toward cookery as an occupation also changed. From the sixteenth century onward (and probably centuries before), the assumption has been that the housewife or female servants did the cookery in all but the grandest households. Until the seventeenth century, it was considered both desirable and normal for even aristocratic women to have practical knowledge of cookery, preserving, confectionery, and distilling. By the eighteenth century, this had become old-fashioned. Except in areas such as Scotland, distant from the influence of London, wealthy women, and even not-so-wealthy women, increasingly withdrew from involvement in the kitchen to become ladies of leisure, leaving domestic matters to housekeepers and servants. To admit to a practical interest in cookery and food became unfashionable.

Baking

Baking was carried out in stone- or brick-built beehive ovens, fired with wood or furze (gorse) which was placed inside the oven, lit, and allowed to burn away, heating the whole structure. The ashes were raked out and the oven floor swabbed before use. The soaking heat this produced was used for a sequence of foods: coarse bread was baked in the highest heat, followed by finer bread, and then as the temperature gradually fell, pastry, cakes, biscuits, and finally things that dried in low residual heat, such as meringues or fruit for drying. Meat was also baked, either as pasties, whole joints enclosed in coarse pastry, or as pie fillings. Baking required good organization if the sequence of bread and cakes was to be maximized. Much preparation was involved—sieving flour, crushing sugar loaves, and picking seeds out of dried fruit. Large stone or brick ovens were built into even quite modest houses and were found all over England and the lowlands of Scotland. Smaller, clay ovens, known as cloam ovens, were used in Devon. Poor people, who had no oven in their own house, would send prepared food to a public bakehouse to be cooked for a small fee. The price and availability of fuel affected the day-to-day lives of the poor, and a scarcity of wood in the southeast was partially responsible for the development of a reliance on bakery produced bread during the eighteenth century.

Flavors

Spices became cheaper as the new sea routes to the Indies became established. Initially they were used with even more enthusiasm than ever as they became more widely available. Sweet-sour flavors, provided by dried fruit, sugar, lemon, and orange juice became typical of late sixteenth-century and early seventeenth-century meat dishes, the acidity tempered with butter. Aromatic herbs such as thyme, marjoram, and parsley, plus onions and garlic, also became more prominent. After the Restoration of the Monarchy in 1660, French cookery began to gain prestige, leading to a distinct shift in flavorings for meat dishes. The taste for sweet-acid sauces, spices, and sweetened meat dishes declined. Savory and sweet were separated, and meat dishes became purely savory, with flavorings such as anchovies and wine, and intensely-flavored meat stocks. A seventeenth-century development was the habit of making *catchups* (ketchup) to add to sauces for meat; these were thin brown liquids concocted from either anchovies, oysters, walnuts, or mushrooms with salt and spices in imitation of fish pickle brought from the Far East. The word *curry* was also introduced at this time, to indicate a spice mixture of East Indian origin for flavoring meat dishes.

Sugar gradually became cheaper. As a crop, it moved westward, cultivated first on the Atlantic islands, then in Brazil and the Caribbean, where the British developed substantial interests in sugar plantations. In cookery, it was used less as a spice and more as an ingredient in baking, and as a preservative; it was also used to sweeten drinks. Sweet foods were perfumed with musk and ambergris in the sixteenth and seventeenth centuries. Rosewater was also popular, and continued to be so into the early eighteenth century; orange flower water also enjoyed a vogue at this time, and remained in use into the mid-eighteenth century.

Meat

Game was still highly valued but was only available for the nobility. By the early eighteenth century, heavy penalties were imposed on poor people caught poaching. Meat from domestic animals became increasingly important at the tables of even the wealthiest. Recipe books contained methods for making beef taste like venison for those whose resources did not run to the real thing. Beef gained status during this period, until the eighteenth century, when it became a symbol of John Bull, a bellicose representation of English nationalism.[12] Most sheep meat was eaten as mutton, from older animals, although young lamb was regarded as a luxury. Pork was most esteemed as sucking pig, roasted whole. Fresh pork from older pigs was also eaten, or made into sausages, while meat from fully grown pigs was salted for bacon and ham. By the eighteenth century, certain areas of the country were recognized for producing good hams. Exotic birds such as peacocks went out of fashion, but chickens, capons, turkeys, pigeons, ducks, and game birds such as pheasants and partridges were much liked. Foreigners noted that all Englishmen who could afford it ate large amounts of meat, and that they could roast it well, but were less apt at made dishes and sauces.

Basic cooking methods were roasting, boiling, grilling, baking, frying, and stewing. Spit roasting was a favored method. It was wasteful of fuel and uncomfortable for cooks as it generated tremendous heat, dissipated into the room or up the chimney. Spits were turned by hand, using a dog wheel (a treadmill turned by a small dog, used in the seventeenth century) or a jack (a mechanical device worked by rising heat, weights or clockwork). The poor, when they had meat to roast, used a piece of string that was twisted to make the meat revolve. Correctly done, spit roasting produced incomparable flavors and textures. Preparation was often elaborate, with complex stuffings, and the meat larded with spiced strips of pork fat, salted anchovy, or orange peel. Game birds were barded (slices of pork fat tied over them), a practice still observed. The meat had to be balanced on the spit and trussed to remain in the correct position. It also had to be at room temperature; too cold, and the inside did not cook by the time the outside was done. It was basted during roasting and the final operation was to dredge the joint with seasoned breadcrumbs or flour, which cooked to crisp coatings. Unlike barbecuing, no smoky flavor was apparent, because it was cooked to one side of the fire, not over it. Slices of tender meat were used for carbonadoes, scored in a criss-cross pattern and grilled, very popular in the sixteenth and seventeenth centuries. Various metal frames were used for grilling chops or steaks or for toasting bread or oatcakes in front of the fire.

Boiling was the other technique of major importance in the British kitchen, used by rich and poor alike. The food was placed in water in an iron pot suspended over a fire of wood, peat, or charcoal, and the resulting dish could range from an elaborate composition of meat and spiced broth to a simple grain-based pottage, depending on the household; by judicious use of nets and bags as containers, vegetables, suet puddings, and meat could all be cooked in the same pot. Large joints of meat were often boiled, a habit which has almost vanished. Meat was also boned, rolled, and bound with tape to make collars that were boiled in salted liquor and served cold.

Made meat dishes changed in nature. The semi-purees of the late medieval period were replaced in the sixteenth century with spiced stews containing dried fruit such as raisins and prunes, hashes of fresh meat sliced very thinly, and cooked with herbs, spices, broth, and wine. Fricassees were made from meat cut into small pieces, fried, and cooked with a little wine in the sixteenth century; during the seventeenth, they developed into meat dishes with thickened sauces. By the eighteenth century, aristocratic houses sometimes had stewing stoves for made dishes, but these burnt expensive charcoal and gave off poisonous fumes, and while they were relatively well known on the continent, were never common in Britain. Pans were still generally placed beside an open fire to heat, although instructions in cookery books hint that more care was taken with cookery processes.

Seventeenth-century books give recipes for dishes "in the French fashion," Turkish or Persian dishes (usually meat with rice), and olios, vast compositions of several meats cooked together, the broth being served as soup and the meat heaped up in a dish. At the end of the seventeenth century, terrines (a dish of birds and other meat in sauce), poupetons (pigeons cooked inside a crust of veal forcemeat), and bisks (stews with thickened sauces, garnished with a raggoo) became fashionable under French influence. Raggoo, from the expression *en ragoût*, originally meant a lavish garnish of truffles, morels, cockscombs, and other savory morsels in rich, highly flavored sauces, but in English came to mean a dish of meat stewed with flavorings and garnishes that vaguely reflected the French original. For much of the eighteenth century, a raggoo of this type represented French cookery for the British.[13] True eighteenth-century French cookery required large quantities of meat such as veal, ham, and poultry, cooked to make cullis (in which the meat was pulverized and strained with the cooking liquid) or gravy (a strongly flavored broth). These in turn were used as liquid flavors for made dishes. These were regarded as hopelessly extravagant by women authors writing for a middle-class audience concerned with economy: simpler, cheaper versions were suggested, or alternatives in the form of lemon pickle or catchup. The new dishes were set alongside plain roast and boiled meats, and older dishes such as fricassees now rich with cream and eggs, and hashes demoted to methods for using up leftover meat. Cream sauces began to appear in recipe books around 1710, and sauces thickened with flour and butter added at the mid-century.

Meat of all kinds was enclosed in pastry to make pasties and pies, noted as an English specialty by the mid-seventeenth century. Some were highly decorative, with elaborate designs of knots, foliage, or birds. Pies of spiced meat sweetened with dried fruit, popular in the sixteenth century, began to go out of fashion, although the Christmas pie of mincemeat—dried fruit, sugar, spices, and meat—survived into the nineteenth century and was the origin of the mince pie still made in December. Pastry was not always intended to be eaten; "huff" pastry of coarse wheat or rye flour was protective, shielding cooking food from the heat of brick ovens; afterwards, it formed a container, preserving it from the air until the crust was cut. Huge pies made with layers of boned poultry and game during the eighteenth century were enclosed in stout rye-flour crusts and sent long distances as gifts. Potting was another method of preserving. Meat was cooked, drained of juices, shredded, seasoned (mace was a favorite spice for this), pressed into shallow pots, and covered with a thick layer of melted butter. This cooled to form a seal that excluded the air and kept the contents good. Small birds could be potted whole.

Fish

Fish gradually lost its importance as fast day food, although Fridays and Wednesdays were declared fish days by Queen Elizabeth I to maintain a tradition of seafaring. Sea fish became increasingly important, especially cod and whitefish, and fishermen ventured increasingly further afield, as far as the coast of Newfoundland for them, but the taste for dried and salted cod declined steadily, as did the habit of eating whale and porpoise. Salmon remained common; it was eaten fresh or preserved by salting and smoking, as were herrings, although the catch of these was affected by competition with the Dutch between the fifteenth and eighteenth centuries. Oysters were enormously popular with all classes; they were eaten raw and, by the seventeenth century, added to meat dishes such as hashed mutton or stuffings for mutton or capons. Lobsters, crabs, shrimps, and prawns were also popular. Soles, turbot, and many other fish were still highly esteemed. The latter were cheap and added to many meat dishes, both for flavor and to stretch a small amount of meat.

Freshwater fish were still eaten; tench, pike, perch, and eels caught in the East Anglian fens were transported live to London in water butts. Some fish were noted local specialties, such as lampreys from the river Severn (made into pies), or char from Lake Windermere in the northwest, (potted in butter for export to other parts of the country). Salmon was cheap and plentiful and preserved by salting, as were herrings, which continued to be food for the poor. Eels were caught in many rivers and made into pies.

Like meat, fish was roasted or grilled before the fire, or cooked in water with added flavorings. In the Elizabethan period, it was cooked with sweet-sour fruit mixtures and put into Lenten versions of pies with dried fruit in the sixteenth century; later, the fruit disappeared, although fish was still baked in a crust until the eighteenth century. Fish cookery followed the change in fashion to bisks and fricassees in the seventeenth century. Parsley and melted butter, thickened with flour, was the usual eighteenth-century accompaniment to plainly cooked fish. Potting, as a preservation method, was applied to fish as well as meat. In the seventeenth century, potted lampreys from the river Severn and potted char from the Westmoreland lakes were sent to London. Pickles based on wine, vinegar, or beer were used for salmon, sturgeon, pike, and eels, while whitefish were marinated, or fried in oil and submerged in wine vinegar for short-term preservation (caveached). During the eighteenth century, one form of extravagant entertainment was a turtle dinner, in which the flesh of the animal was used to make five different dishes, including soup.

Grain, Bread, and Pudding

A preference for white bread made from wheat became apparent in southeastern England during the late sixteenth century and gradually spread northward and westward. Bread was served at all meals, and became more important at breakfast time among the wealthy in the eighteenth century, when it was eaten toasted and buttered. Bread and butter was among the refreshments offered by late–eighteenth-century tea gardens, and the idea of the sandwich also evolved.

Several enriched breads were made. Wigs were often mentioned: these appear to have started off as lightly enriched and spiced breads, probably wedge-shaped—the name is thought to derive from a Teutonic word meaning "wedge"—in the late Middle Ages. By the eighteenth century, when recipes for them appear, they had become rich with cream, butter, and eggs. Other enriched breads were made, some with spices or dried fruit, the ancestors of the various spiced and fruited buns and teacakes still made in Britain.

Puddings also provided another staple food of the seventeenth and eighteenth centuries. By the seventeenth century, several types were known. There were the original black (blood) puddings, now augmented by white ones (cereal or breadcrumbs, fat, sometimes with lean meat), and liver puddings, based on pig's liver. The haggis was also based on offal, but stuffed into the cleaned stomach bag of a sheep or calf. All these survive, although the haggis is now regarded as an exclusively Scottish dish. By the seventeenth century, several other forms of pudding are recorded, including bag puddings made of breadcrumbs or flour and suet (chopped raw beef fat), mixed with seasonings, eggs or milk, and sometimes currants, wrapped in a cloth and boiled, and quaking puddings, made from flour, milk, and egg batter cooked by the same method or poured into a dish and baked. Yorkshire pudding, now a type of baked batter pudding that is traditionally served with or before roast beef, began its career in the eighteenth century as a thick, pancake-type dish, which was cooked underneath roasting meat. Hasty pudding was made by boiling milk and adding breadcrumbs, flour, and eggs, dried fruit, or sugar. By the eighteenth century, the idea of pudding had expanded to include numerous baked dishes, often decorated with pastry. These contained no animal flesh, except, sometimes, bone marrow, but were sweetened and flavored with nuts or fruit, or based on rice or bread with dried fruit. Such dishes were placed on the table with meat. Bag puddings based on suet mixtures could be plain or heavily enriched with dried fruit to make plum pudding. Puddings of all sorts were served as part of the main meal, with roast meat and other savory foods. Rice and sago were also used with milk and sugar to make puddings. Plain rice was provided to accompany curries, recipes for which begin to appear in the mid-eighteenth century. Pasta, in the form of macaroni, was also eaten and considered highly fashionable.

Fruit and Vegetables

Fruit and vegetable cultivation developed considerably. Flemish refugees brought their gardening skills to England in the mid-sixteenth century and settled in the south and east, setting up market gardens to sell produce to London and other towns. The English gentry also began to take more interest in horticulture, establishing gardens to provide fruit and vegetables for their own kitchens. Vegetables introduced in the sixteenth and seventeenth centuries included asparagus, globe artichokes, Jerusalem artichokes, kidney beans, and cauliflowers. The idea of eating young peas fresh and green (as opposed to dried) became fashionable. Salads, including many kinds of herbs and flowers, were popular in the sixteenth and seventeenth centuries. Many vegetables were pickled in vinegar for winter. Ordinary potatoes were introduced in the Elizabethan period. At first, they were known as Virginia potatoes, due to a misconception about their place of origin. They were found to be particularly suitable for the climate in Ireland. They rapidly became a staple food of the poor, while grain was sold for cash. In England, they were first accepted in the northwestern county of Lancashire, where the soil proved to be especially good for its cultivation; they were grown and sold there by the 1680s.

New garden fruit included black and red currants (*Ribes* species) and gooseberries. Cultivated raspberries are first recorded in the sixteenth century. Peaches, apricots, plums, cherries, mulberries, and strawberries were all grown and much liked. Apples and pears were grown both for fruit and for making cider and perry. The appearance of tropical fruits such as bananas and pineapples is first recorded in Britain in the 1630s and 1640s, but neither became regular items of diet. (Bananas were rarely seen until the twentieth century.) In the eighteenth century, pineapples became symbols of status and fashion, grown in special hothouses by the wealthy, whose tables demanded out-of-season and exotic delicacies, forced with great skill by the gardeners on their country estates. All these fruits were eaten fresh or cooked in summer, or preserved with sugar for use in winter.

During the eighteenth century, concern about scurvy (lack of vitamin C), which affected sailors on long voyages, led to experiments with various foods, including many plants that were found to cure it. Eventually it was established that the juice of fresh citrus fruit, especially limes, was very effective in preventing the disease, although the reason why remained unknown until the early twentieth century.

Confectionery and Sweet Pastry

Confectionery also developed. The price of sugar began a gradual decline and several books of "secrets" published in the sixteenth century included recipes for sugar work. In the seventeenth century, a number of recipe books devoted to sweet foods appeared, and eighteenth-century cookery books continued to devote space to them. Tudor and Stuart ladies made preserves, distilled cordials, and concocted medicines in their own kitchens and stillrooms. They made many other confections, including sugar plate (paste made with powdered sugar and gum tragacanth); marchpane (marzipan) modeled into fruits, animals, or made into large flat circular marchpanes, decorated with icing, used to celebrate weddings and other events; flowers candied in sugar; and comfits, spices, or nuts coated with sugar (similar to sugar almonds). Jellies, generally sweet foods by this time, could be made from pectin set fruit juice, or with hartshorn or isinglass, or on a basis of gelatinous stock from calf's feet.

Sugar-preserved fruit were important. Sometimes these were whole, like modern candied fruit, but often they were made into pastes. Marmalade was a favorite item. The name came from *marmelada,* the Portuguese name for quince and for a paste made from it that was imported to Britain as a luxury. Pastes or marmalades were made of many other fruits as well, but in the eighteenth century, the word "jam" began to be applied to many of these. For some unknown reason, the word *marmalade* has been retained to describe preserves made from citrus fruits, especially bitter oranges.

Cakes also began to develop. In the seventeenth century, they were akin to spiced and sweetened breads, yeast-leavened but so enriched with butter and eggs that their relationship to later fruitcakes can be seen. During the eighteenth century, the finest recipes lost their yeast leavening and began to rely on beaten egg for lightness. Another confection of this time was Savoy biscuit, a light mixture of whisked eggs and sugar with flour and caraway seeds folded in, baked at a low temperature. This was a precursor of modern sponge cakes. Meringues were introduced from France at the end of the seventeenth century. Other sweet baked goods included Shrewsbury cakes, made from flour with large amounts of butter and sugar, similar to modern shortbreads. Gingerbread, which was often shaped in decorative molds, went from being a breadcrumb-based confection to one made from treacle (molasses) and flour with spices such as cinnamon and caraway, often with candied peel added.

Sweet foods were stored up for the sugar banquet, an informal collation of sweet foods. This developed from the *voidee* during the sixteenth century, when the hippocras and wafers were augmented with preserved fruit, marchpane, sweet biscuits, jellies (usually a sweet dish by this time), junkets or syllabubs (both dairy-based dishes), and sweet wines. The word *banquet*, hitherto used in the sense of a special formal meal for many people, developed a subsidiary meaning applied to these sugary feasts. Sugar banquets were sometimes taken in special "banqueting houses," constructed in the grounds or on the rooftops of large houses. Witty conversation and relaxed dalliance were part of their attraction. The idea went out of fashion in the mid-seventeenth century, and by the 1680s *dessert* had become the favored term. Tastes changed toward more fresh fruit and less confectionery, served at the dining table, or in an adjacent room.

The English were acknowledged to be excellent pastry makers. Fine pastry crusts included short types made rich with butter, egg yolks, and saffron, used with custards to make tarts. Layered puff pastry developed in the sixteenth century. At first it was eaten alone, but during the seventeenth century, it was used for fruit tarts, and in the eighteenth, it added decorative flourishes to baked puddings. These dishes were served as part of the main dinner, not as dessert dishes. In the eighteenth century, puff pastry was also used for savory patties, the equivalent of modern vol-au-vents.

Dairy Products and Eggs

Dairy products became increasingly important. To the Mediterranean-dominated tastes of the Middle Ages, the northern European dairy tradition had seemed rustic. In the sixteenth century, it became more important, and the use of almond milk declined as fasting did. Cattle emerged as the favored providers of milk in southeastern England by the seventeenth century, although sheep and goats were still milked in remote areas of Wales, Northern England, and Scotland into the eighteenth century. Milk cattle were kept confined in town dairies, and milk was either sold on the spot or carried in pails through the streets. It was often watered as well as being exposed to dirt and dust. Milk was not drunk much by the gentry in southern England, although the Scots continued to use it. It was important in cookery, as an ingredient in batters, pottages, and puddings, and made into "pap" with bread or flour for young children.

Cream went from being food for the sixteenth-century rural poor to a fashionable ingredient in the eighteenth century. There were many ways of using it. Clotted cream was made by heating milk very gently until a thick crust of cream formed on the top. Junket (cream curdled with rennet) appears under the name of "a trifle," although this name was later given to a dish of wine-soaked cake, fruit preserve, and custard, whipped cream or syllabub in the eighteenth century. Syllabubs were mixtures of cream, sugar, and wine. Seventeenth century references speak of making syllabubs "under the cow" by milking her into a pot containing wine and sugar. Recent experiments with this method produced results that were not palatable by twentieth-century standards, unless some cream was added to the wine before milking the cow into it.[14] By the eighteenth century the standard method was to whisk cream, wine, and sugar together by hand to make "everlasting syllabub." Rich dishes of cream flavored with fruit, nuts, chocolate, or rosewater and thickened by heating with egg yolks, are common in early eighteenth-century cookery books. Ice cream is first recorded in Britain in 1671, when it was a great novelty. The first known recipe, "to ice cream" was published in Mrs. Mary Eales' *Receipts* in 1718. Early recipes were simply cream, sweetened and flavored with fruit. Ices remained luxury foods until the latter half of the eighteenth century, and even after that cannot have been food accessible to the poor. But recipes developed, with many different flavors—fruit, chocolate, tea, coffee, nuts, as well as recipes for water ices, appearing in books. Chilling foods became more feasible in the eighteenth century. Winter ice from rivers and ponds was stored in specially dug ice wells for summer.

Cream was also added to savory dishes such as fricassees, and rich possets were made from cream and eggs with beer or wine and sugar.

Butter and cheese became increasingly important. By the seventeenth century, butter was used as a frying medium for many different dishes, added to mixtures for sweet puddings, as a dressing for cooked vegetables, for basting meat, shortening fine pastry, and enriching all sorts of cooked meat and vegetables. In the eighteenth century, it became a breakfast food, spread on toast or bread. Butter for later consumption was preserved by salting, and had to be washed before use. Butter was also employed as a thickener in a form similar to the modern *beurre mainé* (flour and butter kneaded together, added to a sauce at the end of cooking) by the mid-eighteenth century.

Fresh soft cheeses were made at home by many households and farms, but some areas had become noted for hard cheeses. These included the Cheddar area of Somerset, where a cooperative system of using milk resulted in the production of huge, long-keeping cheeses by the seventeenth century. Another noted cheese was made in Leicestershire but sold further south, at the Bell Inn, an important coaching stop at Stilton in Hertfordshire; in this case, the cheese took the name of the place in which it was sold, and is still known as Stilton. Cheshire had become another noted cheese-making area. In some areas, such as Suffolk, cream was taken from the milk for butter and the skimmed milk made into a notoriously hard cheese, considered fit only for servants and laborers. Cheeses from the continent were also known, especially Parmesan and Holland cheese. Cheese dishes are not common in British cookery, but toasted cheese was associated with Wales and became popular in England as well; it was known as a "Welsh rabbit." In the eighteenth century, cheese was also made into potted cheese, pounded with wine and spices. Milk was also curdled, and the solids strained out for use in baked cheesecakes. However, lemon cheese or lemon curd contained no milk products, only lemon peel, eggs, sugar, and butter heated together.

Eggs could be eaten alone, boiled or baked gently. They were also used in many dishes, including "amulets" (the ancestors of omelettes) with cheese or other flavorings. In the late seventeenth and eighteenth centuries, they thickened and enriched custards and creams, and went into rich plum puddings, cakes, and fancy breads. Egg and cream mixtures also began to enrich eighteenth-century fricassees.

Drinks

Tea, Coffee, and Chocolate

During the mid-seventeenth century, tea, coffee, and chocolate were all introduced to Britain. Coffee and chocolate both became breakfast drinks among the fashionable in the eighteenth century, although chocolate eventually gave way to tea.

Tea is first recorded in the 1650s in London. It became the drink to take at home when entertaining guests, served with ceremony, elegance, and specialized, costly utensils. In the early eighteenth century, imported Chinese porcelain cups without handles were used for tea drinking. Toward the end of the century, British porcelain manufacturers began to produce tea services. Other necessaries were silver tea kettles and teapots, lacquer trays and caddies, kept locked because the contents were so expensive. Much of the expense was due to the high level of duty paid on tea, and many people bought it from smugglers. Tea was often much adulterated with other leaves and colorings, and servants in wealthy houses dried discarded tea leaves and resold them. Even the poor took to tea as their main drink in the eighteenth century. It was not normal to add milk, but sugar was usually taken in it. In late eighteenth-century London, tea gardens became places of popular resort, offering entertainment and light refreshment in pleasant surroundings.

Coffee was introduced at about the same time as tea. Although it was taken in the home, it also gave rise to the coffeehouse, a public meeting place where coffee (or other drinks such as tea and chocolate) were available, together with newspapers for a small charge. The first one recorded in Britain was in Oxford in 1650; one was recorded in London in 1652, and by the end of the seventeenth century, most towns of any size had at least one. London and Edinburgh were particularly famous for their coffeehouses. Chocolate also first appeared in Britain in the mid-seventeenth century. It was used as a drink, made from a paste of ground cocoa beans with sugar, water or milk, and sometimes eggs or cream. Cinnamon, cloves, vanilla, or perfumes such as amber or musk were used to flavor chocolate. A few chocolate confections, such as creams and puffs (little meringues) are recorded from the eighteenth century, but it was mostly known as a drink through the late seventeenth and the eighteenth centuries. Chocolate houses were established in the late 1650s. Coffee and chocolate houses were places where men went to discuss business and politics and read the newspapers, were important as places to meet and exchange information, and played a part in the development of the Stock Exchange and Lloyd's of London insurance brokers. Some later developed into gentlemen's clubs.

Other Drinks

Wine continued to be the drink of choice for the wealthy throughout the early modern period. It was imported from many locations in southern Europe. During the eighteenth century, the male aristocracy developed a prodigious appetite for port, some of them consuming several bottles a day. The invention of strengthened glass bottles in the late seventeenth century allowed the development of sparkling wines and ciders. The latter, and perry, were drunk in areas where apple and pear trees flourished. Mead and metheglin (mead flavored with herbs) were also still made, although they went out of fashion toward the end of the seventeenth century. Brewing was also important, and many households brewed their own as a matter of course. Hops were introduced to Britain in the late Middle Ages, gradually replacing other aromatics that had been used for flavoring ale. The word *ale* was used into the seventeenth century for a drink without hops, and *beer* for one that included them. In practice, both names have been retained in English for fermented malted grain drinks with hops. By the eighteenth century, brewing was becoming industrialized. Distilling had also become commonplace. Some distilled drinks were cordials of herbs and spices, overtly medicinal. However, gin (exported to England from Holland by the mid-1570s) became a recreational drink. Distilling became increasingly important in London during the seventeenth century; rises in duty on wine, French brandy, and beer in the 1690s encouraged distilling in Britain. During the eighteenth century, cheap gin became the scourge of the very poor, offering a temporary release from the misery of their everyday lives.

As an antidote to large amounts of food and drink, a fashion for "taking the waters" at spas evolved among the wealthy. Some waters were for drinking, others for bathing in. Spas such as Bath became important social centers.

Meals and Mealtimes

Until the seventeenth century, breakfast consisted of bread and cold meat or fish with a drink of ale. Dinner, the main meal of the day, was taken in late morning or around midday. In the eighteenth century, the impact of new drinks changed breakfast habits; the fashionable took coffee or chocolate with bread rolls or toast at about 10 A.M. During the mid-seventeenth century the timing of dinner slipped later, to one o'clock, and in the early eighteenth century, to two or three in the afternoon among the wealthy and fashionable. It stayed at this time in the middle of the century, and then began to slip later in the afternoon again, to about 5 o'clock by the end of the century. This was only for the fashionable; other people took dinner earlier, according to habit, personal taste, work routines, and whether or not guests were present. Supper was still served in the evening, the timing depending on that of dinner.

Social habits also changed. At the end of the Middle Ages, the master of a large house and his family began to desert the common hall and eat in another room. By the seventeenth century, the idea of a separate room for eating had begun to evolve and in the eighteenth century the idea of the dining room, solely dedicated to dinner, was established. Servants were now confined to a servant's hall for their meals. Dining tables continued to be portable. Only in the 1780s, when tables with removable leaves were devised, did they become fixed.

Dinner continued to consist of a number of dishes placed on the table all at once; this was known as *service a la Française*. Two courses plus dessert was the norm during the eighteenth century, although in practice, the number of courses varied from one to five, depending on the status of the household and the grandeur of the occasion. Lesser gentry and merchants ate simpler meals, perhaps one large joint with a couple of other dishes and pudding (often served alongside meat at this date). The dishes were laid on the table in a symmetrical pattern, with set pieces such as roasts in the middle. The first course was soup or fish, dishes that were then taken away and replaced by "removes"—large, plain roasts, plus a number of smaller entrees, dishes such as fricassees and ragouts. The third course included delicacies such as game, shellfish, puddings and tarts, and vegetables (although the English have never been renowned for their attention to these). In wealthier households, many different types of meat, game, and fish were offered. Puddings could be relatively plain, of the boiled suet or batter varieties, or of the rich and sweet, baked in pastry with almonds, apricots, or other fruit in a pastry case. A mixture of savory and sweet dishes appeared on the table in each course, often augmented with cold beef or ham on a sideboard. Later in the century it became the norm for diners to help themselves and their neighbors to the dishes closest to them. Servants might help diners to dishes from the other end of the table, or to food placed on the sideboard. They also filled and brought glasses of wine to the table when requested, as it was not the custom to leave the glasses next to the diner for sipping.

The meal finished with dessert, which was often spectacular; during the first half the eighteenth century, confectionery, preserved and fresh fruit and little biscuits were built up into tall pyramids, with ices, creams, and cheeses supplementing them. Later, height became less of an object, and dessert was set in the middle of the table to be admired through the meal and eaten at the end. In the mid-eighteenth century, a fashion for elaborate parterres made of sugar work in imitation of gardens developed. These were often ornamented with little sculptures of mythological or rustic subjects, at first made from molded sugar, but later of porcelain from the newly established European factories. After dessert, the ladies withdrew; the men remained in the dining room drinking wine and talking, joining the ladies later for conversation, cards, and tea.

Tableware also changed. By the sixteenth century, the bread trencher had gone out of use, replaced by a wooden one, or, in wealthier households, a plate of pewter or precious metal. Coarse earthenware vessels and plates were made in Britain, but finer ceramic tableware was beginning to be imported from the Far East. It was expensive and highly prized. During the mid-eighteenth century European factories began manufacturing fine porcelain and heavier, but still attractive, earthenware. By the seventeenth century, hosts began to provide knives and spoons for guests. Forks gradually became known in Britain from the end of the sixteenth century onward. At first they were used for sticky foods, such as fruit in syrup, or for carving or serving, but they were gradually accepted for use in eating as well. However, they did not find full acceptance until well into the eighteenth century.

Eating Out

Places to buy food and drink ready-prepared, for travelers and those whose houses lacked a kitchen, had always existed, but the choice became broader after the Middle Ages. The inn replaced the monastery as a place for the better-off traveler to rest. In towns, taverns, once places to buy wine by the jug, now developed as places to eat. In the seventeenth and eighteenth centuries, some taverns, especially in London, gained considerable reputations for good food. Coffeehouses laid the foundations for gentlemen's clubs. Eighteenth-century confectioners served ices and cool drinks at their counters. They also sold high-class ready-prepared food, while cookshops sold roast meat, and street sellers hawked pies, sausages, black puddings, hot peas, gingerbread, and all manner of snacks.

The Poor

The diet of the poor varied considerably during the sixteenth through eighteenth centuries, affected by periods of dearth and the cost of food. Prices of food rose steeply in the late sixteenth century, but wages did not.

One major development was the process by which wheat bread became the staple of even the poorest in southern England during the first half of the eighteenth century. Underlying factors included a shortage of fuel, meaning that both slow cooking of pottages and oven baking were diffi-cult for the poor. Bread, bought from a baker, was a convenience food, made palatable by small amounts of butter, cheese, or bacon. During the same period there was also a decline in the home brewing of beer, and a rise in the popularity of tea drinking. Tea was a high-status drink, but also a convenient one, and sugar, decreasing in price, made it palatable.

Other grains were still grown but reliance on them was diminishing. Rye was grown in some eastern parts of England and used for bread among the poor, but had virtually disappeared by the end of the eighteenth cen-tury. Barley bread continued to be made in the southwest, in Wales and the Isle of Man. Oats, tolerant of cool, damp climates, are recorded in the uplands of Wales, northern England, and Scotland during the eighteenth century. They were used in various types of flat breads and crisp, thin oat-cakes, some varieties of which are still made.

Husked but unground wheat grains were still made into frumenty, al-though this began to have a gradual decline in popularity. The principal use of barley had long been for brewing beer, but it was also used in pot-tages. Oat pottages or gruels were also made. *Llymru* (a word which was Anglicized to "flummery") was a Welsh dish of fine oatmeal and water, thickened by heat and allowed to cool and set. Pease pudding, hasty pud-dings of flour or oatmeal boiled with milk, and other oat- or cereal-based dishes were important to those in the north of England.

The poor ate fresh meat when they could afford it, and kept pigs to make bacon, hams, and salted pork. Mutton and beef were also salted. Vil-lagers pastured geese and cattle on common land, but land enclosures from late Tudor times onward gradually removed this right. Game was only available to the poor through poaching, as increasingly strict laws controlled hunting as a privilege of the wealthy. Preserved fish—red or white herrings and stockfish—were cheap and important in the diet of the poor when fast days were still observed. Fishing rights on inland waters tended to be controlled, but eels, oysters, and salmon were all cheap dur-ing the early modern period, and coastal communities had access to sea fish.

Dairy products remained important for the less well off and rural com-munities during the early part of the period. Butter and cheese were im-portant foods, but the poor had less access to them: less opportunity to keep their own cattle, and less money in real terms to spend on food. Hard cheeses from Suffolk and Essex were sold to laborers and the London poor. Buttermilk and whey were still sold in towns as drinks, but increasingly used as pig food in the country. With the decline of milk products, tea and beer became the main drinks of the southern poor. Drunkenness among the urban poor was perceived as a social problem, but no effective remedy was proposed.

In Scotland, visitors during the sixteenth century remarked on the flocks and herds, and use of meat and dairy products. Scottish highlanders ate rye, wheat, beans, pease, oats, and beef, and those from the region bordering England had flesh, milk, cheese, and "sodden barley" (perhaps a type of broth) but little bread. By the seventeenth century, a trade in droving cattle on the hoof from the Scottish highlands to southern England had developed, the numbers increasing every year. In eighteenth century Scotland, barley broths, milk, oatmeal, and eventually potatoes had replaced meat and dairy products among the poor.[15] The inhabitants of the remotest parts of Britain still pursued a primitive way of life, as Martin Martin observed when he visited the Hebrides in the late seventeenth and early eighteenth centuries, noting the use of seabirds and their eggs on St. Kilda, and butter, cheese, milk, potatoes, cabbage, and oatmeal on the islands in general. Evidence from Ireland shows a greater consumption of grain and increased reliance on potatoes during the seventeenth century,[16] although dairy foods remained important, and sour curds were considered a particular delicacy. A trade in droving cattle from Wales to London also developed.

The reliance on wheat bread led to problems at the end of the eighteenth century, when prices rose rapidly. Grain harvests in Britain were badly affected by poor weather, and imports by war with France. This hit southern and eastern England particularly hard and had a disproportionate effect on the poor, whose diet now relied heavily on wheat bread. The late–eighteenth-century cleric Parson Woodforde recorded eating poor quality bread at his own table and organizing doles of bread for the poor of his parish. An attempt was made to popularize the potato as an alternative to bread among prosperous southerners to reduce the consumption of grain. The idea of charitable soup distributions among the poor evolved, and a system of welfare for the poor, based on the price of bread, was adopted in 1795.

By the end of the eighteenth century, the landscape of Britain was changing rapidly. The open fields of the Midlands were mostly enclosed. Improved roads and newly built canals enhanced communications within England and hastened an already well-established trend toward social and political centralization on London. Industries such as textiles, metalworking, and pottery production were well established in certain areas of the country and undergoing mechanization as the factory system evolved.

The industrial cities of the midlands and the north were growing rapidly, partly because of population growth and partly because of migration from rural areas. Market gardening for vegetables and fruit around the towns had expanded, although transporting food was becoming a problem, only partly eased by construction of canals. In science, the knowledge of chemistry had expanded, and the idea of food requirements in terms of energy had been established. These factors played an increasingly important part in the story of British food culture.

THE NINETEENTH CENTURY

During the nineteenth century, Britain went from being a primarily agrarian society to an urban one. The population rose from about 9 million in 1801 to between 17 and 18 million in 1851, about half of whom lived in towns. The population doubled again in the next 50 years, to 36 million in 1901. The first half of the century was one of great poverty for the laboring classes; the expression "the hungry forties" (actually coined in 1904) came to stand for the conditions of the 1820s to 1850s. At the same time, the wealthy enjoyed great luxury. In between was a rapidly growing middle class composed of the traditional professions, augmented by new ones such as industrialists and engineers. The expansion of this, and the numerous gradations it assumed, were of huge importance socially, as the aristocracy broke ranks just enough to admit a fortunate few who had wealth, beauty, or talent, and the remainder copied upper-class manners and habits as much as they were able.

The British population became increasingly dependent on food imports. The development of rail transport and steamships in the first half of the century aided this. During the late nineteenth century, the British Empire reached its greatest extent. Advances in food preservation—canning, refrigeration, drying—helped to feed the growing population, as did new sources of bulk commodities such as wheat, much of which came from territories subject to the British crown. New processing methods such as roller milling flour also contributed to food habits.

Nineteenth-century ideals of femininity laid emphasis on women in the domestic sphere, but not in any practical capacity in the kitchen, although the mistress of the house would plan or at least approve the menu. All except the laboring classes employed one or more servants to help with domestic work, and many households employed a cook. The British upper classes employed male French cooks and adopted French dishes, devaluing the homegrown English tradition of cookery.

Wood had been the basic cooking fuel of the early modern period (although peat was important in Ireland and the west of Scotland). Coal became important for cooking in the late eighteenth century. The key to this was the development of the coal-fired cast-iron kitchen range, with a central grate, a hotplate above, and an enclosed side oven (and often a boiler for hot water). It was devised in the late eighteenth century, improved by Count Rumford (Benjamin Thompson, born in Massachusetts in 1753), and manufactured in thousands by nineteenth-century iron foundries. "Managing the range" was a perpetual problem of the Victorian kitchen. Gas was introduced as a cooking fuel for commercial kitchens and grand houses in the 1840s but was not used widely until the 1880s, when electricity also made an appearance.

The fire or range was the hub around which the kitchen revolved. The organization of the rest of the room was elaborate or simple according to the wealth and status of the household. In the eighteenth and nineteenth centuries, kitchens in middle-class and aristocratic homes were rooms for the servants (examples can be seen in the great houses preserved as museums). In everyday use, they were hot from the fire or range. A central table and a dresser against the wall provided work surfaces with drawers for storing implements and linen; a rack over the dresser was used for plates and cooking vessels. If piped water was available, it would be pumped up in a separate room, the scullery, where tasks such as washing up, peeling vegetables, and plucking poultry were carried out. During the nineteenth century, a substantial trade in ice from Norway and North America developed. Early refrigerators were first used in about 1900.[17]

Cooking pots were made of iron or copper (needing frequent re-tinning inside) and included saucepans, frying pans, and items such as fish kettles. Elaborate copper molds were used for jellies and pewter ones for ice creams. Spits and roasting tins were needed for meat, and baking tins in various shapes and sizes for cakes, pies, buns, and bread loaves. Horsehair, linen, or silk sieves and tamis cloths were necessary for sieving fine purees. Mixing bowls and kitchen pottery generally was made from earthenware and included bulbous stew jars and basins for boiling or steaming puddings. Kitchen implements included cooking knives, wooden spoons, metal skimmers, cooking forks, and toasting forks. A cook and several maids presided over this arrangement; the scullery maid got the heaviest and dirtiest tasks.

The wealthiest houses had suites of rooms, including a butler's pantry, a cellar, store rooms, and a housekeeper's room. Dedicated rooms such as a confectioner's kitchen, a dairy or a stillroom (originally for distilling alcoholic cordials and medicines, later for cold desserts) might also be included. A large staff of maids, footmen, and a butler worked alongside either a highly accomplished female cook or a chef. A few kitchens requiring servants survived into the 1930s, and they have now all but vanished.

In poor houses, kitchens often doubled as living rooms, the family congregating there in the warmth of the range. Utensils and implements were few and simple: a pan or two, some patty tins, perhaps a pottery mold for jelly or blancmange, and a few bowls for puddings and for mixing. Locally made pottery varied regionally in the nineteenth century: a Yorkshire kitchen would contain a wide, deep bowl for kneading bread, whereas a Lancashire one would have a deep, straight-sided stew jar for making Lancashire hotpot. Scottish, north country, and Welsh kitchens had cast-iron griddles for baking over an open fire. The kitchen table doubled as a dining table, and the housewife did all the cooking herself.

In rural households, the size and extent of the kitchen also depended on the wealth of the family, but in all but the grandest farmhouses, the housewife would probably take some part in food preparation. Specialist food-handling facilities would also be present in some areas, for instance, dairies for handling milk and making cheese and butter in pastoral regions.

Publishing

The eighteenth-century tradition of middle-class cookery books by women for women continued. Mrs. Rundell's *New System of Domestic Cookery* (1806) was typical. It went into numerous reprints with additions by other authors and many pirated editions. Eliza Acton's *Modern Cookery for Private Families* (1845) continued the genre. The trend toward diversity was also apparent. Men published a range of books, from Dr. William Kitchiner's *Cook's Oracle* (1818), covering roughly the same ground as Mrs. Rundell but in a different style, to various works on confectionery, of which William Jarrin's *Italian Confectioner* (1820) summed up centuries of tradition. The chefs Alexis Soyer and Charles Francatelli both published works for the high-class kitchen and small, cheap books on working-class cookery. Trade publications on subjects such as bakery also began to appear.

From 1859 to 1861, a young woman named Isabella Beeton wrote a series of magazine articles. These were published in book form in 1861 as *Beeton's Book of Household Management*. It was being updated and reissued long after the author's untimely death in 1865. The original is a mixture of recipes from earlier authors, such as Acton, and contributions from friends, with an innovative layout, giving exact measurements and timings. Subsequent editions had little to do with the original and were mammoth compilations of everything from the fancies of late Victorian chefs to economical ways of using leftovers. The long life of the title, and the vast print runs (including a much-changed edition in 1888) mean that it has come to dominate the popular idea of Victorian cookery in Britain.

Late–nineteenth-century publications covered all aspects of cookery, from Auguste Escoffier's *Le Guide Culinaire* (1903), for chefs learning the French classical tradition, through George Auguste Sala's *The Thorough Good Cook* (1895), an early example of gastronomic writing, to Cassell's *Dictionary of Cookery* (1875–76), and the monumental *Encylopaedia of Practical Cookery* (c. 1891) by Theodore Francis Garrett. Mrs. Agnes B. Marshall published several works, including one dedicated to ices in the 1880s and 1890s. These promoted her successful cookery school and a shop that sold a huge variety of kitchen equipment, including numerous fancy molds for creams and ices. For the less well off, there were abridged versions of Mrs. Beeton and small, cheaply printed books promoting goods such as beef extract or baking powder, or little books of household hints and recipes. Although they cost only a few pence, even these must have been beyond the reach of the very poor who continued to rely on what little they learnt from family and friends or from observing upper servants at work in better-off households.

Teaching women about food and cookery on a formal level began around the end of the nineteenth century, giving rise to the disciplines of domestic science and home economics. The application of science to food was enhanced by the development of nutritional knowledge. The idea of food providing energy and "flesh forming" substances (proteins) was well established by the mid-nineteenth century, and by 1900, research on the role of minerals and vitamins in health had started. Food purity was an issue throughout the century. In 1820, Frederick Accum published *A Treatise on Adulterations of Food,* triggering arguments about food purity that raged with greater or lesser ferocity for much of the century, also contributing to ideas about healthy diet.

Food for the Rich

In the first half of the nineteenth century, there was a gradual decline of eighteenth-century cuisine as the society that had produced it changed.

Urbanization led to loss of contact with the soil, and although the country estate remained a status symbol, food was no longer seen as an expression of it. The upper classes continued to employ French chefs. In the early nineteenth century, Ude worked for the Earl of Sefton and in Crockford's Club; the Prince Regent employed Carême in 1816 and 1817; Soyer was chef at the Reform Club in the 1830s and 1840s; and Francatelli was in service in the household of Queen Victoria during the 1850s. They produced rich, elaborate food that relied on numerous servants to produce finely textured purées and mousses, sparkling aspic jellies, unctuous sauces, and fiddly presentations carefully built up in repetitive, fancy shapes with precisely cut garnishes. The basis included game of all sorts, especially birds (shooting on large country estates was an important leisure pursuit). Beef, veal, lamb, and mutton were used, although elaborate preparation was favored, for example, cutlets of lamb, trimmed so that only the noisettes of meat remained, were masked with a highly flavored sauce. Chicken, duck, and ham were much used, along with offal such as tongue or kidneys. Fish included sole (usually in fillets), turbot, and lobster. The style was developed by Carême in the 1820s and 1830s and extended (in France) by Urbain Dubois in the 1860s. Variants on this continued to be upper-class food until the First World War. This rich, luxurious style of eating, combined with full enjoyment of wine and spirits, led to a certain rotundity among consumers, epitomized by King Edward VII (ruled 1901–10).

The Condition of the Poor

In contrast to this, the laboring poor, rural and urban, led lives of uncertainty. Staple foods were bread, pudding, or pottage-type dishes made from wheat flour or beans, with barley or oats in areas away from the southeast, plus easily grown vegetables such as potatoes, cabbage, onions, turnips, and beans. Meat was reduced to salt pork or bacon once a week, and fish came in the form of herring. Tea was eked out with burnt crusts of bread. Milk had become rare in their diet, except in the far north of England and Scotland, where a diet of oatmeal, milk, and vegetables was still eaten.

To some extent, the type of employment led to differences: mining communities in the north were relatively well paid and could afford more fresh meat. Factory workers could be reduced to misery by a downturn in trade, such as the cotton famine of the 1840s. Friedrich Engels in his *Condition of the Working Class in England* (1844) noted that better-paid workers, especially when all family members were fully employed, could afford good food, including meat every day, plus bacon and cheese, but if income dropped, the amount of meat consumed was reduced, and the proportion of bread increased. Poorer people could not afford fresh meat, but only a little bacon to add flavor to potatoes; further down the scale, meat disappeared entirely from a diet that consisted of bread, cheese, porridge, and potatoes, and the poorest Irish immigrants ate only potatoes.

Potatoes had become increasingly important in the diet of the poor in certain areas of Britain during the early nineteenth century. They were extensively cultivated in western Scotland, and in Ireland had become the principal food of the people. They were augmented by bacon, butter, or buttermilk when available, providing a monotonous but healthy diet. In the 1840s, the population of Ireland had reached about eight million, when potato blight struck the crop in 1845. The potatoes rotted in the ground, and the population starved or emigrated. A standard private charitable Victorian response to poverty throughout Britain was the distribution of soup, usually based on stock made with very small quantities of meat. On a public level, the destitute were dealt with through a system of workhouses that replaced the issues of small amounts of money and doles of bread given at the end of the eighteenth century. Workhouses provided shelter, a reasonably adequate but very plain diet, but strict, often inhumane living conditions; for most, they were a last resort.

In the late nineteenth and early twentieth centuries, the poor, while still extremely poor, had more access to food, largely due to advances in transport and technology. Wheat from North America, butter and cheese from other European countries and the colonies, plus inventions such as margarine and condensed milk all added to their diet, and canned foods gained acceptance. Imports of frozen meat from Australia began in the 1870s. These foods were sold through small shops and an increasing number of chain grocers. The earliest example was established as a cooperative society in Rochdale in 1844, with the aim of providing good quality basic foodstuffs at reasonable prices to poorer consumers who were members. As a national chain, usually referred to as "the Co-op," this has survived to the present day. Individuals such as Thomas Lipton also established chains in the late nineteenth century. These moved toward prepacked foods, the idea of self service and cutting out the wholesaler, precursors of the modern supermarket.

The poor were not necessarily better nourished. Roller milling brought white flour and bread within reach of most consumers, but removed the most nutritious elements of the grain, further impoverishing diet, and margarine, adopted as a cheap butter substitute, lacked the vitamins that the latter provided. Legislation relating to food standards also helped improve diet, which by the 1850s was often heavily adulterated—bread had alum added to it, milk was watered, and cheap confectionery decorated with attractive bright colors based on toxic substances. Legislation passed in 1860 and strengthened in 1875 laid the foundations of modern food safety laws. During the closing years of the nineteenth century, the effects of inadequate diet on the poor became a cause for concern from the point of view of both social reformers and national security. Many potential army recruits for the Boer War were rejected on the grounds of poor health. The inquiry into this by the Inter-departmental Committee on Physical Deterioration reported in 1904 that many problems were due to inadequate diet, a discovery that lay behind many later moves to improve nutrition.

The Middle Class

Between these two groups lay an expanding middle class. Those who did not aspire to the French cookery of the upper classes continued with the traditions of the eighteenth century, although these were increasingly debased. A trend toward simplicity was becoming apparent. Onions and herbs, plus simple meat stocks or broths and catchups, continued to be used for flavoring meat dishes, but the garnishes and flavorings of the eighteenth-century tradition were much reduced. The standbys of the kitchen became roast or boiled beef, and roast or boiled mutton (served with caper sauce). In the latter half of the century, notions of economy that had preoccupied eighteenth-century women cookery authors became more dominant, and ideas for cheap family meals, keeping up appearances, and the use of leftovers, especially the remains of the large joints of meat, took up more space. Pork was mostly used in winter. Country households kept a pig or two to provide meat for salting as bacon and ham, and made products such as pork pies and sausages. Fish were now mostly those from the sea, as many inland waterways had become too polluted to support much life. The old salt cures had gone out of fashion, replaced by lighter ones such as kippers and bloaters for herrings, and light, cold smoke for haddock. Vegetables, for the most part, were served plainly boiled, and while potatoes were now widely accepted, suet puddings still sometimes accompanied meat. The idea of wrapping meat such as beef steak, mutton, or chicken in a suet crust to make savory puddings had also evolved. Sauces were used with savory dishes, but were slowly being reduced to two basic types: a white sauce and a brown one, based on espagnole sauce.

Meat and Fish

For the first four decades of the century, meat arrived in major towns on the hoof, driven from the distant pastures of Wales and Scotland, as it had been for decades. The railways offered an easier and quicker mode of transport. Major changes also came with the development of new ways of preserving food. Canning had developed at the end of the eighteenth century and by the 1820s canned foods had found a limited acceptance, especially as victuals for the armed forces. By the 1870s, they had been more fully accepted and canned meat from South America and Australia, although uninteresting, was cheaply available. The next development was freezing, and in 1880 the first consignment of frozen meat from Australia arrived in London. Refrigeration, combined with steam trawlers and swift railway transport, helped to deliver vast quantities of cod and haddock caught far from British shores to inland cities. A new institution, shops selling fried fish and chips, emerged sometime during the 1870s, especially in working-class areas of London and the northern industrial cities. Salmon, once a cheap food, became expensive because the fish could not survive in polluted rivers.

The development of the kitchen range led to a change in meat-roasting techniques. Instead of cooking meat in front of an open fire, it was now placed in a tin and cooked in the enclosed oven. Although this was, and still is, referred to as roasting, it is technically baking. This change in method had consequences for the flavor, as the meat now cooked in the accumulated fat and juices that dripped from it. These become very hot and give the meat a different flavor. In addition, the texture of the cooked meat tended to be drier. One theory for overcoming this, which became popular in the late nineteenth century, was the idea that meat should be sealed by starting it cooking at a high temperature, or by frying it first. The idea was that a brief exposure to high temperatures sealed the end of muscle fibers and helped to retain moisture in the cooking meat. Although this has been shown to be a culinary myth, the idea has survived to the present day, and some people believe it is essential to start a roast off at a high temperature, or to seal meat for a stew by frying it before adding vegetables and liquid.

Bread and Grains

The trend toward white bread continued: in the early part of the century, the quality of this was the focus of many worries about food purity. Bakers, it was alleged, added chalk, alum, and even ground-up bones to the dough. Bread in the first half of the century was also affected first by shortages due to poor harvests, and between 1815 and 1845 by the Corn Laws, legislation which protected the price of home-produced wheat and exacerbated the misery of the poor. At times, civil unrest broke out over bread prices. After 1845 a policy of free trade was pursued and much wheat was imported, particularly from North America. The price of bread was further reduced in the 1870s by the adoption of roller milling, which produced fine, white flour. Bread was especially important at breakfast and as an accompaniment to tea. It was eaten alone or toasted; those who could afford it spread it with butter or jam, or ate it with cheese.

Numerous small bread rolls were produced. These varied slightly in their ingredients and shape from place to place—enriched with small amounts of milk, cream, butter, or lard, rounded or flattened, with currants or spice or candied peel. Richer versions included Bath buns (sweet and buttery) and Sally Lunns (larger, rich, but not sweet). Hot cross buns, spiced and fruited, were made for Good Friday. Lightly spiced and fruited loaves were also made for treats and special occasions, such as Christmas. Dough cakes and lardy cakes were made with a portion of bread dough with sugar, spice, and dried fruit kneaded in. Small griddle breads were extremely popular, especially muffins, which were hawked round the London streets by itinerant vendors and eaten toasted for tea.

In Wales, the north of England, and Scotland, small items were baked on an open iron griddle plate variously known as a planc, bakestone, or girdle, heated over the fire. An iron pot in which breads and other mixtures were placed, heated among the ashes with embers heaped over the top was recorded in Wales, Ireland, and southwestern and northwestern English counties and continued in use into the twentieth century.

The old grain-based pottages gradually disappeared; frumenty was considered old-fashioned, and oat porridge and other oat concoctions such as brose became closely identified with Scotland, as did the use of pearl barley in Scotch broth. Suet puddings continued to be important, especially for the less well off; sugar, treacle, or jam was often added to these, and plum puddings became very sweet and rich. Rice, semolina, sago, tapioca, and arrowroot all provided a base for sweet milk puddings, considered good food for invalids and children. Maize never became established as a grain, but cornflour (cornstarch) was found to be a useful addition to the kitchen cupboard.

Fruit and Vegetables

In the early part of the nineteenth century, these were still largely seasonal for those whose means did not run to glasshouses and knowledgeable gardeners. Most towns of any size had market gardens on the outskirts to provide fresh produce. Some areas of the country developed local specialties—cherries, apples, and hazelnuts in Kent, strawberries in Hampshire, asparagus and plums in the Vale of Evesham in Worcestershire, early potatoes in Cornwall and southwest Wales, and forced rhubarb in West Yorkshire. Railways aided transport, and canning helped to extend the season for many items. By the end of the century, the range of food preserved by this method was vast. It also allowed the import of vegetables and fruit from the colonies. One item that was finally adopted for the British table was the tomato. The first published recipe for tomato sauce appears in Mrs. Rundell's book in 1806, and by the end of the century, they were quite widely eaten. Pickling vegetables became a substantial industry, and some dried products such as potatoes and soups were developed in the middle of the century.

Dairy Products

An epidemic of cattle disease in the 1860s led to the gradual disappearance of town dairies. Milk could now be transported from the countryside by railway. Pasteurization was adopted in the 1890s, initially as a preservation method. Milk was used for puddings and custards, perhaps using custard powder. Custard powder, a branded mix of cornstarch, colorings, and vanilla, is an early example of convenience food, invented in the mid-nineteenth century by one Henry Bird, whose wife is said to have been allergic to eggs. Condensed milk also appeared on the market. It was used, especially in poor areas, for feeding babies, although nutritionally it was badly suited to this and the practice also presented hygiene problems. Cream was a luxury, used in desserts, but the flavored creams, syllabubs, and possets of the early modern period went out of fashion. Ice cream, however, became less of a luxury. By the late nineteenth century, cheap versions such as hokey-pokey were sold by street vendors, and the "penny lick" (a shallow, returnable glass from which the confection was licked) were common.

Butter continued to be important as a spread for bread and toast, a frying medium, and an ingredient in baking and pastry, but the old melted butter sauces of the eighteenth century were replaced by béchamel, based on a flour and butter roux thinned with milk, cream, or stock, or the English version of it, white sauce. Margarine was invented in the 1870s and was used by the urban poor as a substitute for butter.

Cheese was still mostly made on farms in specific areas of the country. In the late nineteenth century, the methods for making cheese in various districts were collected and codified, dairy schools established to teach cheese makers, and a move to creamery production begun. Cheddar, in particular, was a successful method that produced a robust product, and by the 1880s, the United States, Canada, and Australia were producing their own variants of this cheese and exporting it back to Britain. Many other local cheeses were made: ones still well known, such as Gloucester, Caerphilly, Cheshire, Lancashire, Wensleydale, Derby, Leicester, and Stilton. Others, mostly soft cheeses with a short shelf life such as Bath, Colwick, and Cambridge or York cheeses, were well known in the late nineteenth and early twentieth centuries.

Confectionery, Pastry, and Baking

Sugar become a cheap bulk commodity by the end of the eighteenth century. Although it was subject to tax until the 1880s, it was now within reach of most consumers; this, combined with a new supply extracted from beet grown in northern Europe, led to the heavy use of sugar in all kinds of puddings, desserts, and sweet baked goods. The introduction of the kitchen range into even quite small houses meant that home baking became more important. Pastry continued to be used for traditional pies and tarts, although the older, coarser types of paste disappeared. French cookery had codified various fine types of paste, including puff pastry and choux pastry, used for desserts.

Chemical leavening agents became available. Sodium bicarbonate came onto the market sometime in the 1840s, quickly followed by baking powder, and was much used in cakes and other baking. Fruitcakes developed into their modern form, heavily sweetened with a high proportion of vine fruits. Cheaper, less rich versions were made for everyday use, and in some places, yeast-leavened versions survived. The Savoy biscuit formula was still used, but cakes based on creamed butter and sugar had evolved. These made plain pound cakes or were sandwiched with whipped cream and strawberry or raspberry jam, a type that became known as Victoria sandwiches or sponges in the late nineteenth century. The basic recipe was adapted by the addition of lemon, orange, candied cherries, coffee, or chocolate to give numerous variations. Madeira cake was a plain, close-textured cake made to accompany Madeira wine. Seed cakes were flavored with caraway seeds. Numerous small buns were made from both cake-type mixtures, more or less plain, and bread-dough mixtures. Scones, a word of Scottish origin, originally meant small griddle baked breads, but a fluffier version based on wheat flour, lightly sweetened, was developed in the early twentieth century. Many gingerbread recipes developed: light cake-type ones, crisp biscuity ones, very thin crisp wafers known as brandysnaps, and parkin, an oat-based northern type of gingerbread.

One sector of baking that expanded dramatically during the nineteenth century was biscuit manufacture. The original biscuits—twice-baked bread, or the Savoy biscuits—had been augmented by other confections such as nut-based macaroons and ratafias and buttery Shrewsbury cakes and shortbread-type confections in the seventeenth and eighteenth centuries. In the first half of the nineteenth century, sweet biscuit (cookie) manufacture became a large-scale industry with companies such as Carr's of Carlisle[18] and Huntley and Palmer's using machinery to cut fancy shapes and traveling ovens for baking. Unsweetened biscuits of the cracker type were also made. All were packed in airtight tins for sale, and they became an important item in the middle-class diet.

Sugar confectionery was industrialized, and cheap sugar sweets (candies) became commonplace. The luxury end of the market was occupied by the development of chocolate as a confection. Eating chocolate was first manufactured by Fry's in the 1820s. By the late nineteenth century, several large chocolate companies were established, including Cadbury's, Rowntrees, and Terrys. Quaker families had a strong presence in both biscuit and chocolate manufacture. All towns had small enterprises boiling sugar for hard sweets and toffee.

Drinks

Tea continued to be the most important British beverage. Until the 1870s, China supplied 85 percent of tea imported to Britain, but India and Sri Lanka were developed as producers. By the end of the 1880s, they dominated the market and tea was then the national drink. Tea also became a weapon in the fight for temperance. Gin drinking had continued to be a scourge into the 1830s, but social reformers introduced the idea of teetotalism with varying success. The development of other drinks, such as cocoa (which became available in the 1820s as a result of innovations in chocolate processing) and fizzy soft drinks, also developed in the first half of the nineteenth century, provided alternatives. Beer continued to be important for the working classes, and wine, as ever, was the aristocratic choice. A safe domestic water supply became an urgent concern after several serious cholera epidemics in the first half of the century, and by 1900, piped water from public supplies was widely available in cities.

Dining

By the 1850s, any house with pretensions to fashion had a separate dining room, perhaps decorated with crimson wallpaper and furnished with table and chairs, plus a sideboard displaying silver or silver plate (suburban houses in Britain continued to have separate dining rooms until well into the twentieth century). A large nineteenth-century house might also have a breakfast room and a luncheon room as well.

The timing of meals also altered. Breakfast became earlier; in country houses it developed into an elaborate meal of hot and cold meats, eggs, and fish, although in town it might be simpler. Dinner became later and later, until it was taken as late as seven or eight in the evening by mid-century. Two developments that encouraged late dining were the advent of gas lighting and the start of commuting to work in cities, especially London: the times of meals now had to fit around business hours of 9:00 A.M. to 5:30 P.M. Two meals, lunch (or luncheon), and afternoon tea evolved to fill the gap between breakfast and dinner.

Another change was in the serving of food at dinner. The system of placing all dishes on the table at once was gradually superseded by one of several well-defined courses—hors d'oeuvre, entrées, roasts, game, dessert—handed round separately by servants. This became known as *service à la Russe* and spread gradually during the nineteenth century, although it was not fully accepted in Britain until the 1890s. *Service à la Russe* cut down on the amount of time spent in dining but required large numbers of servants and also quantities of cutlery and porcelain. Elaborate dinner services and canteens of cutlery with dishes and implements for every conceivable food developed as displays of wealth and taste. Conversation about the food, however, was frowned on.

Children in well-off families ate their meals separately from the adults, usually in the nursery. Plain food was considered appropriate for them, with simply cooked eggs, fish or meat, and an emphasis on "nursery puddings"—soft-textured sweet milk puddings with rice, tapioca, or semolina.

Suppers were often a part of evening entertainments, in both public establishments such as theatres and assembly rooms and in private houses. Food offered in private houses depended on the means of the establishment, but that served at balls appears to have been a cold collation of rich little treats such as salads of fish or meat coated in mayonnaise, cold ham or chicken, savory pastries, and desserts of ices and jellies, washed down with wines or cold soft drinks such as lemonade.

Eating Out

The idea of eating out also developed considerably during the nineteenth century, as the number and types of places to buy ready-prepared foods in grew. One feature of the urban Victorian landscape was the chophouse or eating house, offering an "ordinary," a fixed price, set meal of meat, greens, and potatoes or bread. Such a meal had been served at taverns and eating houses since the seventeenth century; by the nineteenth century it was the midday standby of clerks and other office workers. Another place to eat, for men who were wealthy, fashionable, or aristocratic, was the gentlemen's club. These had developed from the eighteenth-century coffeehouses to become establishments offering food, drink, sitting rooms, and temporary accommodation to their members. Clubs formed centers for particular interest groups, especially certain political or business affiliations. They were not open to women. Hotels also had dining rooms, providing meals to both residents and non-residents. Light refreshments such as fruit, cakes, ice creams, and some drinks could be taken in confectioners' shops.

The word "chef" (an abbreviation of *chef de cuisine*) to indicate a male cook in a professional kitchen came into English in the first half of the nineteenth century and has remained in use ever since. Another concept imported from France during the nineteenth century was that of the restaurant. Most cookery was considered low-status work, although a few chefs achieved wealth and fame: all of continental origin, they include Ude, Carême, Soyer, and Escoffier in the nineteenth century. The latter was responsible for reorganizing the logistics of the restaurant kitchen to give the *partie* system with its hierarchy of chefs.

By the end of the century, two types of establishments existed where respectable women could take meals in public. One was the restaurant: by 1900, London had several elegant restaurants, of which the Trocadero (opened on Piccadilly in 1896) was especially well known. Restaurant cooking depended on a modular system of cooking, which involved a number of standard preparations such as stocks and sauces used with fresh meat, fish, and vegetables to produce variety in a menu. The other was the tea room. Two chains, in particular, opened in the last decade of the nineteenth century: Lyons, and The ABC (which stood for Aerated Bread Company). As well as tea, these establishments sold other hot and cold non-alcoholic beverages, cakes, pastries, and light meals.

INTO THE TWENTIETH CENTURY

Many themes common in the nineteenth century continued into the first four decades of the twentieth. The population continued to rise, reaching about 43 million in 1950, 75 percent of whom lived in towns and cities. Poverty and under-nutrition continued to be a major issue, and getting sufficient food to meet energy requirements was a struggle for many people.[19] Up to the time of the First World War, many poor families lived on about one pound a week, which allowed only the most basic standard of living, and during the 1930s things were not much better. The discovery of vitamins and their role in preventing disease was a major theme relating to food during this time. Much of the essential work on this was done between about 1895 and 1935. It became particularly important during the Second World War, when the knowledge was applied to help make the best of limited food rations.

Food habits remained broadly similar to those of the previous century. Much food was still seasonal, although canned foods such as South African fruit of various types were now widely accepted. More convenience foods were introduced, some of North American origin, such as baked beans and breakfast cereals. But most early twentieth-century ingredients were ones that would have been recognizable and acceptable to generations beforehand. Most cookery continued a solid, conservative tradition of roasted, boiled, and stewed meat served with vegetables and potatoes. For those who wished to express wealth and taste, French cookery continued to be a reference point.

Changes in female employment affected some aspects of food preparation. Up until the Second World War, this affected upper- and middle-class kitchens, as poorer women left domestic service for offices and shops, and the mistress of the house had to learn how to cook. The daily round of meal patterns continued in the nineteenth-century pattern, with a tendency toward formality in dining.

NOTES

1. Paul Mellars, "Revising the Mesolithic at Starr Carr," *British Archaeology* 48 (October 1999), http://www.britarch.ac.uk.

2. Orkney Archaeological Trust, "Skara Brae," http://www.orkneydigs.org.uk.

3. Alan Bowman and David Thomas, "Forts and Military Life: Diets and Dining," Vindolanda Tablets Online, http://www.vindolanda.csad.ox.ac.uk. Oxford University.

4. Ann Hagen, *A Handbook of Anglo-Saxon Food: Processing and Consumption* (Hockwold-cum-Wilton, United Kingdom: Anglo-Saxon Books, 1992, revised 1998), and Ann Hagen, *A Second Handbook of Anglo-Saxon Food and Drink: Production and Distribution* (Hockwold-cum-Wilton, United Kingdom: Anglo-Saxon Books, 1995).

5. Hagen, *Second Handbook*, p. 23.

6. Roy Strong, *Feast: A History of Grand Eating* (London: Jonathan Cape, 2002).

7. C. Anne Wilson, "The Saracen Connection: Arab Cuisine and the Medieval West," in *The Wilder Shores of Gastronomy: 20 Years of the Best Food Writing from the Journal Petits Propos Culinaires*, ed. Alan Davidson with Helen Saberi (Berkeley: Ten Speed Press, 2002).

8. Constance B. Hieatt and Sharon Butler (eds.), *Curye on Inglysch: English Culinary Manuscripts of the Fourteenth Century (Including the Forme of Cury)* (New York: Oxford University Press for the Early English Text Society, 1985).

9. A. Gibson and T. Smout, "From Meat to Meal," in *Food, Diet, and Economic Change Past and Present*, ed. Catherine Geissler and Derek J. Oddy (Leicester, United Kingdom: Leicester University Press, 1993).

10. J. C. Drummond and Anne Wilbraham, *The Englishman's Food: Five Centuries of English Diet* (London: Pimlico, 1991).

11. Gilly Lehman, *The British Housewife: Cookery, Cookery Books, and Publishing in Eighteenth-Century Britain* (Totnes, United Kingdom: Prospect Books, 2003).

12. Ben Rogers, *Beef and Liberty: Roast Beef, John Bull, and the English Nation* (London: Chatto and Windus, 2002).

13. Lehman, *The British Housewife*.

14. Alan Davidson, *The Oxford Companion to Food* (New York: Oxford University Press, 1999).

15. Gibson and Smout, "From Meat to Meal."

16. Drummond and Wilbraham, *The Englishman's Food*.

17. Caroline Davidson, *A Woman's Work Is Never Done: A History of Housework in the British Isles, 1650–1950* (London: Chatton and Windus, 1982).

18. Margaret Forster, *Rich Desserts and Captain's Thins* (London: Vintage, 1996).

19. B. Seebolm Rowntree, *Poverty: A Study of Town Life* (London: Macmillan and Co., 1901); Maud Pember-Reeves, *Round about a Pound a Week: 1913* (London: Virago Books, republished 1999).

2

Major Foods and Ingredients

One thing that can safely be said about ingredients used in Britain at the start of the twenty-first century is that they are changing. Wheat, potatoes, and beef are still important, but the proportions of them in the diet have fallen while intakes of poultry meat, rice, and pasta have risen. Milk remains important, but whole milk has lost ground to skimmed and semi-skimmed milks since the 1970s. Foods almost unheard of 50 years ago, such as yogurt, are now an essential part of daily life, while others, such novelties as kiwi fruit, sun dried tomatoes, and cranberries, have had their moment and then become occasional purchases.

The influences of several generations are apparent in the purchase and use of ingredients. Those whose memories stretch back to before the Second World War might long for the "good plain cooking" from that time. The generation who grew up during rationing and austerity in the 1940s and early 1950s have clear memories of using every scrap of food and have not entirely relinquished this habit. Subsequent generations have become accustomed to abundance of supply and frequent changes in fashions. The most obvious influence in recent decades has been multiculturalism, as cuisines from all over the world are raided for ingredients and cooking techniques in what is sometimes described as the "ethnic pick-and-mix." The beginnings of this process could be seen in the 1950s, and it has accelerated over the years. The growth of vegetarianism, foreign travel, and the influence of chefs and writers inspired by non-British cuisines have also influenced the choices available, as have changes in retailing and an increasing media interest in food. Some chefs and writers have chosen to rework traditional dishes in the light of new approaches and ingredients, in a manner sometimes called "modern British" cookery.

The most important and accessible source for information on food consumption in Britain is the National Food Survey (NFS, 1940–2000) and its successor, the Expenditure and Food Survey.[1] The NFS began in 1940 when the U.K. government collected statistics on household food consumption in England, Scotland, and Wales. Initially undertaken to monitor the diet of the urban working classes (most at risk from poor nutrition at that time), it was extended in 1950 to cover a wide social spectrum, the results published annually. Statistics for Northern Ireland, however, have only been available since 1996. In 2001 the NFS and the related Family Expenditure Survey (which overlapped to some extent) merged to become the Expenditure and Food Survey. The data collected are based on diaries of food purchases kept by household members. The publications resulting from these surveys present overall consumption and expenditure figures; analysis by income, age, and region; nutritional analyses; and much supplementary information. It should be remembered that the figures relate only to food purchased for use in the home (although a little data on eating out is collected in another section), that many foods can be aggregated into one category, and that the results are given as averages. Although the analysis is inevitably broad, it does give clues about food use in certain groups, for instance the conservative element in taste in older age groups who tend to spend more on mutton and lamb and less on processed vegetables and vegetable products than younger age groups.[2]

Statistics in the NFS over the years are not always directly comparable because of changes in data collection and coding methods. They do not tell how the food was cooked and eaten, how it was divided between household members, how much was wasted (although a pilot study on this has been carried out), or how people felt about it and what they might have preferred. Information on purchases of confectionery and food and drink bought outside the home is absent (although recently questions on meals purchased outside the home have been included). But it does provide a broad picture of slowly changing tastes, of increase and decrease in the use of different foods, and hints at some of the issues behind these including cost, received notions about diet and health, changes in marketing of food, fashions, and food scares.

Market research provides supplementary information on food purchasing and eating habits. Several companies are active in this field, including Market Intelligence (Mintel), Taylor Nelson Sofres, Market & Opinion

Research International (MORI), and Keynote. Market research is conducted with the aims of particular clients in mind, and the amount available for free is limited, mostly to indexes of reports, summaries, and press releases. Academic research also provides some insights, though they tend to be diffuse.

Economics, in particular, were and remain important in food choices among U.K. consumers: price is crucial. The amount of money spent on food as a proportion of income, and in real terms, has fallen over the past 50 years. It has also declined as a proportion of household expenditure. Food and drink accounted for about 25 percent of consumers' total spending in 1976, but in 2001–02 was down to about 16 percent.[3]

Religion has relatively little bearing on overall food choice in the general population, although it is highly influential among minority religious groups, and practicing Jews, Muslims, Hindus, and Buddhists are all represented in major urban centers. This principally affects the use of meat, as does vegetarianism, which also has a substantial following among the British population. In 2001, about 4 percent of the U.K. population were vegetarian.[4]

CEREAL AND CEREAL PRODUCTS

Wheat, barley, rye, and oats can all be grown in Britain, though much is also imported. Of these, wheat is most used in baking, as the basis for bread, pastry, cakes, and biscuits, in convenience foods such as breakfast cereal and dried pasta, and in cooking. Rice has become increasingly important in recent years.

Flour

The word flour, unless otherwise specified, always means white wheat flour; other types—wholemeal (whole wheat), rye flour, oatmeal—are stipulated as necessary in recipes. White wheat flour is used in bread, cakes, pastry, biscuits, for thickening sauces, in pancakes, and for dredging food before frying. It is sold in two basic types for home baking: strong plain flour, which has a protein content of 13 to 14 percent, is suitable for bread making; and plain flour, which has a lower protein content, around 9 to 10 percent, and is used for pastry, batter, and cakes. The latter is also sold with added raising agents, as self-raising flour. Industrially milled white flour has an extraction rate of 70 percent (i.e., retains 70 percent of the original grain—the remaining 30 percent comprising the bran and the germ is used in other products). Wholemeal flour is 100 percent extraction, which means that the whole of the wheat berry including the bran and wheat germ is ground and nothing is taken away. It is mostly used for bread. The term "brown" in relation to flour and bread generally indicates something with a less than 100 percent extraction rate, but retaining some bran and wheat germ. Various bread, pizza, and cake mixes are also available, as are special mixes such as granary flour (a brown flour containing a small proportion of malted grains) and flours made from grains other than wheat. The long-term trend in purchasing flour for home use is downward: in the 1970s the NFS showed consumption of about 5.75 oz per head per week, but by 2000, this was down to under 2.5 oz. This is probably a reflection of a decline in home baking since the 1960s.

The fundamental importance of wheat flour in the diet led to the fortification of this with extra nutrients during the Second World War. Extraction rates were also raised so that only brown bread and flour were available. Once white bread became available again, fortification continued, and calcium, iron, and some B-vitamins are added. The only legal addition to wholemeal bread is ascorbic acid (vitamin C), which acts as an improver, making baking easier.

Bread

Bread commonly means white wheat bread in English usage, and the majority of the population purchases this. The white wheaten loaf has been a staple in the British diet from the mid-nineteenth century, and in places, for long before then. Its popularity is best illustrated by a complete reversal in consumption figures for brown and white bread in 1954–55, when the latter became available once again. In 1954, consumption of brown "war" bread stood at about 50 oz per head per week.[5] In 1955, when white bread and other foods were readily available once more, this had dropped to almost nothing, and white bread consumption was between 42 and 43 oz per head per week. Since then overall bread consumption has shown a long-term decline and by 2000, the average consumption was about 25.5 oz per person per week (including a small proportion of brown and wholemeal bread, and bread purchased in rolls and sandwiches). Wholemeal bread is generally a minority choice; consumption was negligible throughout the 1960s and 70s, but rose during the 1980s when dietary guidelines first emphasized fiber in the diet; it now averages just over 3 oz per person per week.

The British expect bread to be white, well risen, and soft, an expectation that developed in the mid-nineteenth century when cheap supplies of high-protein hard wheat from North America became available. Apart from this, the standard British loaf is oblong or square in section, thin-crusted, sold pre-sliced, and wrapped. It is a product of changes in commercial baking techniques that took place during the 1960s. Until then, traditional bulk fermentation methods were used, in which dough was allowed to rise in stages, interspersed with bursts of kneading. In 1961 a method known as the Chorleywood process was devised as a shorter commercial baking method. It uses more yeast but also allows a higher proportion of soft English wheat to be incorporated into the loaves. Ascorbic acid is added to the dough to shorten the process and a short period of very intensive mechanical working replaced the long fermentation time; it is also a continuous process that requires a shorter time and produces a cheaper loaf.

In 1984 the baking industry was also allowed to apply the Chorleywood process to wholemeal bread, using ascorbic acid as an oxidant, and by this time more than 70 percent of the bread produced in the United Kingdom was made by this method. Bread is generally purchased as pre-wrapped loaves made by plant bakeries or from supermarket counters, where prepared dough is finished by baking in-store to give an aroma of freshly baked bread.

During the last three decades, many breads based on southern European and Middle Eastern recipes have become fashionable. Although they do not challenge the market for sliced, wrapped loaves, they are important; some would say they are a reaction to the uniformity of the sliced white loaf. French style batons, croissants, and brioches have been widely available since the 1970s, although the quality is variable. In the 1980s and 1990s, breads of Italian inspiration, particularly focaccia and ciabatta (a tough-textured, open loaf, actually invented in the 1980s[6]), have become extremely popular. Middle Eastern style pita as well as nan (a flat, tear-shaped, puffy leavened bread) and chapatti (thin, circular, and unleavened), both of northern Indian origin, are also widely available.

Use of Bread

Bread and related products—rolls, buns, teacakes—are important as the basis for snacks and light meals. Sliced bread provides the basis for sandwiches (colloquially known as "sarnies" or "butties"), one of the principal convenience foods of twenty-first–century Britain. In the last two decades the sandwich, originally something prepared at home or to order in a shop or cafe, became an industry in its own right, mass-produced and pre-packaged for sale. Sliced bread is also important for making toast, usually thought of as breakfast food but in practice consumed at almost any time by people of all ages and social backgrounds. Toast is usually spread with butter or margarine and jam or marmalade and is also considered an essential support for scrambled or poached eggs, canned baked beans, or cheese.

Breadcrumbs are used in cookery as coatings for fried food and as ingredients in some dishes such as Christmas puddings. Other sweet dishes based on bread include bread pudding, stale bread mixed with spices, sugar, dried fruit, and suet, and bread-and-butter pudding, involving dried fruit, eggs, and milk. Bread sauce, a slow-cooked mixture of breadcrumbs, milk, onions, and spices is a traditional accompaniment to roast chicken or turkey.

Small Breads, Fancy Breads

Apart from the basic loaf, small bread rolls and buns are important. Plain rolls (baked in small, flat discs) are used to make sandwiches, to hold burgers, or served with soup, salads, and at dinner. Teacakes are lightly enriched with a little sugar, dried fruit, and lard or butter, then toasted and buttered as snacks. Hot cross buns are spiced and marked with a cross for Easter. There are numerous regional variations on yeasted rolls and buns, although these are fewer and less distinctive than they were before the Second World War. Sweet Danish pastries, also of variable quality, are widely available, as are doughnuts (which are either spherical, filled with jam, or ring-shaped).

Several breads leavened with baking powder rather than yeast are also made. A plain example is the soda bread of Irish tradition. Most other types are sweetened tea breads, a feature of home baking, mixed with dried fruit, nuts, or bananas, some fat, sugar, and egg; the result is between bread and cake. Another important item is the scone, lightly sweetened and enriched with fat and dried fruit, and leavened with baking powder. In texture and flavor, scones are similar to biscuits as made in North America.

Griddle Breads

Griddle breads include crumpets (round, about four inches across and an inch thick, with a spongy texture) and pikelets (which are similar, but thin-

Crumpets. Courtesy of the author.

ner). They are made from thick, yeast-leavened batters. Muffins are discs of bread dough with about the same dimensions as crumpets; they are also griddle-baked. Confusingly, cupcake-style muffins are increasingly available. Crumpets and pikelets are toasted and spread with butter before eating; muffins are toasted on the outside and then split and buttered, and all are produced in large quantities by commercial bakeries. Several small, distinctive griddle breads feature in the traditions of Wales and Scotland; local bakeries produce them, or they are homemade on a planc or girdle.

Pizza

Pizza was regarded as an exotic novelty in Britain in the 1960s, but is now widely available, both from restaurants and as a convenience food sold ready-to-heat by supermarkets. It is, to a lesser extent, made at home.

Pastry

The basic pastry of the British kitchen is shortcrust. It is made using half the quantity of fat (traditionally lard, although butter, margarine, vegetable fat, or any combination of these can be used) to flour by a method known as "rubbing in": the fat is cut in small pieces and rubbed through the flour with the fingers until a texture like fine breadcrumbs is achieved. A little water is added to make the mixture into a dough. This pastry, or variations of it, is used for sweet and savory pies, tarts, and flans. The word "pie" in the United Kingdom implies something with a double crust; "tart" can indicate a double- or single-crust product (more usually the latter). Flans have single crusts, although they, and tarts, may have strips of pastry laid across the filling for decoration. Richer versions of shortcrust pastry including sugar and eggs are sometimes made, mostly for dessert dishes. Puff pastry (the *pâte feuilletée* of French tradition, or an approximation) is used for topping meat pies, vol-au-vents, and in fine pastries from continental tradition; most people purchase it ready-made. Choux pastry is made but has limited applications, again mostly in items derived from French tradition, such as éclairs and profiteroles. Phyllo pastry has also been available since the early 1980s and is used for wrapping both savory and sweet fillings, and in Middle Eastern pastries such as baklava.

Two types of pastry are characteristically British: suet crust and hot-water crust. The former is flour, shredded-beef suet (the fat from around the kidneys, used unrendered), and water. It is made for wrapping fillings of meat or fruit, which are held in basins or cloths and cooked by steaming to make puddings, or dropped in small blobs onto the top of stews to make dumplings. Hot-water crust is made by heating water and lard until the water boils: this is then poured onto a premeasured quantity of flour and mixed. It makes a malleable pastry, which can be hand-molded while warm, and is used almost exclusively to make pork pies.

Cakes

Purchases of cakes, pastries, buns, scones, and tea cakes have risen slightly (although the long-term trend in purchases of these for home consumption is downward, compared to the immediate postwar years). In 2000, purchases of cakes and pastries stood at just over 3 oz per person per week. Cakes are essential for the British tea table, and they exist in wide variety. Rich fruitcake is regarded as an archetypal celebration food. It contains quantities of currants, raisins, sultanas, and candied fruit. The richest ones are made for weddings or Christmas, coated with layers of marzipan and icing (frosting). Plainer, undecorated versions are made for everyday use by both commercial and home bakers. Fruitcakes are now leavened with beaten egg and baking powder, but yeast-leavened ones, such as Cornish saffron cake, and some north country fruit loaves are still made. The link between bread and cakes is also preserved by lardy cake, made from bread dough folded and rolled with sugar, dried fruit, and lard in many southern counties of England.

The other main type of cake is based on the idea of a sponge cake. Fat-less sponges are whisked eggs and sugar with flour folded in at the last moment. Cake of this type is an essential ingredient for trifle, a celebratory dessert, and ready-made trifle sponges are available in packets. Others involve butter or margarine to make Victoria sandwiches or sponges (the classic formula requires two eggs, plus their weight in sugar, butter, and flour). Flavors added to these include chocolate, coffee, lemon, or orange, and the mixture is sometimes baked as individual buns (cupcakes). Sponge-cake mixtures baked in thin oblong sheets rolled around fillings of jam and cream are known as Swiss rolls. These, too, are often made at home. Plainer cakes involve fewer eggs and less fat and are based on rubbing the fat into flour or melting fat and sugar together as a technique. Ambitious bakers, professional and amateur, make elaborate cakes and gateaux of continental European inspiration.

Other Cereal Products

A wide variety of sweet biscuits (cookies) is also important in British food habits. Some are home-baked, but a huge variety of branded ones are also offered. They can be thin and crisp or thick and crumbly, given texture with wholemeal flour or oats, flavored with ginger or chocolate, nuts or dried fruit, sandwiched with jam or "cream" fillings (industrially produced from cheap fat and sugar). Biscuits are almost always offered with tea or coffee, eaten at any time as a snack, and are hugely popular. Their consumption has remained fairly steady throughout the late twentieth century and stood at about 5 oz per head per week in 2000. (Industry figures suggest biscuit consumption is higher, at around 6.7 oz per head per week.[7])

Categories of cereal food that have increased in consumption include breakfast cereals, pasta, and rice. That of breakfast cereal has risen from about 1.5 oz per person per week in the 1950s to about 5 oz at the present time. Increases in pasta and rice consumption are more recent. Both items are quickly cooked, can be infinitely varied with sauces, and fit in with a perceived time shortage in British life at present. Pasta has been used in various forms since at least the eighteenth century, but consumption was low until the late 1970s. In the mid-twentieth century it was available either as dried spaghetti or macaroni, or as canned spaghetti, macaroni, or ravioli in sauce. Since then the availability of dried pasta in different shapes and fresh pasta packaged to remain moist has expanded dramatically, as has the niche for ready-prepared pasta sauces, bottled or chilled. Figures for fresh and dried pasta (as opposed to canned) were first collected separately in 1998 and have risen 43 percent since then; in 2000, consumption stood at about 6 oz per head per week.

Rice consumption was just over 3 oz in 2000. Short-grain rice has been used for centuries to make milk puddings, and these remain popular. As an accompaniment to meat dishes, plain-boiled, long-grain rice also has a history of several centuries in Britain. It became much more important after the Second World War when Chinese and Indian food increased in popularity. Tastes for paella, risotto, Thai food, and sushi have made consumers more aware of different varieties of rice. Varieties commonly available include Basmati, Arborio, and Thai fragrant rice, as well as ordinary long- and short-grain rice, brown rice, and various convenience products such as boil-in-the-bag rice and flavored mixes.

Consumption of oats has remained steady, at about 0.5 oz per person per week. They are used either as oatmeal (coarse, medium, pinhead), oat flakes, or porridge oats. Porridge as flaked oats heated with water or milk is still made as a breakfast dish. It is widely eaten and popularly considered to have links with Scottish food traditions. Oats are also incorporated into ready-to-eat breakfast cereals, especially those of the muesli type, and into baking, especially in a type of rolled-oat biscuit known as flapjacks. Oatcakes are made in some places. The best known ones are Scottish oatcakes. They are small and dry, usually eaten with cheese or butter, although a northern tradition of baking floppy pancake-like oatcakes survives in the Potteries area of Staffordshire. Oats are also used in sweet biscuits, flapjacks, and in some traditional northern English gingerbreads known collectively as parkins: these vary from small, hard biscuit-like confections to thick, soft cakes.

Barley is most important in brewing and distilling as malt for beer and whiskey. It is little-used in baking: it produces a dense, grayish-brown loaf with a distinctive earthy flavor and crumbly texture, now considered undesirable, although once common in western parts of England and in Wales. A small amount of this grain is used as pearl barley (whole, husked grains), which is added to stews and soups such as Scotch broth, based on mutton stock with vegetables and dried peas.

Rye vanished from the English baking tradition in the early nineteenth century, and although a little rye bread is made once again, it is more likely to derive inspiration from Baltic or central European traditions than anything formerly made in Britain.

Other cereal products available include semolina, coarsely ground wheat that was a popular base for milk puddings from the early eighteenth century until the 1970s but has almost vanished from domestic use (although it remains an important ingredient in the biscuit industry). Couscous and bulghur (cracked wheat) are both available in the United Kingdom and used to a limited extent. Maize is little used. Cornflour (cornstarch) is used in small amounts as a convenient thickener for sweet and savory sauces. As modified starch, it has applications in numerous commercial mixes available on the British market, including items such as custard powder and gravy mix. Other maize derivatives such as corn syrups are also important in the baking industry. A fashion for Italian food has introduced polenta to the British market. Other starchy foods occasionally found include arrowroot (used as a thickener in the same way as cornflour but considered to give a better result), sago, and tapioca. Both sago and tapioca enjoyed considerable popularity from the early eighteenth century until the 1970s, mixed with milk and sugar for puddings, but are now rarely used. Although they are derived from roots, they are considered together with cereal products in British tradition.

PULSES

Dried peas and beans provided the mainstay of the diet of the poor for centuries. A few links with this tradition linger as pease pudding, a puree of dried peas eaten with bacon or ham, and mushy peas, very well-cooked dried peas served in fish-and-chip shops. Dried peas are also used in soups. Growing interest in vegetarianism and curiosity about food from southern Europe and further east led to a renewed interest in pulses in the 1970s. A wide range of canned and dried pulses is now available. Most popular are baked beans, usually eaten on toast. Chick peas are used in hummus (homemade or purchased), popularized through cheap package tours to the eastern Mediterranean; red kidney beans in chili con carne, an Anglicized version of the North American dish; and various types of split pea in dahl recipes, spiced dishes from India. Soybeans are less popular, although tofu is used to a limited extent. Soy derivatives are extremely important in the food industry.

MEAT

For centuries meat has been central to the British diet, eaten by all who could afford it. Attitudes about meat animals, to offal, and now to meat itself show changes, influenced by price, farming methods, and perceptions of health risks. During the eighteenth and nineteenth centuries, domestic animal breeds in Britain were bred to be very fat, a disadvantage when changes in fashion and nutritional thinking favored lean meat in the late twentieth century. Despite this, grass-fed beef from traditional breeds such as Aberdeen Angus, Hereford, Devon, or Sussex cattle is still sought after, and a marbling of fat through the lean is considered desirable.

In the English tradition, roasting has always been the method of choice for prime cuts. Gravy is an important part of the meal; this is not exactly a sauce but a concoction based on the sediment left by the meat in the roasting tin, lightly thickened with flour or cornstarch, and thinned with stock, wine, or water from cooking vegetables. Proprietary mixes such as Bisto are sold for making an approximation of this. It was a habit, not entirely extinct, for housewives to buy a large joint for Sunday, roast it and eat some of it hot, then use the rest of the meat up over the following few days, either cold with salad or made into pies, curries, and other dishes of cold meat cookery. This custom was recorded in a little jingle known as Vicarage Mutton: "Hot on Sunday, Cold on Monday, Hashed on Tuesday, Minced on Wednesday, Curried on Thursday, Broth on Friday, Cottage Pie Saturday," summing up one notion of household economy. Beef, pork, and chicken are now used extensively in stir-frying, and barbecues have become increasingly popular for cooking in summer.

Attitudes toward meat since the 1960s have become complex and ambivalent. Development of intensive farming in the 1960s made poultry relatively inexpensive and more popular, while retail prices for beef and lamb increased. Mutton (meat from sheep of one year or older), once a staple, became almost unobtainable. Scares and scandals connected to animal husbandry, food processing, and public health during the 1980s and 1990s affected public perceptions, especially about beef and eggs (see "Diet and Health"). Figures for carcass meat consumption collected by the NFS have fallen, but this may be partly due to changes in retail practice: butchers increasingly sell boned meat, as opposed to the bone-in joints which were common up until the 1980s, and for several years in the 1990s, beef was only sold off the bone, a public health measure introduced while the possible links between bovine spongiform encephalopathy (BSE) and Creutzfeldt-Jakob Disease (CJD) were investigated further.

Information about nutrition and health also altered attitudes. Red meats—beef, lamb, and pork, once considered valuable sources of protein, iron, and B-vitamins are now perceived as high in saturated fat, while poultry is perceived as lean, and large numbers of consumers claim to eat little or no red meat. Products such as pies and traditional British sausages have also gained a fatty, unhealthy image (although this perception has not affected continental sausages). Meat products generally have developed to utilize the animal as much as possible, disguising sometimes dubious ingredients. The idea of eating meat at all is increasingly questioned by vegetarians.

Beef

There has been a long-term decline in consumption of beef and veal. It began to fall from a post-austerity high of almost 10.5 oz per person per week in the late 1950s. As prices rose, meat consumption generally leveled off, but a Sunday dinner of roast beef was still the benchmark of a proper meal, and a grilled steak a treat. Consumption remained fairly steady at around 8 oz per person per week in the 1970s and 1980s, but had fallen again to under 5.5 oz in 1990. Following the publication of possible links between BSE and CJD, consumption of beef fell back in March 1996, but recovered rapidly later in the year. However, in 2000, consumption was just under 4.5 oz. Despite all the debate over beef and health during the past few years, roast beef remains a celebratory dish for Sunday dinners. Favorite cuts for roasting are sirloin and ribs. Accompaniments include horseradish sauce, mustard, and Yorkshire pudding. Steaks are usually cut from the fillet, sirloin, and rump, although T-bone steaks and rib eye are sometimes available. Boiled salt beef, once a staple, has become a rarity. Thin slices of beef are sometimes made into "olives," rolls of beef wrapped round a stuffing.

The flavor of beef is generally considered better if the meat is roasted on the bone, but easier to carve if it is boned and rolled. Most cooks have their own preferred method; starting the meat in a hot oven and then lowering the temperature to complete cooking is common. The degree of cooking is also a matter of taste: very rare beef is not uncommon, but nor is meat that is extremely well cooked. Moist methods for cooking large pieces of beef, such as pot-roasting and braising seem to be less popular. Steaks and chops are usually cooked fairly plainly, grilled or fried, although marinades of herbs and other flavorings, or sauces based on wine or cream are sometimes used with them.

Beef stews are also popular. At their most basic, these are made by frying onions, then cubed beef (usually dredged with a little flour), and incorporating liquid (water, beer, wine, or stock) and seasonings, followed by slow cooking for two or three hours. Similar mixtures are also used in pies, usually baked in a dish under a puff pastry topping (popular all over the United Kingdom, but especially in Scotland). Pies are also filled with a mixture of cubed beef and ox kidney (oysters, kidneys, mushrooms, or ale are also added, according to the means and tastes of the maker). The same ingredients are also wrapped in suet crust and steamed to make steak and kidney pudding, one of the best indigenous dishes of English cookery. Cornish pasties have a filling of potato, onion, turnip, and beef enfolded in pastry, then baked. Coarser cuts formerly used for braising, such as brisket, now go into minced beef. This is used in large quantities to make meatloaves, burgers, lasagna, and pies. Cottage or shepherd's pie, a dish of minced meat cooked with onion and seasonings baked under a topping mashed potato, can be made with either fresh or leftover cooked meat. Logic suggests lamb in shepherd's pie and any other meat in cottage pie, but ingredients and names seem to depend on the cook. Two dishes based on beef mince that were adopted during the 1960s are spaghetti bolognaise, a sauce loosely based on an Italian *ragù* but served with spaghetti (because no other form of pasta was available at that time) and chili con carne, eaten with rice.

Beef offal is now difficult to obtain; this is partly due to changes in taste, and partly because of legislation relating to BSE. Apart from the use of kidneys in pies and puddings, oxtail provides the base for a classic English soup, and tripe and cowheel were popular in the industrial towns of the midlands and the north, although the taste for them is rapidly vanishing. Suet, beef fat from the kidneys, was once very important for cookery, especially for suet pastry, dumplings, and pudding such as Christmas (plum) pudding, but is of declining importance. Beef dripping (the fat rendered during cooking) has long been an important cooking medium and is still favored for frying fish and chips in parts of England, especially Yorkshire.

Veal

Veal is little used in the British kitchen (many veal calves are exported to continental Europe), and there are few traditional recipes for it: veal and ham pie, to eat cold, is one. Veal is important in dishes derived from French and Italian cookery. Calf's liver is considered a delicacy and became part of the modern British repertoire of the 1980s and 1990s, cooked with bacon or a sauce sharpened with citrus fruit. Veal stock is also important in the classical restaurant tradition, and calf's feet were boiled to provide gelatinous stocks for raised pies.

Lamb and Mutton

Consumption of lamb and mutton rose in the 1950s reaching a high of about 7 oz per head per week, but fell back to about 5.5 oz by 1970 and in 2000 stood at just under 2 oz. Their consumption also tends to be concentrated among older age groups, although they are important to certain ethnic minorities, especially those from Islamic countries.

Sheep meat is traditionally divided by the age of the animal into lamb (applied to animals up to about eight to ten months old) and mutton (more than a year; the best is considered to come from animals between three and five years old). Mutton is now only available from a few specialist butchers, a change which has only come about since the 1950s. In the past it was an everyday meat, served roasted with onion sauce or red currant jelly, or boiled with caper sauce.

Lamb tends to be relatively expensive as the ratio of lean meat to offal is relatively low. Roast lamb is regarded as something of a treat; shoulder, leg, best end of neck, and loin cuts are all prepared this way. Mint sauce (finely chopped mint mixed with vinegar and sugar) is often served with it. Breast of lamb, which tends to be fibrous and fatty, is traditionally stuffed and used as a cheap roast. Loin is also sliced to give chops and best end of neck to give cutlets, both used for grilling. Neck of lamb is the basis for lamb stews, including Irish stew (potato, onion, carrot, and lamb simmered slowly together with water or stock) and Lancashire hotpot (a similar combination, baked in the oven, in which the top layer of sliced potatoes are allowed to brown before serving). Scotch broth is a soup often based on mutton stock. Lamb offal, especially liver and kidneys, is still much liked among older age groups, grilled, fried, or cooked in sauce,

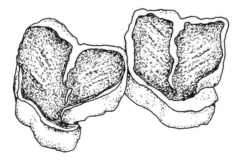

Mutton chops.

and haggis, the national dish of Scotland, is also made from lamb offal. Mutton or lamb is also used to fill raised pies in Scotland.

Both beef and lamb are used in dishes such as curries (a word which indicates dishes inspired by foods of the Indian subcontinent but adapted to British ingredients and tastes), kofta, and kebabs by ethnic minorities, especially Muslims from the Indian subcontinent. An older version of curry is still sometimes encountered. This developed during the period of British rule in India, when curry powders were sent back to Britain and cooks tried to imitate East Indian dishes without the full range of other ingredients. It eventually became a dish based on the meat from a cold joint cooked with onions, apples, sultanas, and curry powder. The newer tradition includes more authentic dishes such as rogan josh, colored red with chilis and paprika, as well as ones that have developed in Indian restaurants in Britain. Lamb is also used in dishes of Middle Eastern origin.

Pork

Consumption of fresh pork also rose after the restraints of rationing were lifted in the mid-1950s and has fluctuated, rising to a high of about 4 oz per head per week in 1980, but falling back again in the 1990s; in 2000 it was just under 2 oz. Preserved pork is also important, although consumption of this has also fallen. In 1970, it stood at about 6.5 oz per head per week, but has gradually declined to 4 oz.

Fresh pork cookery includes the inevitable roasts, cooked so that the skin (usually left on) crisps in the oven to produce crackling. Leg and loin are considered the best cuts. Shoulder and belly are also used; very slow roasting has recently become a popular method for these, with the meat cooked at a low temperature for a long time. Applesauce and sage and onion stuffing are usually served with roast pork. Loin is also cut into chops that are grilled or fried. Pork stews are unusual in the British tradition; those that are made are generally of continental European origin. The meat is also cut in small pieces for stir-fries and other dishes of Chinese inspiration.

Several pork products are made. One is the pork pie, small and cylindrical with a crust of hot-water pastry filled with chopped pork and topped up with jellied stock after baking. Fresh sausages are made from lean and fat pork, ground with seasonings and rusk or breadcrumbs. Grilled or fried, they are served for breakfast or as part of a bigger meal, often accompanied by mashed potato as sausages and mash, a favorite both in the home and as a pub meal.

Ham and Bacon

Salted pig meat has long been an essential in the British diet. An old English saying is that "every part of the pig can be eaten, except the eyes and the squeak." Many country families kept a pig to provide bacon and ham for themselves. It was killed in winter, some of the fresh meat or offal being given to relatives or neighbors with the knowledge that the favor would shortly be returned. The family pig tradition persisted in most rural communities until the Second World War, but it declined in the 1950s and has now almost vanished.

Traditionally, pigs yielded two basic products, hams and bacon. Hams are the hind legs, salted and dried, sometimes smoked (gammon is a leg cured as part of a whole side and then cut off afterward). Several regional ham cures are recorded; the most famous (and debased) is the York cure. All use salt and a little saltpeter; sugar, treacle, beer, and spices are sometimes added. In British tradition, hams were always soaked and cooked before eating, usually cold with mustard and salad, or in sandwiches. Bacon is made by salting a flitch, the side of the animal excluding the hind leg; it can also be smoked. For much of the twentieth century, grocers recognized a preference for smoked bacon in southern England and green (unsmoked) bacon in the north. Grilled or fried bacon is essential for a traditional British breakfast and in bacon butties or bacon sarnies, sandwiches eaten as snacks or quick meals. It is also used in game cookery to bard (wrap) birds such as partridges, providing extra fat during cooking. Bacon boiled in a piece is used in much the same way as ham, but considered more homely. Bacon joints and ham are sometimes roasted, the skin scored and stuck with cloves, or glazed with brown sugar and fruit juice. Both bacon and ham are used to add flavor in cooking stews and soups, bacon fat is used for frying, and stock made from the bones traditionally provides a base for dried pea soup. The British also have a long appreciation of pork products from continental Europe, including prosciutto-type hams, dried sausages of the salami type, Bologna sausages, and various pâtés. Pancetta has also become a fashionable ingredient in recent years.

Methods for coping with the large quantities of offal and trimmings that pig killing brought are still used by traditional butchers. Blood is mixed with oats or barley groats, chopped fat and seasonings, and packed into casings as black puddings. Fat and some meat is used with cereal to make a white version of these. The pluck—liver, lungs, and heart—is chopped, mixed with lean meat and used in various dishes, including faggots (little rissoles wrapped in caul, the fatty membrane that lines the stomach cavity); haslet, a type of meatloaf; or savory ducks, another type of meatball made of oddments of fresh and cured pork, chopped together. Traditionally the head of the pig is boiled and the meat picked off, mixed with the gelatinous cooking liquid, and allowed to set as brawn. The intestines are cleaned and used as sausage casings, or cooked and sold as chitterlings in parts of southern England. Pigs were also valued for lard. Although less important than formerly, it is still used for frying, pastry making, and as an ingredient of lardy cakes.

Meat products is a category under which the NFS includes offal, sausages, pies, corned beef, cooked meat, and convenience meats. They are as popular as fresh meat; in 2000, their consumption stood at about 12 oz per head per week. Within this category, consumption of offal has tended to decline, and traditional British pies and sausages have received adverse publicity relating to fat content and other issues, but various frozen meat products, pâtés, and continental sausages have become more popular, although they are not necessarily any lower in fat.

Chicken, Poultry, and Game

The increase in consumption of poultry, especially chicken, is one of the strongest trends in postwar British food habits. From being an expensive special occasion meat, the development of factory farming turned it into something cheap and ubiquitous. Throughout most of the 1950s, consumption remained level, at around 1 oz per head per week, but then began a rapid and continued rise, to about 5 oz per head per week in 1970, and had reached about 7.5 oz by 2000.

Before the 1960s, chicken was roasted, served with bread sauce, a dish for special days. Coronation chicken, a dish of cold chicken in a lightly curried sauce, was devised for the coronation of Queen Elizabeth II in 1953. Older birds were made into stews, curries, or boiled for stocks and soups. The intensive farming of broiler chickens in the late 1950s altered this. It provided a supply of young, tender chickens, which, while they lacked the flavor of free-range birds, were significantly cheaper. Chicken became a basic ingredient, roasted, grilled, or incorporated into all kinds of dishes, often of French, Italian, or eastern origin. It is especially popular in the curries developed by Indian restaurants since the 1950s. Of these, chicken tikka masala is among the nation's favorite dishes. More recently, Thai chicken dishes, especially green curry, have enjoyed a vogue. Numerous convenience foods use chicken as a base, from supermarket versions of Indian take-aways to reconstituted, crumbed, deep-fried, heat-and-serve nuggets for the children's market. Cold roast chicken is also used in salads and sandwiches (often with avocado or bacon).

Turkey was once confined to the Christmas roast, but became more of an all-year-round item in the 1980s as portions, escalopes, turkey mince, and various convenience products developed. Guinea fowl and quail are also farmed, but consumption is small. Duck is available all year round, usually eaten roasted with a garnish of oranges or in dishes of Chinese inspiration, such as stir-fries and crispy roasted duck. Goose is produced mostly for the Christmas market and has become more popular in recent years, but remains a minority taste. Efforts have been made to introduce novel meats to the British market, including kangaroo, crocodile, and ostrich (some of which is farmed in Britain), but these remain unusual.

Game has always been perceived as high status food. Historically, few wild animals were legally available to the poor. Rabbits were an exception, plentiful, cheap, and widely eaten in the countryside until they were hit by disease in the 1950s; they are still consumed, but in much smaller quantities. Venison, from three species of deer—roe, fallow, and red—was the most sought-after meat. It was usually roasted or cooked in a stew with wine. Deer farming was developed in the late twentieth century using fallow deer, and farmed venison is relatively inexpensive and easy to obtain. Hares have also long been an object of the chase; traditional English methods for them include a meaty soup and jugged hare (cooked with red wine and redcurrant jelly, the sauce finished with the blood of the animal).

Feathered game includes pheasants, partridges, grouse, wild duck, woodcock (all seasonal, confined to the autumn and winter), and pigeon, available all year round. Pheasants are most common. Grouse is an expensive delicacy, raised for shooting on managed heather moorlands of western and northern Britain. This bird opens the shooting season on the "glorious twelfth" of August. As with most other meat in the British kitchen, roasting is regarded as the method of first choice for prime birds, although older ones are cooked in sauces and stews. Traditional accompaniments for roast game include game chips (thinly sliced, crisp-fried potatoes), fried crumbs (breadcrumbs fried in butter until golden), brussels sprouts cooked with chestnuts, redcurrant or rowan berry jelly, and wine-based sauces. Game of all types, cut off the bone, is used to fill raised pies on the same principle as the pork pie.

FISH AND FISH PRODUCTS

Fish has been secondary to meat in the British diet for most of the twentieth century. Fresh fish consumption remained steady through the 1950s and 1960s at about 5.5 oz per head per week, and then declined gradually to about 1.6 oz. This was partly offset by a rise in consumption of fish products, especially convenience items such as fish fingers (frozen breaded fish sticks) and other frozen fish, prepared fish, and fish products, and consumption of these stood at about 5 oz in 2000.

The use of fish in the twentieth century has been affected by changes in taste, overfishing, and the development of fish farming for some species, processes which continue. A basic division is made in the British kitchen between whitefish (low in fat) and oily fish, such as herring. A habit of eating fish on a Friday persisted until recently, despite the fact that Britain had been a Protestant country since the sixteenth century.

At the end of the nineteenth century, large quantities of whitefish (mostly cod and haddock) were landed, much of it used in fish-and-chip shops. Other sea fish included plaice, whiting, sole, halibut, and turbot. Fatty fish, especially herrings, were important, caught in huge quantities in the North Sea, and salted and smoked for preservation. Shellfish such as lobsters and crabs were also much used, but the oyster, once eaten in vast quantities by rich and poor alike, had succumbed to disease and pollution; it has never fully recovered from this and remains expensive. Freshwater fish became scarcer as many rivers were too polluted for them to survive. Trout and salmon were principally available to those with fishing rights on unpolluted rivers.

At the end of the twentieth century, this position was largely reversed. Catches of deep-sea fish fell dramatically, as cod species were overfished. Attempts to source whitefish from the southern hemisphere have been only partially successful. Herrings have virtually disappeared from the North Sea. Trout and salmon, however, have both been farmed successfully and both are now cheap. Salmon, rather like chicken, has undergone a complete reversal in fortune, from being an expensive rarity in the early twentieth century, to becoming cheap and widely available. Some whitefish, especially sea bass, are farmed.

Culinary use of whitefish has altered little over the past hundred years. Basic methods include grilling or shallow frying (in which case the fish is often dredged with breadcrumbs). Batter is generally used to coat fish for deep fat frying (the method universally used by commercial fish fryers of fish and chips). More complex dishes include poaching or baking fish in milk and using the cooking liquor in white sauce, usually flavored with chopped parsley or grated cheese. "Fish pie," in English cookery of the mid-twentieth century meant whitefish in sauce with a topping of mashed potato, although it may now indicate a richer dish with several types of fish and a puff pastry top. Dover sole, turbot, and halibut, always expensive, are usually grilled or served in a sauce. Whitefish, especially haddock, is also salted and smoked. They are cooked by poaching in milk, and served alone or with a poached egg, used in omelettes or in kedgeree, a rice dish of Anglo-Indian origin.

Treatment of oily fish varies. Herrings are dipped in oatmeal and then grilled or fried, or left plain and cooked in a mixture of vinegar and water to make soused herring. This has lost popularity, although raw herring pickled in vinegar, known as rollmops, are still produced. Fresh mackerel is usually grilled or baked, sometimes with Indian spice mixtures. Sauces for cheap oily fish are rare in British cookery, although mustard sauce is sometimes used with herring and gooseberry sauce is recorded for mackerel.

Preserved herring were of exceptional importance in the past. White herring (salted) or red herring (heavily salted and smoked, until they took on a golden-red appearance) were cheap food for the poor, but by the early twentieth century their consumption in Britain had declined, as refrigeration allowed both the transport of fresh fish and the development of lighter cures. One of these is the kipper, lightly salted, cold smoked herrings produced at several locations on the coast. These are usually cooked by jugging (placing the fish head down in a deep pot, pouring boiling water over, and leaving for a few minutes until the flesh has cooked in the heat), or grilling. They are

Kippers. Courtesy of the author.

eaten for breakfast or as a light evening meal. Another herring cure popular during the nineteenth and early twentieth centuries, but now rare, was the Yarmouth bloater (from Great Yarmouth on the east coast); these are salted and lightly smoked without gutting, giving a characteristic slightly gamey flavor. They were grilled or made into bloater paste for spreading on toast. Since the 1960s, mackerel has become available in smoked fillets, eaten alone or used as a basis for pastes.

Wild salmon fished from unpolluted rivers, mostly in Scotland, is a luxury. Since the 1970s, salmon farming has developed in sea lochs on the west coast of Scotland, and salmon has become ubiquitous and relatively cheap. Grilling, poaching, shallow frying, or baking are among the methods used for fillets or steaks of salmon. The classic British method for dealing with the whole fish is to poach it in water or a court-bouillon, remove the skin, and cover the cooled fish with slices of cucumber in imitation of scales. A range of recipes and ready meals based vaguely on French inspiration or using east Indian spices have developed to make the best of farmed fish. Other freshwater fish are little used except by keen fishermen, the exception being farmed trout, which is readily available, and cooked by grilling or frying.

Methods for salting, drying, and smoking salmon were well developed in nineteenth-century Britain. These altered as taste swung away from the heavily preserved foods. Most smoked salmon is now lightly salted in mixtures that may include sugar, spices, or whiskey, then drained and cold-smoked. These are more akin to methods introduced in the late nineteenth century by Jewish immigrants from eastern Europe than to the traditional heavy cures of the past. Smoked salmon, thinly sliced, is used for sandwiches and canapés, and in numerous hors d'oeuvres and snacks such as scrambled eggs with smoked salmon. Trout is hot-smoked. Another smoked fish product that has become popular since the 1970s is cod roe, mostly in the form of ready-made taramasalata (based on a Greek method for a paste of dried fish roe).

Canned fish commonly used includes salmon and tuna (in sandwiches and salads) and sardines and pilchards, often eaten with salad or as snacks on toast. Anchovies, canned or salted, are used as garnishes, in salads, or ingredients in dishes of Mediterranean origin. Two products popular in the nineteenth century, anchovy sauce and Gentleman's Relish (an anchovy paste) can still be bought; the former is used for flavoring meat and fish dishes, the latter is spread thinly on buttered toast. Frozen fish products are more important in volume, if less venerable in tradition; they were introduced after the Second World War and now account for about

20 percent of total fish consumption. Most important are fish fingers (oblong sticks of white fish coated in bread crumbs). Fish cakes made from cooked whitefish or salmon mixed with mashed potatoes are also popular, both in the home and in restaurants.

Of shellfish, oysters are usually eaten raw with lemon juice. They are farmed at a few locations around the coast, but are rarely introduced into meat dishes as they were in the past, as they add significantly to the cost. Mussels are farmed and often made into dishes of the French *moules marinere* type, or cooked with Thai flavorings. Cockles are dredged at various places on the British coast. Scallops are expensive, and tend to be restaurant food. Crabs and lobsters are both much liked, usually boiled and dressed with mayonnaise, although soup and gratin recipes can be found in classic cookery books, and during the late twentieth century they have also found their way into dishes of Italian and Southeast Asian inspiration. Prawns (shrimp) fished from the north Atlantic are used in salads, sandwiches, added to other fish dishes, sauces, sprinkled over pizzas, curried, or stir-fried. They are usually sold cooked and peeled of their shells. Prawn cocktail (shrimp cocktail) became a cliché of restaurant food during the 1970s. Their smaller relatives, brown shrimps, are fished on sandy shores, boiled, and eaten as snacks or potted, preserved under spiced butter, and eaten with toast.

A few fish species remain minority tastes: whelks, once a street food for the poor, are a declining taste. The appetite for eels, either stewed or jellied (boiled and allowed to cool in a gelatinous mass), has also declined, and they are no longer a feature of the working-class food of London. On the other hand, squid, once unheard of in Britain, is now routinely dipped in batter and deep fried in restaurants and fish-and-chip shops. Fresh tuna and shark are also available.

EGGS

Eggs were strictly rationed during the Second World War, working out at less than one per person per week, augmented by dried egg. Once rationing was lifted, consumption rose to about four per head per week in the mid 1950s. It remained at this level until the 1970s, but has dropped steadily since and is now just less than two per person per week. Decline in cooked breakfasts and in home baking probably account for this. Food scares also affected egg use in the late 1980s.

Eggs in some form, usually fried, are regarded as an essential component of a full breakfast. Other cooking methods include boiling, poaching in hot water or over steam (in the mid-twentieth century, every well-equipped kitchen had a special pan for this), or scrambling. More complex egg dishes are few. Omelettes are made as light lunch or supper dishes; one that might be counted as characteristically British is omelette Arnold Bennet, with a filling of smoked haddock and cheese. Another is Scotch woodcock, scrambled eggs on toast topped with preserved anchovy fillets. Other egg-based items found sometimes in snack bars and pubs are Scotch eggs (hard-boiled eggs wrapped in sausage meat and deep fried) and pickled eggs, hard-boiled eggs preserved in vinegar. Eggs are essential for binding stuffings, for coating food so that breadcrumbs adhere, and for glazing pastry to give a golden finish.

Milk and eggs make egg custard, used to fill little tarts (pies) flavored with nutmeg, and a thinner, pouring custard used as a dessert sauce and in ice cream (although powder mix is often used as a substitute). Custard also forms a layer in trifle, a dessert involving wine-soaked sponge and whipped cream. Crème brûlée is a rich mixture of cream and egg yolks with caramelized sugar. Eggs are essential for lemon curd or lemon cheese, a preserve used for spreading on bread or filling little tarts. Savory egg custards were little known in traditional British cookery, with the exception of bacon and egg pie, a double-crust pie filled with bacon pieces, beaten eggs, and a little milk. During the 1970s, the concept of quiche was introduced from France and has now become commonplace, especially as vegetarian food, filled with tomatoes, broccoli, spinach, and other ingredients.

Beaten eggs are important in cake making. The range varies from sponges based on whisked eggs and sugar through fat-enriched sponges to rich fruitcakes, some of which require large numbers of eggs. They are also incorporated into puddings; in several the yolks added to the filling and the whites whisked to meringue and piled on top; examples are lemon meringue pie, queen of puddings (with a custard base), and apple amber, based on apple puree. The inheritance from French cookery includes meringues, mousses, souflées, and sauces such as hollandaise and mayonnaise, which are all used but recognized as belonging essentially to the haute cuisine tradition. The English tradition included a salad sauce based on hard-boiled egg yolks with oil and seasonings, although this is rarely used and purchased bottled salad cream has taken its place.

Batter, apart from coating food for frying, is used for a few other dishes. The usual recipe for pancakes in Britain is based on a runny batter, producing thin pancakes. Small thick pancakes are associated with Welsh and Scottish cookery, and sometimes known as Scotch or Welsh pancakes; the recipes vary slightly, and the proportion of flour to eggs and milk is always much higher than in thin pancakes. Batter mixtures were also used for boiled puddings, but these have died out, though a baked version remains important as Yorkshire pudding; this is served with roast meat, especially beef. It is also used to make a dish called toad-in-the-hole, which consists of meat, usually sausages, baked in a layer of batter in the oven.

DAIRY PRODUCTS

Milk and milk products have long been important in the British diet, and a substantial dairy industry exists. Liquid milk is collected from farms on which it is produced and pasteurized before being bottled or packed for sale. It is sold as whole milk (full fat, about 3.5% fat), skimmed, (half-fat, about 1.5–1.8%) and fully skimmed (virtually fat free, 0.5%). In many urban areas, milk and some other dairy products are delivered to the doorstep in the early morning.

Early in the twentieth century, fresh milk was mostly used by the better off, the poor relying on tinned milk in tea and for infant feeding. Consumption of fresh liquid milk was actively promoted for good nutrition, including provision of milk for pupils in elementary schools. In 1940, consumption was about 3 pints (20 fl oz = 1 pint) per person per week, rising to almost 5 pints in the early 1950s. This level was maintained until the mid 1970s, but has subsequently declined. During this period, "milk" indicated whole milk with richer types (4–5% fat) from Channel Island cattle forming a small but significant proportion. In the early 1980s, concerns about fat intake led to the promotion of skimmed and semi-skimmed milks. In 2000, consumption was about 3 pints per head per week, but only about 18 fl oz was whole milk, the remainder being semi-skimmed and a small proportion of fully skimmed milk.

For much of the twentieth century, cow's milk was used to the exclusion of all other types. In the 1980s the application of an EU quota system to milk production increased interest in sheep and goat milk and their products. Cow's milk, however, still provides the bulk of the liquid milk and the basis of most milk products.

Milk is used as a drink poured over breakfast cereal and eaten with porridge. It is also used for cooking, especially as a basis for white sauce. Dried powdered milk, ultra high temperature (UHT) treated and sterilized milks, and tinned evaporated and condensed milks are all available, mostly regarded as kitchen standbys, although condensed milk, cooked in the tin until fudge-like, is an essential ingredient of banoffee pie, a dessert popular in the 1980s and 1990s. It is also used with custard powder (a similar product with different flavorings is known as blancmange, and was very popular until the 1970s). For much of the twentieth century, milk went into puddings with sugar and rice, semolina, sago, and tapioca (known to generations of schoolchildren as "frogspawn"); these are now regarded as old-fashioned. Junket is a dessert of milk curdled with rennet, now considered old-fashioned.

Cream has always been seen as a luxury and is essential to many desserts. It is sold as half cream (12% fat), single (18% fat), whipping (35%), and double (48%). It is used to enrich savory and sweet sauces and desserts, poured over fruit, sweet puddings, and cakes, and, as whipped cream, decorates many sweet dishes. Sour cream is little used, although *crème fraiche* (a French cultured cream product with a slight sourness) has recently become popular. Clotted cream is very thick and rich with a fat content of 55 to 60 percent. This is a traditional product in the southwest of England, made by heating cream very slowly until it forms a thick crust on the surface, and acquires a rich, slightly nutty taste. It is served with scones or rolls and jam for cream teas and sometimes is added to desserts or ice cream. Concerns over saturated fat in the diet during the 1980s led to the development of various cream substitutes containing a proportion of vegetable oil. Either pouring cream or whipped cream is offered with many dessert dishes, or used to decorate cakes and other sweet foods. Whipped cream is an ingredient of sweet mousses, fools (mixtures of crushed fruit and cream), and syllabubs (cream, wine, sugar, and fruit juice).

Branded, sweetened, and fruit-flavored yogurt was introduced in the 1960s (yogurt was virtually unknown at that time), and consumption has grown steadily since then, to about five fluid ounces per head per week. Plain yogurt is available in low fat (less than 1% fat), full fat (3–4% fat), and richer Greek-style yogurt (10%). Flavored yogurts also come in a range of fat contents, including relatively high-fat, luxury types. Flavors are constantly changing to maintain consumer interest in new products. Yogurt is seen primarily as a convenience food, eaten alone or with fruit as breakfast, dessert, or a snack, although plain yogurt is used in sauces for meat and vegetable dishes of Middle Eastern or East Indian origin. *Fromage frais* (literally "fresh cheese," a cultured dairy product of French origin with a soft, creamy texture) was introduced in the 1980s and shares a similar image to yogurt—a convenient, healthy milk product. *Fromage frais* occupies roughly the same niche as yogurt.

Purchasing figures for ice cream are also given in the NFS, although these only represent that for consumption the home. These have more than doubled since the 1970s, and now are about four fluid ounces per person per week. The products included under this heading are diffuse, including from ice lollies (Popsicles), sorbets, frozen yogurt, luxury or premium ice creams based on eggs, cream and fruit, and wholly industrial products formulated from fats from various sources, by-products of the dairy industry, plus flavorings.

Cheese

There are nine hard, pressed, or semihard cheese types made from cow's milk known as territorials, named for the areas with which they are historically associated: Cheddar, Gloucester (single and double), Cheshire, Lancashire, Wensleydale, Derby, Leicester, Caerphilly, and Stilton, which is a blue-vein cheese. Except for Stilton, whose manufacture has been restricted by law to the east Midlands since 1912, these cheeses are made in most creameries across the country. Cheese consumption has been relatively steady since the 1950s, at 3–4 oz per head per week, although recently continental varieties have been favored at the expense of traditional British territorials.

During the twentieth century, cheese quality was affected by a decline in farm cheese making and the need to maximize food security in the Second World War. Cheese became a uniform product with a dry, hard texture, developed for long keeping. As a reaction to this, to the imposition of milk quotas, and to farm diversification in the 1970s, cheese making became a focus of creativity for artisan food producers. They revived old recipes, used ones of continental origin, or resumed using more traditional methods for territorial types. Sheep's and goat's milk is also used by these "new wave" cheese makers. Although most of these artisans work on a small scale, their products have been important in both raising the profile of British food abroad and at home.

Much cheese, especially the Cheddar type, is imported, especially from Canada and New Zealand, and numerous fine cheeses of continental origin are also available. Parmesan is imported and used for cooking.

Cheese is often eaten with bread or biscuits (crackers) as a snack, or as a course in a large meal, usually served at the end. A few cooked cheese dishes are traditional. The most basic is grilled cheese on toast, a common snack or light lunch. Rarebits, or rabbits, are more complicated versions of this, involving mustard or other spices, milk, cream, wine, or beer; dishes of this type are often known as Welsh rarebit. Cheese is occasionally used in soups, notably Stilton, used with celery or cauliflower. Grated cheese is much used on pasta, for flavoring sauces, omelettes, souflées, and to a lesser extent pastries such as cheese straws, and as an ingredient in salads. Grilled goat's cheese became a fashionable dish in the 1980s.

Soft cheese is also made. Cream cheese has a soft smooth texture, developed from a method of draining sour milk in a cloth; cottage cheese has a lumpy texture, a slightly acid taste, and is not a traditional product. These are used in sandwiches and salads, and in cheesecakes (baked or gelatin-set types), which are much liked but were introduced only in the 1970s. The traditional British type of cheesecake is curd tart, made from milk coagulated with rennet (or some acid or mineral salts), mixed with currants, sugar, butter, and eggs, and baked in a pastry shell.

FATS AND OILS

British taste is generally for salted butter, which has long been a staple food. By law, it must contain about 81 percent butterfat from milk; the rest is water, a little protein, lactose, and salts. Salted butter contains about 2 percent salt. Much is imported from continental Europe and New Zealand. Unsalted butter, and butters of continental origin with a lactic flavor, are also available.

Consumption of butter is affected by price, a preoccupation with slimming, and worries about health. All these have worked in favor of margarine. Initially, price considerations were more important. When margarine was introduced in the mid-nineteenth century, it was a cheaper product that imitated butter closely (to the extent that, legally, margarine must contain the same proportion of fat to water as butter does and is enriched with vitamins to provide similar nutrition). Since the price was lower, it immediately took part of the market share away from butter and has retained it. The share fluctuated depending on the price of butter. After 1954, butter consumption rose sharply and remained at about 6 oz per person per week into the 1970s. Since then butter consumption has fallen to about 1.5 oz per person per week, as perceptions moved away from the idea of it being a luxury food to emphasize the high saturated fat and cholesterol content. In the 1970s, spreadable soft margarines developed their own market niche, followed by polyunsaturated margarines and then low-fat spreads, both trading on a healthier image. Consumption of margarine, which had remained at about 2 oz per person per week through the 1960s and 1970s rose and stabilized at between 3 oz and 4 oz per person per week in the 1990s. Figures for low-fat spreads, which became available in the 1990s, show that these occupy a substantial share of the margarine market. Name-branded products based on vegetable oils mixed with dairy-derived products are marketed, with claims that they combine the flavor of butter with the health benefits of margarine.

Butter was always favored for spreading on bread and toast, although many people now choose a polyunsaturated margarine on health grounds. It also has numerous culinary applications, used as a base for sauces, dotted over fish or chicken before baking, as a medium for shallow frying, to dress boiled vegetables, and as a fat for cakes and pastries. It provides the essential flavor in fine cakes, biscuits, and shortbread (a mixture of flour, butter, and sugar, lightly baked).

The British kitchen also relied heavily on animal fats until recently. Lard, dripping (rendered beef fat), and suet were all used in cookery. Their consumption remained steady at about 1.5 oz per head (mostly lard) from the end of rationing until the 1980s, and then began to decline; in 2000, it was down to about 0.3 oz. These fats are heavily saturated. The interest in health, combined with an obsession with body weight, a tendency toward vegetarianism, and changes in fashion toward dishes of Mediterranean and eastern origin has led to a decline in their use.

Butter and lard, or lard alone, were important for pastry and in baking (small amounts are often required in regional bread recipes). Dripping, from beef, was also used in plain pastry and cakes and sometimes on bread or toast. Both lard and dripping were used for frying. Suet is essential in traditional pudding and dumpling recipes. However, solid white vegetable fat for pastry making and a vegetarian substitute for suet are both available, showing that items made with them still have symbolic importance.

Use of vegetable oils in cookery and for salads is a recent development. Until the 1960s olive oil was a minority taste, available from a few Italian delicatessens or pharmacists (it was used for treating earache). Throughout the 1960s and 1970s, consumption of vegetable oils was about a tablespoon per person per week; since then it has risen, although it is still only about 2.5 fl oz. Interest in oils, however, has increased, and the British have come to recognize olive oil in different qualities (cold-pressed, extra-virgin, etc.) and from different countries (Spain, Italy, and Greece). It is a fashionable ingredient in salads and salad dressings, in vegetable dishes from southern Europe, and for dressing pasta. Corn, sunflower, peanut, and colza oil are all used, mostly as frying oils. Perceived health benefits have influenced their popularity. Sesame oil is used to flavor Chinese recipes; walnut and hazelnut oil in salad dressings, and almond oil in baking and confectionery.

VEGETABLES

Potatoes

The most important vegetable in the British diet is the potato. In the 1950s, consumption was about 55 oz of fresh potatoes per person per week. This has gradually fallen, and in 2000 it was down to about 25 oz. Since the 1980s, though, consumption of processed potatoes and potato products has risen, and in 2000 it was about 7 oz per person per week. Reliance on the potato as a staple was a development of the early nineteenth century in most places, although it goes back further in Ireland. Meat and potatoes were an essential component of main meals for most of the twentieth century.

Several areas are recognized as being good for producing potatoes: fine early potatoes are traditional crops in the island of Jersey, Cornwall, and Pembroke, while main crop potatoes are grown in many places throughout the United Kingdom. Potatoes, especially new ones, are also imported. New potatoes are generally boiled with a sprig of mint and served with butter; early potatoes from Jersey, Jersey Royals, are considered a delicacy and priced accordingly. Main crop, or old, potatoes are usually peeled before boiling or steaming (after which they may be mashed with butter and milk). Jacket potatoes are baked potatoes, cooked in their skins in the oven. Roast potatoes (peeled and baked in hot fat) are an essential part of a traditional Sunday meal. Deep-fried chips (french fries) are extremely popular, prepared from scratch at home, bought as frozen chips ready for frying, or baking as oven chips, a more convenient and lower fat alternative. Together with fish, chips have been an important fast food in Britain since the late nineteenth century. Shallow frying can be used to cook raw potatoes, but is also popular as a method of reheating left-over cooked potato. Mashed potato and fried cooked cabbage is known as bubble-and-squeak; in Irish tradition, champ is a mixture of mashed potato and spring onions (scallions), and the Scots make clapshot (potato and turnip mashed together). Potatoes are also used in hotpots and Irish stew. Dishes of French inspiration such as gratins are well liked.

Mashed potato is used in baking, mixed with flour and fat to make potato scones, which are griddle baked and eaten with butter. These are traditional to Lancashire, Scotland, and Ireland. Potato products are also extremely popular, from crisps (chips), and other potato-based snacks to numerous pre-prepared heat-and-serve items. Another, more old-fashioned potato convenience product is dehydrated powdered potatoes, for reconstituting as mashed potato.

Other Vegetables

Until the 1980s, fresh vegetables were mostly seasonal. Green vegetables, mostly belonging to the cabbage family, were most important, and consumption of these remained steady at about 10 oz per person per week until the mid 1980s; since then it has declined a little, to about 8 oz. The consumption of other fresh vegetables also stood at about 10 oz but began to rise in the 1980s, and is now about 17 oz per person per week. This category includes all kinds of root vegetables, tomatoes, and numerous items that were novel and exotic on introduction but are now quite commonplace. Supermarkets have played a large part in the development of a trade for exotic vegetables. A complex chain involving production in third-world countries, air freight, and retail competition have all encouraged this. Salad leaves and herbs are also imported. However, the number of varieties within the traditional home-produced vegetables such as cabbages and potatoes has diminished, as seed merchants and growers concentrate on a few strains best suited to the handling techniques and cosmetic appearance demanded by supermarkets. Both fruits and vegetables are the focus of much attention, as their protective qualities in the diet are currently the subject of a government campaign to encourage higher consumption.

The British are stereotyped as unimaginative cooks when it comes to vegetables, notorious for serving them overcooked by unimaginative methods (usually boiled) and without a dressing, except perhaps butter. Things have improved—overcooking is less common—but plainly boiled vegetables are still the norm with roast meat and stews, generally carrots or a member of the cabbage family, probably the most important category after potatoes. Hard white cabbages, loose-headed dark green spring cabbage, and Savoy, with crinkly green leaves, are popular. They are usually boiled for a short time. White cabbage is also used in salads, particularly coleslaw. Red cabbages are stewed gently with vinegar and apples or pickled in vinegar (traditionally served with Lancashire hotpot). Brussels sprouts are winter food, usually served for Christmas dinner, although many people profess dislike for them. Broccoli is available all year round, as is cauliflower; the latter is often served with cheese sauce. Cauliflower is also an ingredient of piccalilli, a mixed vegetable pickle with mustard and turmeric. Curly kale, loose-headed with a strong flavor, is a traditional pot herb for soups, especially in Scotland. The cabbage family also provided sea kale (*Crambe maritima*), a rare but distinctively English vegetable—the only one which they can be said to have truly developed for cultivation. The plant is native to shingle seashores, but in the nineteenth century, a method for blanching was devised. It is now uncommon, cultivated on a very small scale.

Summer vegetables include green peas, which are often cooked with mint. They are grown on a large scale for commercial freezing. Mange-tout peas became common in the 1980s. Several varieties of green beans are available. Together with mange-tout peas and baby sweetcorn, these are often grown in countries such as Chile or Zimbabwe and air-freighted to Britain. Asparagus is another much-imported vegetable. The season for home-produced asparagus runs from late March to early June. It has always been a luxury, boiled and served with melted butter or hollandaise sauce, in soup, or, recently, roasted with olive oil. Spinach is also used, either simply boiled, in soup, or as an ingredient of Mediterranean or eastern dishes. Celery is chopped and added to the basic mix for stews, used in soup, or gratinéed in cheese sauce. Raw, it is chopped and added to salads, or eaten with cheese. Vegetable marrows, once a challenge for gardeners to see who could grow the largest, have lost ground to their relative, the courgette (zucchini).

Onions are important for flavoring. Large ones are sliced or chopped for almost all meat stews and pies and pasties. They are also sliced and used raw in salads, and occasionally cooked alone (usually by baking) as a vegetable dish. Very small onions are grown for pickling in vinegar; shallots are used for pickling, and also for a more subtle onion flavor, especially in dishes derived from French cookery. Garlic, like olive oil, has gone from being much disliked in the 1950s to an essential ingredient. It is now a basic flavoring for numerous meat and vegetable dishes.

Root vegetables are winter staples. Carrots, turnips, and parsnips are often added to soups or beef stews, or used alone as vegetables. Parsnips have a distinctive sweet flavor and can be boiled and mashed or oven-roasted, and curried parsnip soup is a modern British classic. Beetroot are boiled or baked and used either hot as a vegetable or cold in salads; they are also pickled in vinegar.

Since the 1960s, various exotic vegetables have become commonplace. These include peppers (capsicum and chili types), aubergines (eggplants), fennel, sweet potatoes, yams, courgettes, and various squashes. Aubergines, sweet peppers, and courgettes came onto the market during the 1960s for newly fashionable recipes such as ratatouille, peperonata, and baba ganoush. Fashions for curries and other eastern dishes have led to an increase in the availability of hot peppers. Avocados also arrived in Britain during the 1960s, usually as a restaurant hors d'oeuvre, with vinaigrette dressing or prawns in mayonnaise; they are now popular in salads, sandwiches, and guacamole. Sweetcorn is also used as a vegetable, eaten as corn on the cob, baby corn, or canned sweetcorn. Greengrocers serving various ethnic groups stock numerous other vegetables almost unknown outside their communities.

Unusual vegetables that have a long history in the British kitchen include cardoons (members of the thistle family, eaten for their stems), globe artichokes (which are boiled and eaten with butter or oil and vinegar, much as in southern Europe), and Jerusalem artichokes (which are generally made into soups or eaten as gratins). In some coastal areas, samphire, a plant of salt marshes with fleshy green stems, is used, and a few communities also gather seaweed, especially in south Wales.

Many species of edible fungi grow in Britain. Field mushrooms (*Agaricus campestris*) were the species most commonly used in the past, fried or cooked in cream and served on toast, made into soups, or added to meat dishes. A cultivated variety is now widely sold. All other species were referred to as toadstools and were usually regarded as poisonous, an attitude which has not completely disappeared. An interest in Japanese food has led to cultivation of oyster mushrooms and shitake, and Italian recipes have raised awareness of porcini (*Boletus* sp).

Salads include lettuce, cucumber, tomatoes, spring onions (scallions), and radishes. For a summer meal, all these items would be prepared separately, and arranged in a bowl with halved hard boiled eggs or ham, tinned fish, or cold meat. Lettuce leaves and other salad vegetables are also used as a garnish for cold dishes, as is mustard and cress, sprouted seeds grown in punnets. Another traditional salad is watercress, grown in clean spring water in southern England. It has a peppery flavor and is also used for a creamy soup. In the last 20 years, numerous varieties of lettuce and other salad leaves have become popular in Britain. Some, like mizuna, have been introduced from other cultures; others, such as rocket, were popular in the early modern period, but vanished, only to be reintroduced as exotic novelties in the 1990s. Tomatoes are baked, grilled, or fried for breakfast. Skinned, pipped, and chopped fresh tomatoes are also added to sauces, fish, and meat dishes, although these recipes are usually of French or Italian origin. Preserved tomatoes in various forms—sieved and bot-

Watercress. Courtesy of the author.

tled, tinned or pureed—are also much used in both meat and vegetarian cookery, and sun-dried tomatoes were a fad of the mid-1990s. Both ripe and green tomatoes are made into sweet-sour spiced chutneys, products of the Anglo-Indian tradition.

The last 20 years also brought renewed interest in fresh herbs. In the early twentieth century, the British depended on fresh parsley, mint, sage, thyme and chives, mixed dried herbs, and horseradish root grated raw into cream as a pungent accompaniment for roast beef. A revival of interest in herbs generally, plus the interest in French, Italian, and Middle Eastern cookery that began in the postwar period, stimulated a taste for novel flavors. Fresh herbs gradually became easier to buy; basil and green coriander (cilantro) became especially popular. The taste for the latter, which has little history of use in Britain, was stimulated by the interest in East Indian and Thai cookery, and it is now easily available.

Vegetable Products

This includes a miscellaneous selection of dehydrated, canned, and frozen products, including dehydrated potato and green peas, canned peas, and frozen vegetables. Canned tomatoes and related products—purees and sauces—are much used in meat and vegetable dishes generally. Other canned vegetables are generally regarded as standbys, although canned sweetcorn often finds its way into everything from pizza to salads. Frozen vegetables other than potatoes include peas, beans, sprouts, and spinach. Vegetable soups are also available in dehydrated, canned, and fresh (chilled and packed under aseptic conditions). Onions, cabbage, gherkins, and beetroot are all sold pickled in vinegar. The growing interest in vegetarianism has also led to interest in ready-to-heat vegetable dishes, the development of texturized vegetable protein (a soy-based meat substitute), and mycoprotein, sold under the brand name Quorn.

FRUIT

Marketing of fruit, like that of vegetables, has been affected by developments in preserving and transport and by fashion. In the 1970s, total fresh fruit consumption was about 18 oz per head per week; by 2000, it was about 26 oz. Consumption of fruit products has also risen; in the 1970s, it was about 7 oz a week (mostly canned and dried fruit), and in 2000 was around 11 oz. Much of this was accounted for by a rise in purchases of fruit juices, which was almost negligible in the 1970s but had reached about 10 fl oz per head by 2000. Fruit products apart from juices include canned fruits (berries, pineapple, tropical fruits), frozen products (mostly berries), pie fillings, and bottled sauces based on various fruits such as mango (statistics on preserves are categorized separately by the NFS). Until the Second World War, much orchard fruit and all berries were homegrown and production was closely associated with specific areas of the country, mostly in southeastern England. Since 1980, fruit consumption has recently been affected by the same factors as vegetable consumption—campaigns to encourage the consumer to eat healthily, including more fruit in the diet, and wider availability of more varieties, encouraged by air freight and retail competition. Many southern European members of the European Union export fruit to the United Kingdom.

Apples

Apples are the quintessential British fruit. Consumption has fluctuated around 7 oz per person per week since the 1970s, although recent trends have been slightly downward. Only a few of the numerous apple varieties known in the United Kingdom reach the market, as commercial growers concentrate on a handful of popular, easily handled varieties for super-markets (although a wider range are available from growers). Recently, older and more unusual apples have been given more publicity for their history and local interest.[8] Some varieties have been known for centuries, but most were developed in the last 150 years. The late nineteenth century was a time of especial interest among both commercial and amateur growers. Recently, many ancient orchards containing unusual varieties have been destroyed, although Apple Day in late October has been insti-tuted to raise awareness of apples in particular and orchards in general. Apples are also imported from France, Spain, New Zealand, South Africa, Chile, Canada, and the United States.

For the British market, apples are classed as early, mid-season, or late, and subdivided into eaters or cookers. Homegrown early apples open the English apple season in mid-August, but do not keep well; late keepers ex-tend it into the spring of the following year. Pippins, fine-flavored, late-keeping varieties, are a particular specialty, intended as dessert fruit. The best known variety is Cox's Orange Pippin. Such apples are generally eaten raw, as dessert, snacks, or in salads, although they can be cooked, and some people prefer their flavor and texture in tarts and other dishes.

The concept of apples specially for cooking is a largely British one. Cookers are generally acid and need sugar. The best known variety is Bramley's Seedling (colloquially known as Bramleys). These collapse to an acid, fluffy purée. Few other cooking varieties are now marketed except locally. There are numerous cooked apple desserts. Favorites include apple pie, baked apples, apple dumplings wrapped in pastry, and basic stewed ap-ples (applesauce). Crumble (fruit topped with a mixture of flour, sugar, and butter) is also made. Grated apple is sometimes added to other sweet dishes, such as Christmas mincemeat. Apple preserves include jellies, es-pecially one made with small acid crab apples, which has a deep orange-red color, and apple butter, apple purée cooked with sugar until it will set in a stiff mixture. Apples are also used in a sweet-sour spiced chutney, made for eating with cheese or cold meat.

Drinks made from apple are important. They are pressed for juice, gen-erally blended, but some is marketed as single variety apple juices. Certain varieties are grown for cider (always a fermented drink in Britain). This is important in the west midlands, the southwest, and East Anglia, and is made both by small farmers and large companies. Cider is used mostly as a drink, although it is also added to meat dishes, especially those with pork or chicken. A very small amount is distilled to make apple brandy, and some is made into cider vinegar.

Pears

Pears are grown for both eating and cooking. Consumption is relatively low, at just under 2 oz per person per week in 2000. Production of home-grown pears has declined, as they are at their northernmost limit of culti-vation (at least for commercial purposes). Many are now imported from the same countries that provide apples. Varieties typically include Williams, Comice, and, more recently, Portuguese Rocha pears. The dis-tinction between cooking and eating pears is not as marked as that found in apples, but the Conference variety is often used as a culinary pear. Methods for cooking pears include poaching in sugar syrup or red wine with spices; they can also be used in many apple recipes, and are some-times baked in tarts with an almond filling. They are pickled in vinegar and sugar. Pears, too, are crushed for their juice, which is fermented to make a drink called perry. Production of this is limited, with one company producing it as a branded drink and a smaller amount produced mostly on farms in the west Midlands.

Stone Fruit

Consumption of stone fruit (plums, cherries, peaches, and apricots) has risen since the 1970s, when it was only about 0.3 oz per person per week, to about 2 oz per person per week in 2000. This must be in part due to in-creased imports of these fruits, which are now available all year round.

Many varieties of plums are traditional to the United Kingdom, but few reach the market. Those that do include Victoria, Majorie's Seedling, Czar, Early Rivers, and greengages, mostly grown in the south and east. Out-of-season fresh plums are imported from several other countries. Plums are eaten as dessert fruit, raw, or stewed, or made into puddings such as pies and crumbles. Plum jams and chutneys are also made. Damsons are a small, acid, juicy plum. Unusually, they are grown over much of England and Wales but reach the market in relatively small quantities. They grow easily, are tolerant of wet and cold, and were often planted in gardens as well as commercial orchards (a proportion of the crop was actually used for dyeing cloth). Culinary uses are similar to those for other plums; traditionally they are also pickled in spiced vinegar.

Cherries are cultivated in the southeasternmost corner of England, but many are imported. They are mostly consumed fresh. Fruit such as apri-cots, peaches, and nectarines are all imported from southern Europe in summer and from Chile, South Africa, or the United States. They are mostly eaten fresh, or used in tarts, compotes, or ice creams. Pears, peaches, and apricots are also sold canned, eaten either alone with custard or cream or used in trifles and other puddings.

Soft Fruit

Strawberries, raspberries, redcurrants, blackcurrants, and gooseberries are all popular in summer; strawberries, and to a lesser extent, raspberries, are imported during the winter. Since the 1970s, consumption has fluctuated at just under an ounce per head per week. Although imports have made these fruits more widely available, most consumption must be during the summer months when locally produced supplies are available in many parts of the country.

Strawberries and raspberries are both eaten with cream and sugar for dessert. Eton mess is a dessert made from whipped cream, crushed meringues, and crushed strawberries. Raspberries are also popular with meringues. Both fruits are used to make jams, which are served with scones and cream, spread on bread and toast, used for filling cakes, and used in sweet dishes and desserts generally. Red and blackcurrants are grown commercially in limited quantities. They are mixed with strawberries and raspberries in summer desserts, especially summer pudding. Currants are made into jellies and jams, and blackcurrants are grown for commercial use in cordials and confectionery. Gooseberries (*Ribes grossularia*, small, hard, acid, yellow, green, or reddish berries) grow easily

Gooseberries.

and are common in gardens everywhere from Cornwall to the Shetland Islands. A few are cultivated to produce raw dessert gooseberries; otherwise, they are stewed or made into pies and crumbles. Another dish commonly made with gooseberries, although other soft fruit are also used, is a fool: this is a mixture of pureed fruit (cooked and sweetened if necessary) mixed with custard or whipped cream.

Other berries that are cultivated on a limited scale include tayberries, boysenberries, blueberries, and blackberries; they are all used in similar ways to those mentioned. Blackberries are also collected from the wild, as are bilberries (*Vaccinium myrtillum*), related to blueberries. Cranberries were little known until the 1980s, when they became increasingly popular in sauce for turkey, as juice, and as an ingredient in baking. Rhubarb is usually classed with soft fruit, although it is actually the stem of the plant that is eaten. It is always cooked—stewed or made into puddings. Pink forced rhubarb is a delicacy only available in the late winter and early spring.

Citrus Fruit

Citrus species are very important in British culinary traditions and have been imported fresh or preserved for centuries. Always imported, they were virtually unobtainable during the Second World War, but once they became available again, oranges returned to being one of the three most popular fruits available in the United Kingdom (together with apples and bananas). Since the 1970s, the consumption of oranges has remained at about 7 oz per person per week, and consumption of other citrus fruits (including satsumas, clementines, and grapefruit) has risen slightly from about 1.5 oz to about 2.5 oz in 2000. Most of these fruits are consumed raw, as dessert fruit, or, in the case of grapefruit, for breakfast or as appetizers. Limes are also imported and used for flavoring meat dishes, in desserts, and to garnish drinks, especially gin and tonic. Citrus fruit, especially oranges and to a lesser extent grapefruit, are important for juicing.

Fresh citrus fruit are also used in cooking. Lemons have numerous applications in savory and sweet dishes. Their zest is added to stuffings and used to flavor meat; the juice is squeezed over fish and chicken, and lemon wedges are used as a garnish. Juice and zest are used in sweet dishes such as lemon meringue pie, lemon curd, syllabub, mousses, and ice creams and are added to many other desserts for flavor. The use of oranges in savory dishes is more limited, the classic example being duck a l'orange. Bitter oranges are grown in southern Europe for the British market and imported for making orange marmalade, found on most breakfast tables. This is made both at home and by several large companies.

Bananas

Bananas were first imported in the early twentieth century. By the time of the Second World War, they were extremely popular and much missed during rationing. In the 1970s, their consumption was about 3 oz per head per week, but this began to increase in the 1990s, and is now about 7 oz. They are mostly eaten raw, but also used as an ingredient in making banana cakes, baked for a dessert dish, and sliced into custard as a children's pudding.

Other Fruit and Tropical Fruit

Grapes and melons are mostly imported from southern Europe, and mostly eaten as dessert fruit. Consumption of grapes has also risen, from about 0.3 oz per week in the 1970s to about 1.6 oz in 2000. Tropical fruit imports include pineapples, mangoes, papayas, and more unusual items such as lychees. Pineapples have been known in Britain since the late seventeenth century, when a few were imported as novelties from South America. Throughout the eighteenth and early nineteenth centuries, they were grown by the wealthy in special hothouses, a sign of status which they have never quite lost. Tinned pineapple came onto the market in the mid-to-late nineteenth century; imported fresh pineapples became available with the development of refrigerated transport. They are mostly eaten as dessert fruit, although tinned pineapple is sometimes combined with sponge cake in puddings or served with ham; candied pineapple is used in confectionery and occasionally as an ingredient in fruitcakes. Mangoes, papayas, and other tropical fruit were expensive luxuries until the 1990s, when increasingly large quantities were imported by air. Kiwi fruit (Chinese gooseberries) were heavily promoted in the early 1980s, when they were used as a garnish for almost everything over a period of two or three years. Few specific dishes exist for the use of these fruits, although any or all of them may be put into fruit salad or ices, and some, such as mangoes, have become popular as sauces and ingredients for other dishes. Mangoes also form the basis for imported mango chutney, eaten with curries. Melon is often served as an hors d'oeuvre; traditionally, sugar and powdered ginger is offered with it, although port or a sauce made of some other fruit is more likely to be offered now.

THE STORE CUPBOARD

Dried Fruit and Nuts

British baking relies heavily on dried fruit: sultanas, raisins and currants (all forms of dried grape), prunes, and dates. Candied orange, lemon, and citron peel are imported and are an essential store cupboard item for anyone who makes fruitcakes, traditional enriched breads, plum puddings, and mince pies. Currants are used alone as a filling for pastry to make currant slices and several traditional pastry-wrapped cakes of regional origin such as Eccles cakes and Banbury cakes. Dates are also used with pastry, or in date and walnut cakes. Currants, raisins, and sultanas are added to teacakes and the plainer types of fruitcake. Christmas mincemeat is made from currants, raisins, sultanas, candied peel, sugar, and suet all chopped together, and the same mixture goes into Christmas puddings. All dried fruits are used in traditional steamed suet or sponge puddings. Prunes, stewed and served with custard, were a much disliked standby of twentieth-century nursery food and school meals, and are now used to a limited extent in desserts. Candied cherries and angelica are also used; cherries go into cakes and both items are used to decorate sweet dishes and cakes.

Nuts are also essential in baking. They are imported from many countries: hazelnuts, almonds, walnuts, Brazil nuts, pistachios, pine nuts, and peanuts are all available (pecans and macadamias are more unusual). Almonds are the most important. Ground, they are used in marzipan, important for decorating cakes, in the cakes themselves, in macaroons (little biscuits), and in other sweet dishes. Almonds are also used for decoration, whole, flaked or chopped, raw or toasted. The flavor of bitter almonds, historically very important in British food, now comes from almond essence: only sweet almonds are imported because of worries over the potential toxicity of bitter ones. Pistachio nuts are traditionally used chopped as a garnish for sweet dishes. Nuts generally are used to flavor confectionery and biscuits.

Roasted and salted nuts, especially peanuts and cashews, are favorite snacks. Peanut butter is used as a spread and an ingredient in dishes such as satay. Nuts are added to salads, dishes from Middle Eastern and East Indian traditions, and in nut roast or nut rissoles for vegetarian cookery. Chestnuts are also used. Roasted and eaten with salt, they are a traditional street food; cooked and shelled they go in stuffings for game and poultry, garnishes, and purées for sweet dishes. Dessicated coconut (the flesh, shredded and dried) became popular as an ingredient for sweet dishes in the late nineteenth century and is still used to flavor cakes and make coconut macaroons. In the last 20 years, coconut milk or cream, either made from fresh coconut or pre-prepared, have become popular as ingredients for curries.

Sweeteners and Preserves

A sweet tooth was a British characteristic for the nineteenth and most of the twentieth centuries. Sugar provided cheap energy; it sweetened tea and coffee, fruit dishes, and desserts, was added to cakes, used in preserving, and sucked and chewed in confectionery of all sorts. Cane sugar is imported from tropical countries, but a proportion of U.K. sugar is refined from homegrown sugar beets. It was severely rationed during the Second World War; consumption subsequently rose to more than a pound per head per week in the mid-1950s. Since then, sugar purchases have declined to a point where they are lower than wartime levels, at about 3.75 oz per person per week. Drinks are taken unsweetened, and home baking and preserving has declined, although sugar is sprinkled on breakfast cereals. However, while use of packet sugar has declined, there are many sources of hidden sugar among purchased foods, and sugar consumption from processed food and confectionery keeps the overall intake much higher. Of the 2.25 million tons of sugar consumed in the United Kingdom every year, about 75 percent goes into industrially produced food, notably soft drinks and confectionery.[9]

White (refined) sugar is available as granulated, caster (equivalent to superfine), and icing (confectioner's) sugar; brown (unrefined) as Demerara, soft light brown, soft dark brown, and muscavado sugar. Jam sugar (with large crystals) and sugar with added pectin are sold for preserving. Granulated white sugar is used unless another type is specified. It is used for baking, preserving, and on the table (although Demerara is usually offered with coffee). Caster sugar is used when a finer crystal size is required, especially in baking. Icing sugar is used for frostings, and decorating desserts. Unrefined sugars are used in traditional cakes and biscuits, especially gingerbreads. Black treacle and golden syrup are by-products of sugar refining; black treacle, similar in taste and color to molasses is used in some fruitcakes and gingerbreads. Golden syrup is pale gold, the residue from the final stage of refining. It is also used in cakes and gingerbreads, as a sauce for sponge puddings (by lining the basin with it before the sponge mixture is added) and in treacle tart, a mixture of syrup, breadcrumbs, and lemon in pie crust.

Preserves include many types of jams and jellies. Figures on honey, golden syrup, and treacle are also collected under this heading for the NFS. Their consumption has shown a slow decline for the last 25 years, from about 2.5 oz per head per week in the 1970s to just under 1.5 oz in 2000.

In the late nineteenth and early twentieth centuries, cheap industrially produced jams were poverty foods that helped to make the large quantities of bread in the diet palatable. Changes in eating habits have affected their consumption: nowadays less bread is eaten, so less jam is required to spread on it. Home preserving is also less important than it was. Honey is used as a spread on bread and toast, and a little in baking and in sweet dishes such as Scottish cranachan (cream, honey, and toasted oatmeal). It is also used with lemon or whiskey to soothe sore throats. Large amounts of honey are imported and sold either as runny or set without any further qualification. Home-produced honey is also widely available; heather honey from the moorlands of the southwest, Wales, Northern England, and Scotland is one of the most prized types. Golden syrup was also used as a spread, and with treacle it is an ingredient for home baking, especially in gingerbreads.

Artificial sweeteners and sugar substitutes are available, but their use in the home is relatively small, principally for sweetening tea and coffee, or in households with diabetics. They are, however, used in many low-calorie purchased foods.

Vinegar

Vinegar is an essential souring agent and pickling liquid. Strongly flavored, brown malt vinegar is used to pickle onions and other vegetables, eggs, and in chutneys and is routinely sprinkled over chips, fried fish, and other foods. Where the flavor and color are undesirable, colorless spirit vinegar is used instead. Wine vinegar, red or white, or cider vinegar is used for salad dressings and dishes in which a gentler flavor is required. Balsamic vinegar, sherry, and rice wine vinegar are all available.

Flavoring Agents and Spices

Spices include cinnamon, nutmeg, mace, ginger, vanilla, saffron, allspice, cloves, curry powder, chili, turmeric, mustard, juniper, white pepper, and black pepper. Some of these have a very long history of use.

Cinnamon, nutmeg, cloves, and allspice are primarily regarded as sweet spices, mostly used in baking; together they compromise mixed spice for buns and cakes. Nutmeg is grated over egg custards and junket. Cloves are often added to apple dishes. There is a residual tradition of baking with saffron in the southwest. Vanilla is used for flavoring sugar, custards, and ice creams; pods, essences, and substitutes are sold. Ginger is also used in sweet baking, especially in biscuits, gingerbreads, and parkin. It is also sold as stem ginger, candied ginger preserved in thick syrup: this is chopped and added to cakes and gingerbreads.

On the savory side, pepper is ubiquitous in sauces and stews. Nutmeg is used in béchamel sauce, mace in potting recipes, and cloves in bread sauce. Pickling spice for vegetables is a mixture of black and white peppercorns, mustard seeds, and whole dried chilies. Allspice and pepper occur in spicing mixtures for salting meat. Turmeric is used in picalilli and dishes of East Indian origin. A little chili powder and mustard are often added to cheese dishes such as cheese straws or rarebits. Few items classified as spices grow successfully in the British climate, and mustard is the only one that has been grown commercially in recent times. English mustard is ground to a fine, pungent yellow flour and mixed to a smooth paste with water (ready-mixed mustard in jars or tubes is also available). It is eaten with cold ham and beef and is a traditional accompaniment to brawn. Recently, milder coarse-grain mustards have been developed, and French mustards have become popular.

Curry powder, based on spice mixtures sent home by the British in India, have been made for over 200 years, initially in the home, but later as branded products produced by spice blending companies. Immigration to Britain from the Indian subcontinent brought new spicing mixtures. Best known is *garam masala*, a phrase which simply indicates a mixture of spices made up to the maker's taste and ground together according to the company producing it and the dish for which it is intended. It is generally less aggressive in flavor than curry powder, and several brands are sold. Numerous ready-made sauces and pastes, bottled or chilled, are sold as convenience products for meat, vegetables, and rice or noodles. Varieties include the flavors of the Indian restaurant—tikka or tandoori pastes, rogan josh, Kashmiri spices, and more recently, Thai curry pastes. Chinese mixtures such as sweet-and-sour and spices such as star anise, five-spice, and Sichuan peppercorns are also widely available. Italian-inspired cook-in sauces include ones based on tomatoes, cream, and cheese or pesto.

Bottled sauces include various brown sauces; the best known brand is HP, thick, sweet-sour, and spicy, used with meat, fish, cheese, or egg dishes. These originated in the nineteenth century and are still hugely popular. Thin, dark, spicy sauces such as Worcestershire sauce or Yorkshire Relish are also standbys for flavoring meat stews and cheese dishes, as are mushroom ketchup (a thin dark sauce made from spices and fermented mushrooms) and anchovy sauce (a liquid puree of anchovies). Tomato sauce (ketchup) is also much used. During the latter half of the twentieth century, soy sauce and *nam pla* (Thai fish sauce) also became kitchen standbys. Gravy browning, a dark liquid caramel, is used for coloring anemic gravies and stews. Preserved anchovies, pickled or salted capers, and chutneys or pickles such as Branston (a commercial product based on diced vegetables in a spicy brown sauce) are also stocked, as is Marmite, a branded product based on yeast extract, which is eaten on bread or toast.

Other miscellaneous products include gelatin, in powder or leaf form, for mousses and cold desserts; packaged jellies, which are colored, flavored gelatin cubes; and perhaps cornflour based custard powder and blancmange mixes; and possibly angel delight mix. Mixes for sage and onion stuffing, bread sauce, and gravy also feature among the selection of dry goods, together with bouillon cubes; mixes for cakes, breads, and pizzas are other possibilities. There may also be quantities of snack food, including potato-based snacks, especially crisps (potato chips), and items such as salted nuts or pot noodles.

Beverages

The British taste for tea and coffee (and to a lesser extent, cocoa and drinking chocolate) sweetened with sugar is a major subject in its own right. These crops played a substantial role in the development of trade between the British Isles and the tropical world. Their basic importance in British culture—the ritual of the cup of tea, coffee for the casual visitor, a milky drink as a nightcap—means that very few households in Britain are without at least one of these drinks. Despite this, purchases of tea for use in the home have dropped from about 2.5 oz per head per week in 1975 to just over 1 oz in 2000. Those for coffee have remained more or less even, at about 0.5 oz a week.

Tea is closely identified with British food culture. It is drunk after meals, at any time between, and has given its name to two meals, afternoon tea and high tea. Most tea is black tea of Indian origin, purchased as teabags, although fine loose-leaf teas from India and China are sold. It is little used as an ingredient in cookery (the most common use is for soaking dried fruit for some types of cake). Most coffee is purchased as instant coffee, although coffee beans are widely available, whole or ready ground. Apart from its use as a drink, coffee is a popular flavor in cakes, desserts, and confectionery, alone, with chocolate, or with walnuts.

Cocoa is the solids left after cocoa butter has been removed when manufacturing block chocolate. It is sold as powder and mixed with hot milk and sugar for drinking, or used as a base for drinking chocolate. In baking it is added to sponge mixtures to make chocolate cakes or puddings, or used in desserts or chocolate sauces. Chocolate itself is also used in baking, especially in patisserie recipes of continental origin. Much chocolate sold in Britain is sweet, low in cocoa solids, and includes a little noncocoa butter vegetable fat (a source of discord at the EU level), although some fine bitter types are available. Other hot drinks include name-brand mixes based on such substances as malted milk.

Finally, the store cupboard might contain alcohol specifically for cooking: sherry, to add to trifles; rum or brandy, for Christmas foods; and possibly a liqueur such as Cointreau for flavoring desserts. Until the 1960s, wine was a vehicle for a display of connoisseurship, not an everyday part of life in Britain, but it has become more important in cookery and as a beverage since then.

Other Drinks, Confectionery

Recent trends in household consumption include a decrease in purchases of soft drink concentrates and an increase in those of ready-to-drink products (not including fruit juices), and low-calorie, ready-to-drink ones, to about 1 3/4 U.K. pints per person per week as reported by the NFS in 2000. Consumption of lager, beer, and wine was about 8 fl oz, 4 fl oz, and 3 fl oz, respectively, although the averaging effect of the study over the population sample must disguise relatively large purchases in some households and none at all in others. Even so, it is worth noting that these are all increases on previous years. Mineral water consumption, almost unheard of in the 1970s, was about 5 fl oz per person per week in 2000. It must also be remembered that these figures exclude drinks purchased for consumption away from home. Industry figures show the consumption of soft drinks to be around 217 liters per person per year (equivalent to about 7.3 pints per person per week). These figures include bottled water, which account for about 13 percent of the market. About 50 percent is carbonated drinks, and the remainder is cordials and squash for dilution, and fruit juices.[10]

Chocolate consumption as recorded in the NFS stood at 1.7 oz per person per week, and mints and other boiled sweets at 0.4 oz in 2000.

However, because of the way in which figures for the survey are collected, much confectionery consumption goes unrecorded. Information from industries based on sales indicates that consumption is actually much higher, with chocolate confectionery estimated at about 6.7 oz per head per week, and sugar confectionery at about 3.7 oz.

Neither drinks nor confectionery are seen as food in the sense that meat, bread, and potatoes are, but (with the exception of mineral water) they contribute energy, and sometimes other nutrients to the diet.

NOTES

1. All figures in this section are taken from the National Food Survey 2000 unless otherwise stated.

2. Peter Atkins and Ian Bowler, *Food and Society* (New York: Arnold and Oxford University Press, 2001), p. 265.

3. Bev Botting (ed.), *Family Spending: A Report on the 2001–2002 Expenditure and Food Survey* (London: HMSO, 2003).

4. "Summary of Realeat Polls," Web site of the Vegetarian Society, http://www.vegsoc.org.

5. See David H. Buss, "The British Diet since the End of Food Rationing," in *Food, Diet, and Economic Change Past and Present,* ed. Catherine Geissler and Derek J. Oddy (Leicester, United Kingdom: Leicester University Press, 1993).

6. Atkins and Bowler, *Food and Society*, p. 278.

7. Biscuit, Cake, Chocolate, and Confectionery Association, "Our Industry: Industry Statistics," http://bccca.org.uk/figures.htm.

8. Joan Morgan and Alison Richards, *The Book of Apples* (London: Ebury Press, 1993).

9. "Sugar: Introduction," Department for Environment, Food and Rural Affairs (DEFRA), http://defra.gov.uk.

10. The 2003 Sucralose Soft Drinks Report, *UK Market Review,* http://www.splendaingredient.co.uk.

3

Cooking

In the early twenty-first century, many people would suggest that British consumers have partially or wholly given up cooking in favor of pre-packaged meals. This is an exaggeration, but the provision of ready-to-cook food and convenience ingredients is an important aspect of contemporary food culture, and it is useful to consider where U.K. consumers buy their ingredients and other foods from. And what makes people buy particular items? The traditional networks of local supply that underpin peasant economies have long since vanished, and information about food and how to prepare it comes from a vast array of sources. At the present time, food retailing in the United Kingdom is dominated by a small number of supermarkets, a concentration of retail power in food that is not matched anywhere else in the world. This situation has developed only in the past 40 years. The most successful companies act as market leaders and influence both food prices and consumer choice in the goods they offer, their layouts, and the locations they choose for their stores. The companies concerned are undeniably successful in economic terms and achieve extraordinary logistical feats, although debates frequently break out over their effects on prices, food choice, and the environment. A recent publication, *Not on the Label* (Felicity Lawrence) provides a good summary of this. Supermarkets also provide recipes and magazines about foods as a promotion tool, but this is only a fraction of a much larger media interest in food aimed at all sectors of society.

CHANGES IN RETAILING FOOD

For most of the early modern period, people who did not grow their own food obtained supplies from street markets and a range of traditional specialist suppliers—grocers, butchers, bakers, and delicatessens. Well into the nineteenth century, fresh milk came from town dairies, in which cattle were kept in confined spaces all year round. Many fresh foods were "cried" on the streets, hawked in small quantities by itinerant vendors who sold perishables such as soft fruit, fish, shellfish, and milk in the larger towns. By the early nineteenth century, provisioning in the growing cities had developed into a complex system of importers, wholesalers, street markets, and shops. Retailing food in the early nineteenth century was characterized by numerous small shops run by individuals—grocers, butchers, bakers, Italian warehousemen (forerunners of delicatessens), fishmongers, and fruiters. With the exception of those serving the luxury market, small grocers and provision merchants carried a relatively narrow range of goods that formed the basis of the working class diet—flour, oatmeal, sugar, butter, cheese, and bacon being especially important. In the second half of the century, several factors made this trade more profitable, notably a small but significant rise in the standard of living for the mass of the population and the effects of the removal of import duty on most essential foodstuffs (during the late 1840s and into the 1850s), changes which themselves took place against a background of rapid population increase and improvements in transport by sea and rail.

The Co-op and the Chain Grocers

The first chain grocery in Britain originated from a movement to secure a relatively inexpensive and pure food supply for the poor. This was the Co-operative Society founded in the 1840s by a group of poor workers in Rochdale, Lancashire, to purchase basic foodstuffs at wholesale prices for their members; the profit made on retailing the food in smaller packages was returned to members as dividend. The Co-op movement grew throughout the nineteenth century as a provider of food and other household goods, establishing shops in many towns. It has survived to the present day and still has a strong presence in food production and retailing.

In the second half of the century, several individuals founded grocery stores that flourished and went on to become chains. The best known included Lipton's, founded by Thomas Lipton, who began with a shop in Glasgow in 1971 and established a name that remained a force in British food retailing until the 1970s, and J. Sainsbury, founded in 1869 and still among the most important food retailers in Britain. Lipton was an entrepreneur whose policies relating to market penetration and advertising foreshadowed the twentieth-century supermarket. He actively sought vertical integration in his business, buying meat-packing plants in North America and tea plantations in Ceylon (now Sri Lanka), as well as bakeries, sausage and pie manufacturers, and jam factories. Industrial products such as margarine and condensed milk became important in his stores. Economies of scale in buying were translated into lower prices at the point of sale. Lipton's and other chains, such as The Home and Colonial Stores and Maypole Dairies, offered basic goods such as bacon, butter, and tea at prices a little below those of their competitors. Such chains were established in shopping areas where the large working-class populations of industrial towns did their shopping.

Chain grocers were important at the national level by the late nineteenth century, but took their place alongside street markets and numerous other small food shops, from specialists to general village stores. Fresh food was weighed and wrapped individually for the purchaser by the shopkeeper or an assistant. This mix of chains and small independent retailers came to typify British "high street" food provision in the first half of the twentieth century. Underlying these developments from the mid-nineteenth century until the Second World War was a policy of free trade and the possession of a huge empire. This allowed Britain access to large reserves of basic foods such as wheat, beef, mutton, cheese, and butter. These supplies of relatively cheap food went especially toward sustaining the urban poor. Canned fruit and other staples of the British kitchen such as dried fruit, tea, coffee, and cocoa were also produced by the countries of the empire and imported in large quantities. Choice was limited by factors such as food preservation, transport techniques, and the size of the family budget.

The outbreak of the Second World War immediately threatened imported food supplies on which Britain had become dependent. During the years from 1939 until 1954 (from the start of the war to the end of rationing), the wartime government was concerned with ensuring adequate nutrition for a predominantly urban population from a limited supply of food, some home produced and some imported under difficult conditions. Imposition of rationing by the newly formed Ministry of Food ensured most people had enough to eat, but choice was severely limited, although the concept remained in the points system, which allowed the consumer freedom to choose a limited quantity of items considered non-necessities. It is often claimed that wartime diet was scientifically planned for opti-

mum nutrition with resources available, but this has recently been chal-
lenged.[1]

Postwar Developments

After the war ended, government intervention in the food industry
continued until 1954 (rationing actually became more severe for a while
in the late 1940s, because of poor harvests). Policy was dominated by the
idea of freedom from want and a concern with affordable, safe food for the
largely urban population. During this period, domestic agricultural interests in the shape of the National Farmers' Union (NFU) developed a powerful political lobby and close relationships with one government
department, the Ministry of Agriculture. The NFU also supported policies
such as intensification of agriculture, which tallied with national policies
concerned with ensuring food security as far as possible. In the late 1940s,
government legislation provided a privileged position for the NFU in ne-
gotiations with the government over food. Farmers were given guaranteed
prices and an assured market for their produce. Domestic food production
was protected by subsidies and national purchasing boards, which provided guaranteed prices to producers.

The end of rationing brought challenges for food retailers. The first self-
service grocery shop in Britain opened in the late 1940s. The small premises of traditional grocer's shops were unsuited to the idea, but it spread.
By 1962, there were over 800 self-service shops, some of which had a selling space in excess of 2,000 square feet—in effect, supermarkets. One factor that encouraged the growth of early supermarkets was the abolition of
Retail Price Maintenance, which had allowed manufacturers and suppliers to dictate prices. Supermarkets could now dictate prices to suppliers.
Another factor was the rapid growth in car ownership among the population. The idea of supermarkets spread rapidly during the 1960s and 1970s,
and by the 1980s, they had come to dominate food retailing in the United
Kingdom. During this decade a handful of companies competed for a limited market by investing increasingly large amounts of capital in fixed assets and information technology systems.

This "store wars" era had several repercussions. One was to alter the
basic access to food for much of the population. Opening a new store was
a major capital investment (a cost of about £25 million in the mid-
1980s—approximately $38 million at 1987 exchange rates). For maxi-
mum returns, favored sites were on previously undeveloped land on the
edge of cities or large towns, with ample parking, good road access, and

minimal competition. By 1990, five retailers—Sainsbury, Tesco, Argyll (the Safeway chain), Asda, and Gateway (the Somerfield chain)—controlled 60 percent of the total U.K. grocery market, or 40 percent of a more broadly defined food market including independent suppliers. Inevitably this affected other food retailers, leading to a decline in the traditional town center or suburban nucleus mix of small food retailers scattered among other shops. It is possible that supermarkets simply exacerbated a process of decline that had already begun. The combination of small shop closures and movement of large food retail stores to the edge of towns, however, favored certain sectors of the population, especially the relatively affluent and car owners (car ownership increased rapidly in the 1980s, and three-quarters of supermarket customers travel by car[2]). It disadvantaged women, the elderly, and the disabled (all generally less mobile).

It also affected the development of retail techniques. High capital costs led to a preoccupation with effective use of resources, logistics, and the supply chain. This was particularly evident in the application of information technology. The introduction of electronic scanning devices in the mid-1980s yielded a huge amount of information about consumer behavior and preferences, which in turn generated ideas for product innovation. This affected the concept of the own-label (retail brand) product. In the 1960s and 1970s, own-label products generally had a cheap, generic image. In the early 1980s, retailer own labels accounted for about 23 percent of the packaged grocery market in the United Kingdom; by the early 1990s, it was 36 percent, with a higher penetration in leading suppliers. Own labels had developed to offer the consumer innovation and high quality, and the retailer higher profit margins combined with total control over manufacture and the opportunity to take more risks over the type of products they developed. Pre-prepared meals, frozen or chilled, and part-processed ingredients are important in this sector, as is the careful use of packaging technology. Lines include ones sold as slimming foods, healthy eating ranges, or dishes of exotic origin. In particular, the chilled ready meals sector, which scarcely existed in the early 1980s, had expanded to a market worth over £300 million (about $480 million) by the early 1990s. One chain, Marks and Spencer, whose stock is entirely own label, were pioneers in this sector. Innovation is just one method supermarkets use in an attempt to keep their market share; others include price competition, diversification into other goods and services, and loyalty schemes. The introduction by supermarkets of loyalty cards (offering redeemable points on each transaction) has extended the collection of information about consumer behavior. One novel idea, Internet shopping, has been slow to take off in Britain despite the fact that all grocery chains offer a service, as do many specialist retailers.

Another innovation was the development of just-in-time logistics, in which products are rapidly transferred from a few centralized depots as and when needed. This, coupled with the large distances that food travels to and from depots (from one end of the country to the other and back, or from around the other side of the planet to the United Kingdom) have led to concerns about "food miles." A characteristic of major supermarkets is vertical integration, with purchasing power reaching back down the food chain to manufacturers and producers, who find themselves having to meet increasingly stringent specifications at short notice. Concerns have been expressed over the effect this has on suppliers, especially farmers, who find their crops rejected by buyers at the last minute. Other sectors of the food industry express different concerns, for instance, craft bakers who claim that the huge discounts supermarkets offer on loss leaders such as bread undermines their market.

Figures illustrate the changes in retailing: in 1961, there were about 150,000 independent food retailers; by 1999, this was down to 25,000. In 1971, the independents had a market share of 30 percent and the multiple retailers about 50 percent. Market-research figures show that this has continued to increase; in 2001, multiple retailers had 89.5 percent of the grocery market shares, and of this, 67.8 percent was controlled by four companies. Co-ops had 5 percent of the market share, and independent shops 5.5 percent.[3] The long-term decline of independents and smaller chains has continued, despite the establishment of purchasing organizations that aim to give independents some of the advantages of multiple retailers. Supermarkets had come to rival multinationals in their economic importance; for instance, Tesco in 2002 had the largest share of the market, had 730 U.K. stores, with a turnover of £25.7 billion ($37.3 billion) and 200,000 employees.

Concern over the concentration of retail power has been expressed at the national level, with only limited effects. In the 1990s, tightening of legislation controlling land use, plus competition from continental European discount stores, led to a reevaluation of out-of-town sites. One response of major chains was to devise compact store forms that were more suited to city-center sites and smaller towns. In 1999, a government inquiry investigated competition, or lack of it, in supermarket retailing; the final report illustrated a complex monopoly situation, some of which worked against public interest. In spite of this, a few supermarkets remain hugely powerful in food retailing in the United Kingdom, offering the promise, if not the actuality, of cheap food. This situation seems likely to continue for the foreseeable future, despite attempts to create local food networks through projects such as Farmer's Markets and vegeboxes (a weekly delivery, by arrangement, of vegetables and fruit from a local supplier).

THE MEDIA

Media interest in food is a continuing phenomenon in British food culture. Recipe books existed for centuries, often haphazard in layout and unreliable in detail, collections stitched together from older books and oddments from family and friends. The nineteenth century brought increasing precision in recipe writing, particularly in the form of *Beeton's Book of Household Management*, which includes details such as precise quantities of ingredients, timing, cost, and portions. The long and successful history of this book overshadowed numerous other nineteenth-century cookery writers. Publishers such as Warne's and Cassell's produced compendia of recipes in the early twentieth century, but there were many smaller publications, from leaflets promoting new products—the Be-Ro book, produced by a baking powder company, was especially popular—to collections nostalgic for a supposed golden age of English domestic life. Manufacturers of gas and electric cookers started to produce cookery books for use with their appliances. Even in the 1930s, books such as Mrs. Beeton's compilation remained the benchmark for middle-class housewives in the 1930s. In addition, the idea that girls should be taught to cook was introduced into schools in the early twentieth century, leading to textbooks of Domestic Economy that included information on the emerging science of nutrition and basic cookery—baking, boiling, roasting, frying, and recipes for puddings, pies, and cakes, and devices for using up leftovers.

Magazines have been increasingly influential.[4] Periodicals for women have a history that stretches back to the 1690s in Britain, but they did not emphasize the domestic sphere until the early Victorian period. In the mid-century, Mrs. Beeton's work was first published as a series of articles in *The English Woman's Domestic Magazine*, published by her husband Samuel Beeton. By the late nineteenth century, there were several women's magazines on the market that included recipes and information on cookery. Those aimed at lower-middle-class women displayed an obsession with economy and an assumption that cookery was a burden, with recipes for "plain but wholesome" English food—meat and vegetables, savory or sweet puddings, with a reliance on suet and dripping as cooking fats. Advertisements for prepared foods such as shredded suet and custard powder (mix) also began to appear in magazines at this time, providing yet another source of information about food.

After the First World War, women's magazine publishing expanded, especially for the less well-off. For the professional middle classes, a British edition of *Good Housekeeping* magazine started in the early 1920s. Middle-class women had to think more about cookery, as domestic servants were fewer. During the Second World War, rationing led to a campaign to educate the consumer in making the best of both the conventional food available and of novel ingredients such as dried egg. Magazines, leaflets, and books were used to inform people in how to make the most of the food available. Radio was also important: the BBC was established in the 1920s, and radio broadcasts had begun in 1922. A five-minute radio cookery broadcast, "The Kitchen Front," went out once a week after the morning news. Culinary educators such as Marguerite Patten and Ambrose Heath did their best to provide inspiration, including ideas from foreign traditions.

When rationing ended, convenience foods such as cake mixes, powdered soups, and quick-cook pasta became available and were heavily promoted in magazines. By 1962, a complete convenience meal was being advertised—a dehydrated beef curry. Among books, updates of Mrs. Beeton's book continued alongside manuals by authors, such as Constance Spry and Marguerite Patten, who continued to provide a solid grounding in the good plain cookery tradition of English food. During the 1950s, an interest in food from other countries slowly became apparent; one well-known exponent of this was Elizabeth David, whose recipes influenced several generations of postwar home cooks and restaurant owners, and inspired shops to begin stocking French and Mediterranean kitchen equipment.

Television made its debut in Britain in 1936, and the first TV cook appeared shortly afterward, when the restaurateur Marcel Boulestin made a series of appearances. It was not until the 1950s that TV really become an important broadcasting medium. In this decade, the chef Philip Harben broadcast a series of highly influential programs; his articles in magazines also included instructions for dishes of exotic origin. He was followed by "The Galloping Gourmet," Graham Kerr. Commercial TV also began in

the 1950s, and the advertisements it carried immediately provided another source of knowledge about food.

1960s Onward

Cheap full-color printing, introduced in the 1960s, enhanced the at-
tractions of cookery books and articles. Major daily and weekly newspapers began to feature cookery articles, especially in their weekend color
supplements; some of the authors of these, such as Jane Grigson, amassed
a substantial body of work. Radio and television also took an increased interest in the subject. On radio, the Food Programme, an investigative program broadcast weekly, which was begun by Derek Cooper in 1979 and is
still running, has been highly influential. A trend toward more cosmopolitan and adventurous recipes had developed, and by the 1980s a sense of
excitement about food was apparent in both printed and electronic
media. In particular, cookery on television became increasingly popular.
Presenters ranged from Delia Smith providing precise and foolproof
recipes for those in need of guidance, to chefs from the best restaurants,
such as Anton Mossiman and Albert and Michel Roux, demonstrating
dishes beyond the scope of all but the most ambitious domestic cook.
Other presenters, such as Ken Hom and Madhur Jaffrey, exploited their
ethnic backgrounds, presenting series on Chinese or Indian cookery. Such
programs were increasingly tied in with publishing, each series yielding a
recipe book. The amount of time dedicated to broadcasting cookery programs increased slowly but steadily during the 1970s and 1980s until it
stood at about three hours a week on each of the four main channels. The
trend continued into the 1990s, and opinion is divided over whether it is
slowing or simply becoming more diffuse, as more television channels become available. Some organizations develop a whole portfolio of food-
related interests: for instance, the BBC, in addition to broadcasting programs relating to food on radio and television, publishes a magazine on
the subject, organizes a national food and drink exhibition every year, and
has a Web site dedicated to food and food-related issues.

Little information on the cumulative effect of media influences is available. The sheer volume, and the amount spent, for instance, on cookery
books, suggests that this must be considerable, if only by providing a standard to aspire to. One study that compared the 10 most popular women's
magazines from 1967–68 and 1991–92[5] suggested that they have both
practical functions (as deliverers of technical information about cookery
and food, especially in the form of recipes), but also fuel the imagination

on ideas about food, style, and pleasure. In 1991, it was estimated that the five bestselling weeklies and the five bestselling monthly magazines were seen by approximately 29 million people. On average, the amount of space in these magazines devoted to food articles was about 12 percent, and another 13 percent was given to food advertisements. Over this time, the appeal of technological novelty (mixes, etc.) in food declined, but more attention was given to ethnic recipes, European and non-European, in what might be seen as "routinization of the exotic." Many recipes required ingredients originating in several continents, and year-round variety is taken for granted—something the current British food system, dominated by supermarkets, has enabled.

During the late 1980s, magazines aimed at a wider audience and dedicated solely to food appeared on the market; one of the more successful is published by the BBC and features the personalities and chefs involved in its radio and TV programs. Most newspapers also produce columns explicitly related to food (in addition to the large number of items relating to food production and safety that appear in the mainstream news pages); these include a mix of recipes, discussions of ingredients and cuisines, restaurant reviews, descriptions of the work of chefs and suppliers, and items relating to health and safety. Cookbooks are one of the most profitable sectors of publishing, and those bearing the names of a handful of TV cooks consistently top the bestseller lists. Even though sales figures have fallen recently, the best-known TV chefs can expect to sell hundreds of thousands of books. However, the emphasis placed on food and cooking by the media, resulting in massive viewing figures for certain cooking programs and high sales figures for magazines and books does not necessarily translate into a practical interest in cooking at home.

WHO COOKS: THE DOMESTIC SPHERE

Background

In British culture, domestic cooking is women's work, and high-status professional cooking is usually a male preserve. The gender divide between female (domestic) cooking and male (professional) cooking disguises both nuances in the status of male cooks and much female employment in catering, especially those that deal with large numbers of meals on a relatively low budget, such as schools and hospitals. Restaurant chefs are often male, although more women enter the profession now, but the most prestigious paid work is still seen as the preserve of the male chef. The high profiles that the latter often enjoy disguise a much larger number of poorly paid catering workers in pubs, fast-food outlets, and institutional kitchens. In addition, there are numerous people employed in the industrial production of pre-prepared and packaged convenience foods.

The stereotype of women cooking in the home has remained remarkably untouched by the social changes of the last hundred years. Key changes that might be expected to affect responsibility for domestic food preparation include the disappearance of the domestic servant, the rise in the proportion of women economically active in the labor force, a rise in disposable income, changes in household composition, and the development of alternatives to home-based leisure. In particular, women's participation in paid employment gradually increased; in 1911, about 10 percent of married women worked outside the home; by 1991 about 50 percent did so. The figure for economically active women (full- or part-time work) in 2001 was 12.8 million. The number of single-parent households with children also increased, reaching 1.5 million in 2001, and 9 out of 10 of these were headed by women.

The nineteenth century had been an era of plentiful domestic labor. Rich households had numerous servants, but even modest ones employed one or two, usually female. Skills were not necessarily well developed; servants were often very young, poorly trained, and sometimes incompetent or dishonest. This, combined with a general lack of interest in food as a subject for polite conversation, and a late–nineteenth-century obsession with economy led to some inferior food being served. Paid cooks were the norm in even quite modest houses, at least to do the heavier work, although the wealthier the household, the more likely it was that a male cook would be employed.

In poor households, the burden of cooking almost always fell to the woman. The first systematic investigations into the lives of the poor, in the early twentieth century, described a household pattern consisting of husband, wife, and children in a family unit. It is clear from the work of investigators such as Maud Pember-Reeves that food shopping, preparation, and clearing up afterward were done by women. At the same time, such surveys highlighted the gross inadequacy of cooking facilities among the poor—lack of efficient stoves, few and poor utensils, little space, no facilities for storing food, and lack of piped water supplies in the home.

During the First World War, the mobilization of troops to fight on the continent opened up jobs in offices and factories. Women chose these in preference to domestic service, a trend that continued through the 1930s

and the Second World War (when many young women who might otherwise have entered service chose women's units in the armed forces). In
1931, 4.8 percent of households in England and Wales had one or more
domestic servants, and 1,332,224 women and 78,489 men worked in service; by 1951, this figure was down to 1.2 percent, representing 509,728
women and 28,933 men. Among other household tasks, middle- and
upper-class housewives found themselves having to cook, whether or not
they had the inclination and training for it. Domestic cooking continued
to be the responsibility of women throughout the difficulties of the Second World War. From the late 1950s on, the growing interest in exotic flavors and novel ingredients indicated a change in attitudes toward food,
but not toward the domestic division of labor.

Since the 1970s, evidence for who cooks has come from two main
sources: social-science researchers, often investigating the effects of low
income on families or looking at possibilities for influencing dietary change;
and market researchers, commissioned to investigate specific market sectors. Social-science researchers paid considerable attention to domestic
division of labor in the final three decades of the twentieth century, especially in poorer socioeconomic groups. Their findings reinforce the stereotyped view of domestic cooking as a female occupation, demonstrating
that in families composed of a couple and children, the shopping, planning, storing, cooking, serving, and clearing up of food was mostly done
by women. There is a clear perception of gender divisions of tasks, even if
they are sometimes carried out by the "wrong" sex.[6]

In the 1980s, housewives were found to undertake most cooking, especially that which was boring and routine, and expected little positive help
from husbands or children. Women are more likely than men to do almost
all food preparation, including routine tasks such as assembling packed
meals for husbands and children. Studies of time spent on meal preparation by gender revealed the inequalities in division of labor in the household. The main meal on a Sunday showed the most inequality, with
women spending 14 times longer than men and children combined on
this task. Time spent on breakfasts and snacks (which both involve a high
proportion of convenience foods) was less unequally divided, suggesting
other members of the household are involved more in preparing these.[7]
Almost all raw foodstuffs are purchased, not grown, and items such as
bread, cake, and beer bought rather than made at home. One study investigated a list of more involved food preparation tasks and found that in
households that bothered with these, women were more likely to bake or

make jam, but men were more likely to cook on barbecues or to brew beer or wine; they were also more likely to collect takeaways.[8] One task that was more equitable was food shopping, which about 30 percent of households reported sharing, although women were more likely to undertake local top-up shopping—a task that became less easy as neighborhood shops closed.

Researchers consistently remarked on how cooking, viewed as potentially enjoyable and creative, became reduced to a matter of supplying food to the rest of the family because of other demands on women's time. Meals were often common-denominator compositions, planned to contain foods that no one in the family disliked. Women sacrificed their own preferences to those of husbands and children.[9] Making routines in cooking was seen as a method for relieving the chore of cooking, and family meals were usually quickly prepared. More effort went into them when guests were present.

Female participation in paid employment was a significant determinant for who cooked; if the woman had a job, the man was more likely to share the cooking. Decisions about shopping and preparation were mostly made by women, but preferences of men and children were significant in food choice. Age group also had an effect, with couples under the age of 40 more likely to express an egalitarian ideology.[10] However, it was rare for men to cook on a regular basis. Market research indicated some social-class differences, with men in higher socioeconomic groups more likely to help out with cooking and shopping.

These findings came mostly from white working-class communities. Some studies argued that an appreciable change in domestic division of labor took place in the 1980s, but there seems to be little evidence to support this. Sometimes, especially in wealthier areas, an ideology of sharing was expressed, but evidence for it in practice was limited. Even in the southeast of England, an area from which social trends generally diffuse, women were still reported as doing the bulk of shopping and cooking, although a greater degree of task sharing was reported than in other parts of the country. Work in the north of England noted that the women cooked and the resulting meals were eaten by all the family together, a pattern which could probably be extended to much of the country.[11] It was also considered important for women to be able to cook. One survey in the 1990s reported that 66 percent of employed women and 86 percent of unemployed or economically inactive women claimed to prepare meals for the family everyday; the respective figures for men were 14 percent and 36 percent.[12] Another survey cited about 80 percent of women cooking all meals and 16 percent of men never cooking at all. Market research in 2002 found that more women than men prepared the midweek evening meal, and that the 25–34 age group, single people, and those living in the northwest of England spent the least time cooking and were more likely to use prepared foods. A very small percentage of adults (between 4–6%) said they never cook.[13]

It is not unusual for men in mainstream British culture to boast that they cannot cook. Observers studying conventional households in which men do cook found that they tended to do so out of choice,[14] as a non-routine event, whereas women cooked out of necessity, and that level of education was a strong factor in whether or not the man cooked (the higher the education level, the more likely they were to cook).[15] A study of a cookery class for men found little evidence of a desire to learn to cook through a desire to become a symmetrical family in which tasks were equally shared.[16] The men concerned were learning because they were in womanless households. Two clear categories were noted. One was the absolute beginners, heterosexual men, who through divorce, widowhood, or the loss of a mother or sister who had cooked for them, found themselves needing to develop their skills. The other group, more advanced cooks wishing to learn specific skills or dishes, were mostly homosexual, and therefore unlikely to find themselves in a household with a female cook.

Convenience Food

Perceived time shortage is a significant factor affecting meal preparation in homes in which both partners work. Swiftness is seen as a positive in food preparation. This is apparent in both magazine articles, which by the early 1990s laid emphasis on ease of preparation and food that could be prepared in advance for reheating, as well as planning ahead, for instance, for Christmas.[17] In supermarkets, the vast range of semi-prepared ingredients and precooked meals provides another solution to this problem. The ease with which a food product can be acquired, prepared, stored, served, and eaten all count in a society that perceives itself as time-pressured. According to market research, the market for convenience foods grew dramatically over the years from 1991 to 2001, with the total spent on convenience food rising from £9.39 billion ($15 billion) in 1991 to £15.59 billion ($22.6 billion) in 2001.[18] Women who work outside the home have less time for complex recipes and meals that take only a few minutes to prepare are favored.

Ethnic Minorities

There is little information available about food shopping and preparation patterns in ethnic minority communities. A study in Glasgow, comparing Italians and Asians with the general population, did note some
significant differences. These included the observation that both minority
groups engaged in hospitality more often than the general population and
made more elaborate meals. There was also continuing emphasis on
home-prepared traditional food made from fresh ingredients for evening
meals, although Asian women were observed to utilize western convenience foods such as fish fingers and pizzas at midday meals. A smaller proportion of Asian women worked outside the home than in the general
population; among the Italian community, more women worked more in
paid employment but were still expected to run the home, sometimes rising early to prepare food in advance of the evening meal. A division between the private and public sphere was found to affect food shopping for
the Asian women, with men undertaking much of this. There was also a
greater adherence to a culture's food traditions in the minority communities. This contrasted with the diversity exhibited by the majority culture,
who were observed to incorporate foods from non-British traditions, such
as pizza, lasagna, and curry into meals for family hospitality.[19]

Another study in the south London borough of Lewisham, with a high
population of people of Afro-Caribbean descent, found that older Afro-
Caribbeans were more likely to continue cooking traditional West Indian
food than the young. An age difference was also noted, with older white
inhabitants tending to view British or English food as plain, wholesome,
nourishing, and healthy. They were less likely to incorporate new items
such as pasta, rice, and curries into their diets. Those younger than 50
considered it a dying concept, bland, boring, and unhealthy, involving
the stereotypical dinners, meat and vegetables, and preferred "a new form
of creolised cuisine" incorporating foods of Italian, Chinese, and Indian
origin.[20]

THE KITCHEN AND ITS EQUIPMENT

Up until the 1950s, kitchens were either utilitarian rooms for food
preparation, or, in less wealthy houses in which coal-fired ranges had survived, the room in which the family lived for most of the time because the
range kept them warm. The ideal of the postwar kitchen went through
several changes. In the 1950s, it became a streamlined room in which the

housewife displayed her technical skills against a backdrop of Formica and the latest consumer goods; by now, these might include a fridge, a cake mixer, and a coffeemaker. The idea of the fitted kitchen replaced the older notion of moveable furniture such as dressers and freestanding cupboards. The kitchen was not generally a room for lingering in once the cooking was done; a separate dining room was usually the norm, even in quite modest houses. During the 1960s, a growing informality and a new interest in cookery as a skill led to the idea of the kitchen as a place to eat as well as to cook, and the kitchen table began to double as a dining table. Since then, possession of a well-designed and fitted kitchen making use of fashionable materials—from Italian tiles to industrial work surfaces of stainless steel—has become a status symbol, even if in practice, little cooking is undertaken in there.

The technology of cookery in Britain has undergone major changes within living memory, from a solid-fuel-based enterprise, sometimes without facilities such as running water, but perhaps with the presence of one or more servants, to a situation in which a household could exist entirely on purchases of pre-prepared food that only need reheating. The volume of precooked meals on the market suggests that reheating, as much as cooking, is an important element of twenty-first-century food preparation. Even so, consumers obviously recognize different cookery techniques as giving results they like or dislike, and most people still cook occasionally. Cookery operations characteristic of the British kitchen include roasting (or technically, now, oven-baking) for meat and boiling (now principally for vegetables). Stewing, frying, and grilling are also important, and poaching and braising to a lesser extent. Traces of regional habits relating to fuel types and cooking technology can be seen in a few baked goods.

Fuels and Ovens

Coal-fired ranges continued to be used until well after the Second World War, especially in mining areas and rural areas. The concept lives on in large enameled iron stoves, the best known of which is the Aga, patented in Sweden by Dr. Gustaf Dalén in the 1920s. Agas and other solid-fuel stoves were mostly used in rural homes where gas was not an option, but they became increasingly popular and fashionable in the 1980s. These are now usually fired with oil, gas, or electricity, and the image (although not necessarily the reality) is still closely identified with rural life. The idea of wood-fired brick or stone-built ovens was virtually abandoned

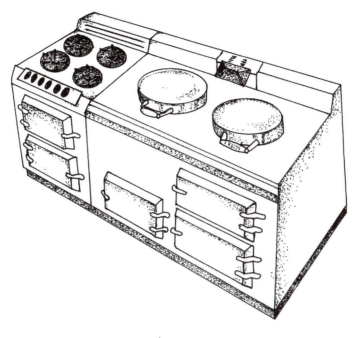

Aga stove.

in Britain after the Second World War, but has recently begun to reappear in the special context of pizza restaurants and a few high-class restaurants using recipes of Mediterranean inspiration.

Gas and electricity are now by far the most important fuels for cooking. The change to these began in the late nineteenth century. Gas had been used for cooking as early as the 1820s, but only in professional kitchens. In the 1880s, its use as fuel for domestic cooking began to accelerate; the form of the cooker—four burners above an oven—became fixed, and shortly afterward, the introduction of pay-as-you-go meters also helped to popularize it. Cooker thermostats were introduced in 1923. Gas cooking spread rapidly in towns. In 1898, one in four households with gas supplies had a gas cooker; in 1901, the figure was one in three, and by 1939, it was estimated that three-quarters of all families had a gas cooker.[21] Progress in the countryside was limited by availability of supplies, and it is still a less common option in rural areas.

Electricity as a cooking fuel was introduced in 1890. Slower to spread than gas, it was also relatively expensive, and heating elements were slow and unreliable. Electric cooker design improved, and prices fell, in the

1920s, and they gained in popularity, but as late as 1936 only 6 percent of families had an electric cooker. By 1948, this had risen to 18 percent, and in 1980, it was 46 percent.[22]

Gas or electricity is now preferred for cooking and are standard fittings in most British kitchens. A few minor additions have been made, such as timers and automatic ignition systems, although rotisseries have never become popular. For electric cookers, controllability of the heat for the hotplates has always been an issue, partially solved by the introduction of halogen rings. The other major innovation in cooking appliances has been the microwave cooker, which developed during the 1950s as a spin-off from radar technology. First marketed for domestic use in the early 1980s, ownership rose rapidly, and in 2002 about 86 percent of U.K. households owned one, or a combination oven that could be used either as a microwave or a conventional electric oven. It is debatable how much real cooking they are used for; defrosting food and reheating pre-prepared meals seem to be their principal uses in the British kitchen.

Other Kitchen Equipment

At the start of the twentieth century, devices for storing perishables included the fly-proof meat safe (which had no facility for chilling), and, in large houses, a special larder or pantry with small north-facing windows and stone shelves, which maintained a lower temperature than the rest of the house. Refrigeration was uncommon, but not unknown. Artificial refrigeration came into use in the 1870s for transporting and storing food in bulk. Domestic ice boxes, chilled by ice bought from the ice man, were introduced in the late nineteenth century for keeping small amounts of food chilled for short lengths of time but remained uncommon. The uptake of fridges was relatively slow to begin with, but they were swiftly adopted after the Second World War, and by 2002 the vast majority of British households owned one. Home freezers became popular in the 1970s. Limited space in British kitchens means that fridges and freezers are often combined in one unit. These play their part in the logistics of the weekly one-stop shop.

Labor-saving devices were slowly adopted in Britain. The availability of servants up until the First World War is often cited as the reason behind this, although the evidence is not clear-cut. Small appliances such as electric kettles and toasters were taken up quickly. Quick and convenient ways to produce the essential British snack of tea and toast, these items were readily available by the 1930s. In the second half of the twentieth century, they became kitchen essentials. One item that undoubtedly is used, although the market was slow to become established, is the dishwasher, which about 27 percent of U.K. households owned in 2002.[23]

Other items of electronic kitchen equipment come and go. Food mixers are one of the most enduring. They began to appear on the market just after the Second World War. The best known of these, the Kenwood Chef, was invented in 1947, and became more common in the 1950s, together with liquidizers. In the 1970s, they were replaced to some extent by food processors, which began to appear in the 1970s. Hostess trolleys, with electrically heated hotplates and cupboards, became very fashionable in the 1960s and 1970s, but lost popularity as entertaining became increasingly casual in the 1980s. A plethora of smaller appliances such as slow cookers, soda streams (for carbonated drinks), sandwich toasters, table-top grills and deep-fat friers also became available. The 1990s brought ice-cream makers, espresso machines, rice cookers and steamers, and bread makers. It is unclear to what extent any of these are used.

Other items of small non-electronic kitchen equipment include pressure cookers (first marketed in 1949) and "chip pans" (for deep fat frying; as the name suggests, they are mostly used for frying potatoes). Since the 1960s, ethnic cookware has become increasingly popular, partly inspired by the kitchenware range stocked by the chain of Habitat furniture shops. Chicken bricks (terracotta vessels for baking a whole chicken) and fondue sets had their moment in the late 1960s and early 1970s. Woks became increasingly common in the 1980s as interest in Chinese food and stir-frying increased; around 65 percent of British households now own one.[24] Pasta machines were a must-have of the early 1990s. Barbecues have also become much more popular as a means of summer cooking and entertaining.

More traditional small items include the usual range of pans, casserole dishes, cake tins—shallow ones for sandwich cakes, Swiss roll tins and deep tins for fruitcakes; roasting tins and baking trays; whisks, knives, and usually a potato masher; mixing bowls, perhaps two or three pudding basins; and maybe a pie funnel, a china or earthenware funnel that, placed in the center of a pie, supports the crust in the middle during cooking. A recent phenomenon relating to kitchenware is the effect of a cooking host recommending an ingredient or item such as a specific make of omelette pan, leading to a national shortage of the item. This is known as "the Delia effect," named after the presenter Delia Smith.

Until the last few years, the British kitchen has relied on imperial measurements of ounces, pounds, and the 20 fl oz pint. Measuring cups as understood in the United States are available, but recipes (unless of North American origin) rarely state measurements in these terms. Older recipes occasionally call for the use of various types of drinking cups, which are slightly smaller than measuring cups (teacups, breakfast cups). Tablespoons and teaspoons are frequently quoted for small quantities; measuring spoons are fairly common, although in practice the cook will just use spoons out of the cutlery drawer. Imperial measurements are still widely quoted both in food purchases and in recipes, but membership in the European Union means the United Kingdom officially uses metric measurements of grams, kilograms, and liters, and these are increasingly found in practice.

WHO COOKS: THE COMMERCIAL SPHERE

Professional cooks in relatively high-status situations, such as restaurants, are more likely to be male than female, although much preparation, clearing up, waiting, and lower-status commercial cookery (institutional settings) is likely to be done by women. Foreigners have also been important as kitchen staff in Britain, especially in London, for at least the last 200 years. This was sometimes because they were exceptionally skilled (for instance, French chefs) or because kitchen work and waiting offered an open labor market, as it did to Italians at the end of the nineteenth century. More recently, the structure of the industry in Britain, with few skills required at the basic level, makes it a field in which recent arrivals can easily find work, although it is often poorly paid.

The Celebrity Chef

A few names, such as those of the great nineteenth-century chefs, became well known in the past. From the 1960s onward, television began to influence the status of chefs (and a handful of female cooks). Combined with an intense interest from the media and publishing, a few of those working in London restaurants have become well known through magazine and newspaper columns, and a number have seen their books top the bestseller lists. Despite constant assertions that the cult of the celebrity chef appears to have peaked, it shows little sign of declining. The phenomenon has led to more interest in cooking as a profession among teenagers, but the image of the celebrity chef is frequently at odds with the real world. One study showed many young cooks leaving the profession before they reached the age of 20 because of long hours, authoritarian regimes, and low pay. Equally, the antisocial hours, late-night work, and stamina required mean that few older people (in their thirties or forties) remain in the profession.[25]

NOTES

1. Derek J. Oddy, *From Plain Fare to Fusion Food: British Diet from the 1890s to the 1990s* (Rochester, N.Y.: Boydell and Brewer, 2003), pp. 162–68, 229.

2. Lucy Michaels and the Agriculture Project, "What's Wrong with Supermarkets 3," http://www.corporatewatch.org.uk.

3. "The Evening Meal," *Mintel Report* (London: Mintel International, April 2002), p. 21.

4. Stephen Mennell, *All Manners of Food: Eating and Taste in England and France from the Middle Ages to the Present* (New York: Basil Blackwell, 1985).

5. Alan Warde, *Consumption, Food, and Taste: Culinary Antinomies and Commodity Culture* (London: Sage, 1997).

6. Stephen Mennell, Anne Murcott, and Anneke H. van Otterloo, *Sociology of Food: Eating, Diet and Culture* (London: Sage, 1992).

7. Roy C. Wood, *The Sociology of the Meal* (Edinburgh: Edinburgh University Press, 1995), pp. 69–70.

8. Warde, *Consumption, Food, and Taste*, p. 141.

9. Nickie Charles and Marion Kerr, *Women, Food and Families* (New York: St. Martin's Press, Inc., 1988), p. 63.

10. Pat Caplan, Anne Keane, Anna Willetts, and Janice Williams, "Studying Food Choice in Its Social and Cultural Contexts: Approaches from a Social Anthropological Perspective," in *The Nation's Diet: The Social Science of Food Choice*, ed. A. Murcott (New York: Longman, 1998), p. 174.

11. Charles and Kerr, *Women, Food and Families*.

12. Spencer Henson, Susan Gregory, Malcom Hamilton, and Ann Walker, "Food Choice and Diet Change within the Family Setting," in *The Nation's Diet*, ed. A. Murcott, p. 186.

13. "The Evening Meal," *Mintel Report 2002*, pp. 32, 35.

14. Charles and Kerr, *Women, Food and Families*, p. 41.

15. Charles and Kerr, *Women, Food and Families*, p. 176.

16. Wood, *The Sociology of the Meal*, p. 58.

17. Warde, *Consumption, Food, and Taste*.

18. "The Evening Meal," *Mintel Report*, p. 16.

19. Annie S. Anderson, Hannah Bradby, Helen Bush, Mike Lean, and Rory Williams, "Food Choice and Culture in a Cosmopolitan City: South Asians, Italians and other Glaswegians," in *The Nation's Diet*, ed. A. Murcott, pp. 267–86.

20. Caplan, Keane, Willetts, and Williams, "Studying Food Choice," in *The Nation's Diet*, ed. A. Murcott, pp. 168–82.

21. Caroline Davidson, *A Woman's Work Is Never Done: A History of Housework in the British Isles, 1650–1950* (London: Chatto and Windus, 1982).

22. Davidson, *A Woman's Work Is Never Done*, p. 71.

23. Bev Botting (ed.), *Family Spending: A Report on the 2001–2002 Expenditure and Food Survey* (London: HMSO, 2003).

24. "Cookware," *Mintel Report* (London: Mintel International, June 2003), p. 23.

25. Roger Dobson, "Young Chefs Just Can't Stand the Heat," *Independent on Sunday* (London), 13 July 2003.

4

Typical Meals

Eating habits are affected by age, life-cycle stage, and social class, with the elderly and the less well-off socioeconomic groups displaying the most routine eating habits, and the most wealthy and young married couples without children the least routine. The latter group could be seen as an adventurous stage between the eating conservatisms of childhood and old age. Tastes also change with age, from sweet to savory, and the middle-aged are more conscious of their weight.

In the daily food cycle of British households, eating is organized into several named meals. Through much of the twentieth century, the names given to these and the times at which they were taken were indicators of social class and regional background. Using time markers, running from first thing in the morning, midday, late afternoon, and early-to-mid-evening, one sequence followed the pattern of breakfast, lunch, (afternoon) tea, and dinner. This implied a middle- or upper-class background, or a life influenced by high-status habits, and by London fashions. The alternative—a sequence of early breakfast, midday dinner, and (high) tea in the late afternoon—implied a lower-middle-class or working-class background, or origins remote from the influence of London and metropolitan habits, in the countryside or from the north. By the late twentieth century, it also tended to be a pattern associated with older people.

In each pattern, the word *tea* was used but referred to quite different types of meal. This was indicated by the use of the qualifiers "afternoon" or "high," although most people simply said "tea," whatever type of meal they anticipated. The word *supper* was also used by people of all backgrounds to denote an evening meal of a varying time and size according to the habits of the speaker. Sometimes it replaced dinner or high tea, but often it denoted an additional, light, late meal.

Despite social changes in recent years, these two basic schemes still underpin British eating habits, even though they are not adhered to as strongly as formerly, and the two varieties of tea meal are in decline. Who eats what when depends to some extent on age, social group, and geographical location. The two patterns crystallized in the mid-to-late nineteenth century and still provide a basis for the way in which people think about the timing and structure of meals. However, they contain elements that are confusing to those whose background is not British: in particular, the application of names to midday meals and the presence of the two entirely different types of meal both colloquially known as tea. The roots of this confusion lie in changes in the timing of meals over the past 200 years.

THE STRUCTURE OF MEALS

Before examining the changes in timing and implications for the meals concerned, it is useful to consider the question "What is a meal?" in British food habits. Throughout the twentieth century, social scientists gathered information describing and quantifying meals, and latterly, considered more deeply the implications of their structure. Name and timing are two elements that help to define meals. Other factors that can be used to define the concept include the presence or absence of companions, tableware, seating, notions of etiquette, and their structure. While the latter has recently shown changes, much continuity can be traced, and it is also the element of meal-taking that has received most attention from researchers into contemporary culture.

From the 1970s onward, there were several studies of meals, mostly within the context of traditional, urban, working-class communities (dense settlements with a history of several decades and a reliance on blue-collar employment in industries such as steel production, mining, and shipbuilding). The work that laid the foundation for this in the 1970s was concerned with theorizing the structure of meals.[1] A basic observation is that meals and drinks are contrasted categories in British food culture. Meals are structured events and have names (breakfast, dinner, etc.); in addition to food, they involve eating implements, tables, seating order, rules about sequences and combinations of foodstuffs, and contrasts in fla-

vor, texture, and temperature. They are often, but not invariably shared—
meals are sometimes taken in isolation because of different work sched-
ules or household composition.

Drinks do not have these things and are more democratic, easily shared
with a wider circle (meals are usually shared only with intimates and honored guests). Snacks, while involving food, were not considered meals, as
the social complexities were fewer and the food items tended to be self
contained (as opposed to the combinations of foods deemed suitable for
meals). The boundaries, however, were flexible, depending on individuals, and the basic work was done before changes in eating habits accelerated in the 1990s.

THE "PROPER MEAL"

Research attention focused on microstudies of working-class food
habits in the 1970s and 1980s, especially the unspoken consensus that exists about the main meal of the day. It was variously referred to by those
being surveyed as a "proper meal" or a "cooked dinner." Fresh meat (beef,
lamb, pork, or chicken) was a priority, with vegetables, always including
potatoes. A sweet pudding often, but not invariably, followed. The savory
course could stand as a meal on its own, but not the sweet. In colloquial
speech, this meal is often called "meat and two veg" (vegetables). Most
studies were undertaken in working-class communities and families, usually traditional nuclear ones of husband, wife, and children. Some work
extended to middle-class families and showed that the concept of the
cooked dinner was also important here; in fact, it was a notion held by
most women, irrespective of age, class, or religion.

An influential study undertaken in the late 1970s assumed that working-
class diet involved two staple carbohydrates, potatoes and cereals (upper-
and middle-class diets included a wider range of cereals, beans, and roots).
Three types of meal were identified: a "major meal," including potatoes,
taken around 6 P.M. on weekdays and in the early afternoon at weekends,
and a "minor meal," bread based, taken at 9 or 10 P.M. on weekdays, and
5 P.M. on weekends. The third meal type consisted simply of a biscuit
(cookie) and a hot drink, available at any time. From this research, it was
concluded that the archetypal meal followed a specific pattern, epitomized in the major meal, of a first main course, hot and savory, based on
the staple potato plus a centerpiece of meat, fish, or eggs, with additional
vegetables and a semiliquid dressing, usually gravy, which links all the
elements and forms a "plateful." A sweet second course repeated these

rules, this time with a cereal staple (pastry, sponge cake), plus fruit and a dressing of custard or cream. The presence of potatoes in the first course was deemed essential to the definition of this meal. Other distinguishing features included the order of sweet to savory, hot to cold, and large amounts to smaller amounts of food in the two courses.[2]

Although later researchers regarded some of the assumptions in this pioneering work as problematic, work in the early 1980s bore out the notion of meat, potatoes (not as chips), an additional vegetable or two, and gravy as being of fundamental importance, considered central to the well-being of the family. The idea of a proper dinner is most developed in the "roast" or "roast dinner." This may be eaten during the week but is most closely associated with Sundays. Amplified with special festive foods, the basic plan also serves for Christmas dinner, and such meals are fundamental to the ideology of the family.[3]

Roast Beef and Gravy

To say everyone knows how to roast beef is an exaggeration, but it is a method rather than a recipe, the success of which depends on well-reared and well-matured meat and the right cut. Grass-fed beef from a traditional breed such as Aberdeen Angus or Hereford is the best, although many farmers raise leaner continental European breeds. Sirloin and rib are popular for roasting, preferably on the bone. The joint should weigh at least 2 lb, preferably more. Dust the fat of the meat with a little flour, pepper, and mustard powder before cooking. Put it in a roasting tin and start it in a very hot oven, 475°F for about 20 minutes. Then turn the temperature down to 375°F and cook for 15 minutes per pound (rare), plus 15 extra minutes (for medium-rare), plus 30 minutes extra (for well-done). At the end of this time, remove the meat from the oven and put it on a heated plate in a warm place. Leave to rest for 30 minutes before carving.

To make the gravy, take the tin the meat was cooked in and pour off most of the fat and any juice into a small bowl. The fat will form a layer on the surface. Spoon off as much as possible, and reserve the juices underneath.

Add about a tablespoon of flour to the tin and stir well over gentle heat to take up the remaining fat. Then stir in the juices from cooking the meat, plus stock (or water from cooking the vegetables) and any juice that is in the plate the beef is on. Cook gently for a few minutes, adjust the seasoning and serve with the beef.

The preparation of cooked dinners appears to have a symbolic role in the validation of women's roles in the family and marriage. Researchers argued that such meals do this because they are important in accommodating the food preferences of the husband or male partner, and women were shown to give priority to male food preferences over their own tastes.[4] The expectation in working-class cultures is that "good wives" have a hot meal on the table upon the return home of the male wage-earner. Over the past century, researchers consistently noted that high meat consumption is associated with men. In the early twentieth century, in households in which food was in short supply, the mother would deny herself food to allow the maximum to the (male) breadwinner and then to her children. In working-class households with limited resources, the man would receive most of the meat purchased in any given week, a habit still noted in the 1980s.[5] There is some indication that the cooked dinner dietary system is primarily a male system, and women on their own choose different, less formal patterns.[6]

In recently married couples, the evening meal was found to be shared, with both partners striving to coordinate activities so that they could share this meal.[7] Considerable emphasis was laid on its importance as time together, relaxing, and it was seen as a meal requiring care and attention, and time for both preparation and consumption. Midday meals (more influenced by work patterns) were rarely shared, and breakfast was a quick, light meal, not necessarily eaten with a partner. In households with children, a proper meal was cooked by the woman and eaten by the whole family sitting round the table together, establishing relationships between family members, important for socializing children and teaching them table manners and food tastes.[8]

Older people were observed to eat in a more structured way, with set mealtimes, eating at the table, at least one cooked meal a day, and little snacking. They were also more likely to cook a Sunday dinner with a roast, while younger families had abandoned this or only did so intermittently, partly because of the time involved in preparing it. Sometimes this habit was revived when older children who could help with the preparation were present, or because it served as a focus for a dispersed family.[9] Young people, especially those living away from the parental home, were more likely to eat snacks, convenience foods and takeaways (purchased, ready-cooked hot food); they are also more likely to be inexperienced cooks, and this is possibly a life-cycle phase that changes with marital and parental status.

The cooked dinner model appears to cross boundaries of social class, but it is flexible and varied according to factors such as availability and taste preferences. Researchers in the early 1990s concluded that the middle-class diet is more varied than that of the working class, a reflection of long-standing social inequalities.[10] Nevertheless, studies of working-class diets showed an aspiration, even if financial constraints prevented it being fulfilled, toward "good" food, seen as quality cuts of meat and fresh vegetables. Women in higher social classes were more willing to make use of eggs, cheese, beans, and other pulses in meals in place of meat, without this being seen as social deprivation; they might use pasta- or rice-based meals to replace a meat-and-two-veg meal. Whether this division will survive the constant introductions of novel foods, the influence of foods from other ethnic groups and the constant pressure for change from supermarkets and the media remains to be seen. Recent evidence is conflicting: in 2003 less than half of those interviewed for market research said they ate a roast every week, but 40 percent still considered themselves "traditionalist" diners who regularly eat meat and two veg.[11] Subsidiary meals, even if they involved food preparation such as making toast and boiling eggs, were not classified as cooking by the interviewees in one study.[12]

MEAL TIMES

The concept of meat and two veg as the proper meal or main meal of the day helps in understanding the confusing patterns of times and names used for meals in everyday usage. These have arisen from a shift in the time of the fashionable hour to eat a proper meal, a process which took place over about 200 years. In early modern Britain, the times of meals were the same for all, irrespective of status or wealth. Some type of breakfast was taken early in the morning, followed by dinner, the main meal of the day (and, although different in structure, the forerunner of the twentieth-century proper meal), at noon or just after. A light meal or supper was taken in the evening, shortly before retiring to bed.

The pattern changed in the eighteenth century. Dinner slipped to later in the afternoon and by the end of century it was taken at about 4 P.M., or later among the very fashionable. The time continued to slip to six or seven o'clock in the evening, and in the mid-nineteenth century, Queen Victoria dined at about 8 P.M. For men in business and the professions, working days began to include a rail commute to work in city offices, with only a short break in the middle of the day. Since then, 7 or 8 P.M. has remained the time for dinner among the leisured and wealthy. As the time between breakfast and dinner got longer, other meals evolved to fill the gap.[13] One was lunch, or luncheon, sometimes a simple collation of leftovers, sometimes more elaborate, taken about midday. The other was afternoon tea, a light meal of bread and butter or cake with tea to drink, taken between about 3:30 and 5 P.M. Very late evening suppers were also served, especially at balls, when they could be very elaborate.

This pattern had relatively little effect on the working classes, the rural population, and those in parts of the country distant from the influence of fashionable London society. A pattern of an early breakfast and a large midday dinner continued to be the norm, although a cooked meal might be provided in the evening for a male breadwinner who could not get home at midday. The evening meal continued to be known as supper until another late afternoon meal, also confusingly known as tea, evolved in the nineteenth century (exactly when is not clear, but evidence from novels suggests it was known by the 1840s). Taken about 5 or 6 P.M., it is distinguished from afternoon tea by being much more substantial, often involving cooked food. People who routinely ate it referred to it as tea, without further qualification, but when it was adopted in the early twentieth century by those more accustomed to an evening dinner, it became known as high tea to distinguish it from afternoon tea.

The idea of a substantial, hot midday dinner became institutionalized in the twentieth century through canteen catering in the workplace, hospitals, and schools, but this aspect of institutional life has declined over the past 30 years. Meals in such places are now more flexible, and sometimes amount to little more than snacks.

Both the lunch/evening-dinner and the midday-dinner/tea pattern have survived, although the latter became less common toward the end of the twentieth century. Until recently, an invitation to tea could leave guests unsure in advance what type of meal they were being invited to share, and to discover that much more, or much less, food was on offer than anticipated. The differences between high tea and a late dinner have now been eroded somewhat by social change, and the use of a particular term may serve more to distinguish the background of the speaker than the content of the meal itself.

INDIVIDUAL MEALS: FORM AND CONTENT

Breakfast

This is the one meal in the British day whose time has remained reasonably constant over centuries of social change. Although the content may vary, there is a consensus over both the time of day to eat breakfast (generally between 7 and 9 A.M., perhaps earlier on a weekday, and later at weekends), and on the ideal foods to be eaten. At the present time, most people who eat breakfast take a light meal of cereal with milk, or toast, butter, and marmalade or some other preserve, and drink orange juice, tea, or coffee with it; oatmeal porridge is also eaten, as is yogurt. Patisserie such as croissants and Danish pastries have become popular in recent years. Anything more complex is unlikely to be cooked in the home on a working day, although a bacon sandwich or a fried breakfast might be eaten in a cafe.

The "full English" (or Scottish, or Irish, or Welsh, depending on which part of the British Isles one is in) breakfast is mostly encountered in hotels or bed-and-breakfast establishments, and only features in private homes at weekends and holiday times. The basis of this meal is fried bacon and eggs, but it is usually elaborated with the addition of any or all of the following: sausages, tomatoes, mushrooms, fried bread, baked beans, fried potatoes, black pudding (blood sausage), potato bread. In some places the pudding may be hog's pudding (a pale sausage-type item, made from cereal and pork, sometimes with dried fruit in it), or, in Scotland, mealie pudding (a sausage based on oatmeal and beef suet) or fruity pudding (similar to mealie pudding, containing dried fruit). This "fry-up" is frequently offered by cafes, especially those for travelers and workmen at any time, as an "all day breakfast." Poached or scrambled eggs sometimes replace fried eggs, or are chosen as a lighter alternative to the full breakfast, as are boiled eggs. Fish is also sometimes offered for cooked breakfasts, especially kippers, smoked haddock, or kedgeree (a dish of smoked fish and rice).

Kedgeree

A dish that developed through the interaction of British and East Indian cultures.

- 12 oz cooked smoked haddock (whitefish or salmon can also be used)
- 6 oz cooked rice
- 1 large onion, chopped
- 2 hard-boiled eggs, shelled and cut in quarters lengthwise
- 3 oz butter
- salt
- a little curry powder or cayenne
- chopped parsley

Melt half the butter and fry the chopped onion gently until soft and lightly browned. Remove any bones and skin from the fish while it is hot and flake coarsely with a fork. Melt the rest of the butter and stir in the onions, fish, and rice. Season to taste. Pile on a hot dish and garnish with chopped parsley and the eggs. Serve with mango chutney.

Porridge, cereal, and perhaps fresh or stewed fruit may precede the cooked element of a full breakfast, and toast, butter, and marmalade or jam are invariably offered after it. Tea or coffee is always offered with breakfast; chocolate- or cocoa-based drinks are unusual in Britain. The breakfast-lunch combination of brunch is known in Britain, but it is regarded as a transatlantic import. It is available in some cafes, and sometimes served in private homes, but has not eroded the affection for the British breakfast and often depends on the same foods.

This type of breakfast developed in the context of nineteenth-century country-house life, when a fashion for house parties developed and the idea of a large breakfast evolved. Food was kept hot over spirit burners and everyone helped themselves. At its most extensive, the meal might include items such as deviled kidneys, curry, mutton cutlets, poached fish, and cold cuts of meat such as ham or tongue. It was a breakfast intended to keep people going during days of hunting or shooting in cold weather.

Dinner

The structure of dinner, as well as the timing, has shown change over the past 200 years. In grand houses, *service à la Française* gave way to *service à la Russe*, with its sequence of dishes handed separately. Edwardian dinners were elaborate with sorbets to cleanse the palate in between the earlier courses and a savory at the end of the meal—a small portion of a dish based on cheese, offal, or meat, highly flavored. After the First World War, dinner became a simplified meal, as the large numbers of servants needed to cook, serve, and clear up the food and clean the china, glass, and silverware for an elaborate sequence of courses disappeared to work in other jobs. Dinner was reduced to three or even two courses, unless it was a formal occasion with guests present. A simplified form of starter (appetizer), main course, and sweet or pudding has become the standard three-course meal of late–twentieth-century entertaining and eating out; the appetizer is usually dropped for family meals.

The Poor

Out of necessity, the poor always maintained a much simpler pattern, eating meat when they could afford it, with pudding or potatoes and a vegetable such as cabbage at dinner, and relying heavily on bread for subsidiary meals. In the two decades before the First World War, this pattern was consistently recorded by socially concerned observers.[14] Breakfasts showed a reliance on bread and butter or margarine and tea, although housewives made efforts to provide bacon, especially for the male bread-winner. Their evening meal repeated the bread-and-butter pattern, possibly with the addition of watercress, a little fish, cold meat, or cake if finances allowed. During the 1920s and 1930s, novel foods such as breakfast cereal were gradually incorporated into the diet. Well into the 1950s, more than half the population said they ate their main meal at lunchtime; a survey published in 1958 noted that 60 percent of the population took their main meal in the middle of the day and called it dinner, eating a tea meal in the evening.[15] Even in 2002, a lingering preference for this remains among households with older, retired occupants, but more than 50 percent of the population eat their main meal in the evening.[16]

Weekday Dinners

The routine weekday cooked dinner does not stipulate particular forms or preparation methods for meat. Standard meals involved steaks, chops, stews, pies, sausages, or offal such as liver, while dishes based on fish, cheese, or eggs were regarded as acceptable on occasions. Potatoes were likely to be plainly boiled, or boiled and mashed; chips (french fries), while sometimes served, were not generally seen as part of such a meal by those interviewed in research during the 1980s. A typical weekday family dinner on the mid–twentieth-century pattern would be a stew, grilled or baked chops, or leftover meat from a roast served with potatoes in some form and a simply cooked vegetable such as cabbage or carrots, followed possibly by pie, crumble, a milk pudding, or stewed fruit with custard or cream.

Crumble

One of the simplest and best-loved puddings, made with many different fruits: apples, apple and blackberry, gooseberries, pears, plums, or apricots. Serve with cream or custard.

- 1 1/2 lb apples (preferably a tart cooking variety such as Bramleys)
- sugar
- 6 oz plain flour
- 3 oz butter
- pinch salt
- 3 oz sugar

Peel, core, and slice the apples. Put them in a pan with a tablespoon water and cook gently until they are just beginning to soften. Taste and add enough sugar to take off the tartness, but don't make them too sweet. Pour into a shallow oven-proof dish.

Rub the butter into the flour until it resembles breadcrumbs. Stir in the sugar and salt.

Sprinkle the crumble mixture in a thick layer on top of the fruit. Bake in a pre-heated oven at 400°F for 30 minutes until the top is golden and crisp.

For quick meals, bacon and eggs or fried egg and chips (fries) might be chosen (or possibly purchased fish and chips). Other options were burgers, pies, or pasties (pastry folded over meat and vegetables, sealed and baked), eaten with chips and vegetables. Meat left over from Sunday dinners, eaten cold or made into some other dish might also be used. Salad was rarely served at dinner, either as a side dish or as the main component of the meal, except in very hot weather. Figures on family expenditure showed that wealthier households ate more and better cuts of meat, and more expensive types of fish. In the early-to-mid twentieth century, they were also more likely to eat more than two courses.

By the twentieth century, a basic two-course pattern of savory followed by sweet became the norm. School dinners, based on this pattern, probably played a strong part in ideas about the proper meal in the second half of the twentieth century. From around the time of the Second World War until the 1980s, a hot two-course midday meal was a standard part of school life for the majority of pupils. The concept of the proper meal has only recently shown signs of breaking down as the impact of longer working hours, more women working outside the home, pre-prepared meals, and ideas about food from other cultures have become influential.

The Sunday Roast

The paradigm of a proper dinner is the main Sunday meal. In the weekly round of the mid-nineteenth to mid-twentieth century, the Sunday dinner or Sunday roast became the most important meal. Sunday was the day of rest, the one day that factory workers had to themselves. Exactly how it was spent depended on the individual, but it offered an opportunity to relax and eat together as a family. Also, it was relatively close to the weekly payday (usually Thursday or Friday), so even poor families had the means to purchase a slightly more expensive piece of meat.

The format of the Sunday roast is relatively stable, built around a large piece of meat. Beef is the first choice, although lamb, pork, and poultry are all acceptable. Most importantly, the meat should be roasted (which now always means oven roasting). It should also be properly accompanied. This invariably means gravy, and usually some other condiment. For beef, horseradish sauce and perhaps mustard would be expected. With lamb, mint sauce is the traditional accompaniment. Pork is generally roasted to ensure the skin forms crisp crackling, and is served with both applesauce and sage and onion stuffing. Poultry is an acceptable alternative for a Sunday dinner. Until the 1960s, a roast chicken was considered an expensive treat; since then, intensive production methods have made them cheap and ubiquitous. Properly, a roast chicken is served with bread sauce and stuffing (usually sage and onion, but sometimes sausage meat or chestnut). Game is also acceptable, though a minority choice. Redcurrant jelly is often offered with both furred and feathered game, and bread sauce with game birds and turkey.

It is not traditional to offer any form of hors d'oeuvre or starter before a Sunday dinner, although wealthier households, or those influenced by continental or restaurant practices might offer a soup or another light dish. The exception to this, and one that is purely British—or more specifically English—relates to Yorkshire pudding (a baked batter pudding). This is the classic accompaniment to roast beef (although it can be served with other meats as well). In northern English tradition, the pudding was cut up and served with gravy before the roast. The idea is traditionally said to be a device for taking the edge off hunger, and has given rise to the saying "him who eats most pudding gets most meat." Alternatively, the pudding can be eaten on the same plate as the meat and gravy.

Yorkshire Pudding

Often served with roast beef, or sometimes before it, with gravy. Mix the batter a couple of hours in advance.

- 4 oz flour
- 2 eggs
- 10 fl oz milk and water mixed
- salt

Put the flour in a basin and add a pinch of salt. Break in the eggs and stir until well amalgamated. Add the milk and water slowly, stirring well to eliminate lumps. Stop adding liquid when the batter has reached the consistency of light cream.

To cook the pudding, take a roasting tin and add about a tablespoonful of beef dripping from roasting the joint. Put this in a hot oven, 450°F, to heat for a few minutes. It should be smoking hot. Remove the tin from the oven and pour in the batter (wear oven gloves, as the fat may spit—it should hiss as the batter is added). Put the tin back in the oven and bake for about 30–40 minutes, until golden and cooked (there should be no soft batter in the middle). Cut into squares for serving.

The vegetables served with a roast normally include roast potatoes, cooked in hot fat in the oven until they develop a crisp crust. Potatoes cooked in some other manner, usually boiled, may also be offered. In summer, boiled new potatoes might be offered instead of any other form, especially with lamb, and those following late–nineteenth- or early–twentieth-century practice would offer "game chips" (straw potatoes) with roast game birds. Parsnips, roast or mashed, might also be offered with beef or game; they are generally considered winter food. Other vegetables depend to a certain extent on the season, although boiled carrots and boiled cabbage are commonly served at any time of year, as are peas, since they are now mostly purchased deep frozen. Broccoli, cauliflower, green beans, and in recent years, courgettes (zucchini) are also options.

The other essential component of a proper Sunday meal is a pudding, or something that in other countries would be regarded as a sweet dessert. The usage of the word pudding in British English is confusing for foreigners. It applies to several different groups of dishes, some sweet, some savory, as well as acting as a portmanteau word for any sweet item considered suitable for ending a meal, and when it indicates anything from plum pudding to fresh fruit. This relates to the development of various types of puddings as a staple food in early modern Britain: the evolutionary tree included sausage-like black or white puddings of offal and cereal, boiled puddings of suet and flour or breadcrumbs, batter puddings (of which Yorkshire pudding is the sole survivor), suet puddings with savory fillings, and numerous sweet steamed or baked puddings. The latter were frequently fruit-based, trimmed with pastry, and began to elide into the pie or tart categories of food. Other types included soft-textured puddings made from a sweetened combination of milk and cereal such as rice or semolina. Until the mid-nineteenth century, puddings, plain or rich and often sweetened, were often served in the same course as roasts of meat, and plum pudding and roast beef are mentioned as foods for Christmas celebrations.

In modern English, pudding had become equated with sweet dishes and assumed the sense of dessert. Sometimes this course is known as a sweet, although, as with everything to do with deportment in British society, terminology is riddled with social nuances, and this term tends to be regarded as lower class. In current usage, a pudding (or "pud") for a Sunday dinner would generally be something slightly more elaborate and celebratory than that for a weekday. Puddings, apart from being sweet, were usually hot and filling. Standard choices in mid–twentieth-century practice included fruit pies or crumbles, steamed sponge puddings, or perhaps a trifle. Other choices, especially in the early twentieth century included jelly, custard, and tinned fruit.

Bread and Butter Pudding

A dish that probably evolved as a method for using up leftover bread and butter from tea meals. By the mid-twentieth century, it was considered plain and old-fashioned, nursery food. In the 1980s it was revived as a dessert worthy of the best restaurants.

- 3 slices white bread, buttered
- 1 pint (i.e., 20 fl oz) whole milk, or milk and cream mixed
- 3 eggs, beaten
- 1 oz sultanas, soaked in water
- 4 oz sugar
- nutmeg

Cut each slice of bread and butter into four triangles. Arrange in a buttered oven-proof dish. Drain the sultanas and sprinkle over the bread slices. Bring the milk to boiling point and remove from the heat. Stir in the sugar and then the eggs and pour over the bread. Leave for half an hour to allow the bread to soak up the custard mixture. Bake in a moderate oven, about 350°F, for half an hour, until set and lightly browned. Dust with nutmeg and serve.

Serves 4.

Summer Pudding

- about 6 oz white bread, preferably a couple of days old
- 8 oz raspberries
- 8 oz red currants
- 5 oz sugar
- 2–3 tbsp sugar

Mix the sugar and water in a pan, bring to the boil and add the fruit. Cook gently until the juice runs.

Cut any crusts off the bread and cut in thin slices. Use most of this to line a pudding basin. Pour the fruit mixture in and cover with a layer of bread. Place a saucer on top and put a weight of about 1 lb on this. Chill for several hours or overnight. Turn out and serve with cream or custard.

Trifle

Packet "trifle sponges" are sold in Britain for making this. Sponge finger biscuits or a small sponge cake cut in fingers can be used instead. Ingredients of trifle are a matter of personal taste: some people add fruit, fresh or canned, instead of jam; others add a layer of jelly (Jell-O) over the sponge, and some use a syllabub instead of cream.

- 8 trifle sponges
- raspberry jam
- 6 macaroons or ratafias
- sherry
- 15 fl oz custard
- 10 fl oz whipping or heavy cream

Split the sponge cakes and spread them with jam. Arrange in a glass bowl and pour 2–3 glasses of sherry over. Crush the macaroons or ratafias and sprinkle over. Pour over the custard. Leave in a cool place until almost ready to serve, then whip the cream and spread this over the top.

Decorate with flaked almonds lightly browned in the oven, or glacé cherries, halved, with candied angelica leaves.

A Note about Drinks

One characteristic of British food culture is that drinking and eating are viewed as essentially separate activities. Wealthier households might offer sherry or gin before a Sunday roast, and perhaps wine to drink with it. Wine with meals, especially dinner, was essentially an upper- and upper-middle-class habit until the 1970s, but has become more widespread since then. In many communities the men would decamp to the pub for a pint (of beer) before the midday meal on Sunday. Alcoholic drinks are less likely to be served with food during the week. Beer or cider might be offered with a meal, but this has never been an especially strong habit. Water, milk (for children), and soft drinks of various types might also be offered. Tea or coffee is normally drunk after meals, although they are sometimes served throughout, especially at meals of the high tea type.

Recent Changes

The idea of what is allowable at the main meal of the day has seen considerable change in the last 30 years. Ideas about timing have also relaxed, as traditional patterns of employment and homemaking have been eroded. Eating a main meal in the evening is no longer an upper-class phenomenon, but although the timing has changed, the old pattern of names may be adhered to so that the person eating it calls it "tea." In 2002, market research reported that the evening meal was a "key eating occasion" in U.K. households, but that it was being influenced by social change, in particular, that less preparation time was being spent on it. This was due to pressure of work (especially on women) and conflicting interests in other leisure pursuits. Six out of 10 adults were reported to spend less than three-quarters of an hour preparing their weekday meal; the majority spent between 16 minutes and half an hour; and about half the respondents took no more than 30 minutes to eat it. Only 2 out of 10 cooked from scratch, but conversely, only 1 in 10 relied heavily on prepared foods, the rest being somewhere in between. Household structure also influenced meals—single-person households were less likely to eat a main meal in the evening, and families with children more likely to do so. Lower socioeconomic groups reported more snacking and a less formal pattern of eating.[17]

Food considered suitable for the evening meal now includes pizza, pasta in several forms, kebabs, curries, and stir-fries and other Chinese-influenced food. In the 1990s, many households, especially wealthier ones and those in the mid-range age group with children present, began to experiment more with these exotic foods. Recently, Thai food has become popular, chiefly among younger, higher-income metropolitan groups.[18] Purchased desserts, especially dairy-based items such as yogurt, fromage frais, and ice cream also became more popular in place of heavier, cooked sweet dishes. One study suggested that knowledge about and consumption of exotic food is one way of establishing distinctions between social groups, and that it has status currency in groups with less ability to compete in purely materialistic terms.[19]

However, food, including exotic items, may as easily be purchased pre-prepared, either cook-chilled from a supermarket, or hot from a takeaway (hot food shop), as prepared at home. Between 1991 and 2001, the amount spent on ready meals went from £0.81 billion ($1.3 billion) to £1.70 billion ($2.5 billion), and the amount of money spent on takeaways and eating out also showed large increases.[20] The market for convenience ethnic food also increased from £1.25 billion ($2 billion) in 1991 to £2.80 billion ($4 billion) in 2001. Market research showed a growth in purchases of complete Indian or complete Chinese ready meals, up from about a quarter of respondents in 1999 to about a third in 2002.[21] Markets for pizza, pasta, and rice also grew, as did that for packaged desserts. This was attributed to the activities of grocery chains, which have been developing take-out ethnic meals and ready-to-bake pizzas. The uptake of such foods, however, varied according to employment participation, social class, and age group. The largest take-up was among better-off and professionals, with the poorest least likely to indulge, though whether this was through lack of money or innate conservatism was not explored.

Lunch

Lunch is always a midday or early afternoon meal. The composition has always been variable; in the mid-nineteenth century, it was an informal collation of cold items and leftovers set out on a help-yourself basis. Toward the end of the nineteenth century, more formal lunches of two or three courses evolved, but they would be unlikely to involve the heavy roasts and meat dishes made for dinner. A family lunch might follow the two-course pattern, consist of a light egg, meat, or fish dish, a salad or soup, followed by fruit or some light dessert or cake. In the late twentieth century, as the pattern of taking larger meals in the evening became dominant, the idea of lunch became much more variable. Packed lunches made at home are a common option for schoolchildren. They usually consist of a sandwich, plus crisps (potato chips), or some other savory snack and a carton of fruit juice or juice-based drink. Fresh fruit and yogurt or fromage frais are frequently included as well. For working adults, lunch at the office could be a sandwich (purchased or brought from home), baked potato or soup, or possibly something more substantial in a works canteen (cafeteria). A business lunch in a restaurant, however, might be a large, expensive meal with heavy food and substantial amounts of wine.

Salmon Fishcakes

Originally a method for using leftover cooked whitefish, fishcakes are now often made with salmon and appear on pub and restaurant menus.

- 10 oz potatoes, cooked and mashed roughly
- 10 oz salmon, cooked and flaked
- about 2 tbsp parsley, chopped
- a little dill, chopped
- grated rind of half a lemon
- 1 egg
- about 4 fl oz double cream

- 1/2 tsp salt
- dry breadcrumbs
- oil for frying

Mix the potatoes, salmon, herbs, lemon rind, and salt gently but thoroughly. Whisk the egg and the cream and stir in. Divide into eight and form each piece into a neat disc about an inch thick. Chill until firm, then dip each one in bread-crumbs.

Heat the oil in a frying pan and cook gently for about five minutes on each side until golden brown.

Serve with tartar or hollandaise sauce.

Tea

Both afternoon tea and high tea involve drinking tea, and there the re-semblance ends. Not only are there implied social nuances and variations in timing; the structures of the meals are also quite different. Both meals are also considered old-fashioned, and disappearing from British life, al-though some cafes and hotels offer elaborate teas.

Afternoon tea has always been a light meal. Food is often minimal and dainty, but presentation is elaborate. In the nineteenth century, bread and butter was the normal accompaniment. This developed into tiny sand-wiches filled with cucumber, cress, or perhaps potted meat or fish. Toast, muffins, or crumpets (small, very thick yeast-leavened pancake-type items) might be served in winter. Some type of cake is usually offered with afternoon tea: a sponge cake or a fruitcake are the standard choices. Scones are also considered a tea-time specialty, usually served with whipped cream and jam. In the southwest of England, this might become a "cream tea," with clotted cream.

Scones

- 1/2 lb flour
- 1/2 teaspoon salt
- 1/2 teaspoon bicarbonate of soda
- 1 teaspoon cream of tartar
- 2 oz butter
- milk to mix (about 5 fl oz)
- beaten egg to glaze
- 2 oz dried fruit—currants, raisins, sultanas or chopped dates (optional)

Sieve the flour, salt, bicarbonate of soda and cream of tartar into a basin and rub in the butter. Stir in the fruit if used. Stir in enough milk to make a light dough, just firm enough to handle. Turn onto a floured surface and roll out lightly to about an inch thick. Cut into rounds and place on a floured baking sheet. Brush the tops with beaten egg and bake in a hot oven, 450°F, for 7–10 minutes. Cool on a wire rack.

Serve with strawberry jam and whipped cream, or, if available, clotted cream.

Although less emphasis is placed on porcelain tea sets and silver teapots nowadays, most British households can muster a kettle for boiling water, a tea pot and cups or mugs, testimony to the continuing importance of the drink in British culture. One item developed specifically for after-noon tea is the cake stand, a tiered stand of three dishes one above the other, used for serving cakes, scones or other teatime delicacies.

High tea involves much more food and simpler presentation. (The name "high tea," which indicates a tea at which meat was served, seems to have evolved when the meal was adopted by the relatively wealthy as an alternative to dinner on the servant's afternoon off.) At present, the only difference between one person's tea and someone else's dinner may be one of nomenclature, but high tea did have a distinct identity from the late nineteenth to the mid-twentieth century. It was distinguished by the pres-ence of meat or something considered nearly equivalent. Sausages, kip-pers, herrings, smoked haddock poached and served with an egg, pork pie, ham salad, cold meat, mushrooms on toast, egg dishes, baked beans on toast were all possibilities. Bread and butter (or margarine) was always placed on the table, often with a choice of two or three different types—a standard white household loaf, perhaps a teacake or some other small enriched rolls, or crumpets in winter.

Another distinguishing feature was the presence of numerous cakes. Among these would be found at least one, and possibly two large cakes—perhaps a plain fruitcake, plus a sponge, and smaller buns, jam or lemon curd tarts, and any number of plain sweet pastry or cake-type items, recipes for which were popularized by manufacturers of baking powder and flour millers in the late nineteenth century.

Lemon Curd

- 4 lemons
- 5 eggs
- 4 oz fresh butter
- 1 lb sugar

Cake stand. Courtesy of Bettys & Taylors of Harrogate, Ltd., North York-shire, U.K.

Wash the lemons, then grate the zest finely. Squeeze the juice. Beat the eggs, and put them with the lemon zest, juice, butter and sugar in the top of a double saucepan. Stir until the sugar has dissolved and the mixture thickens. Once thick, strain into small sterilized jars, cover and store in a cool place.

Use as a spread on toast, bread, to fill small tarts, or serve with ice cream.

As the preserve contains large quantities of egg, it should not be kept for more than a few weeks.

The food was all placed on the table at once. Hot items being consumed first, then individuals selected from the rest to make up their meal. In this respect, the structure of high tea bore some resemblance to the eighteenth century dinner with its removes and wide range of foods to which the diners helped themselves. In the popular consciousness high tea was generally connected with farmhouses and rural life. The tableware and linen associated with the idea was more rustic than anything that would have been expected at dinner.

A few special variants of teas developed. One was the fried "ham and egg" tea, which seems to have been a phenomenon of the 1920s and 1930s. Another was a connection with north country traditions, and with the county of Yorkshire, which was considered to produce particularly excellent and ample teas. Scottish tradition also developed a special type of high tea, involving a hot course such as sausage and chips (fries), followed by a cake stand of sweet items. Sunday teas, common in the 1950s, were more elaborate than weekday teas, with foods regarded as a treat, such as tinned salmon or peaches. The word supper has also been retained as a name for an evening meal, but exactly what that meal comprises depends on the speaker. It can indicate a full-blown proper meal, a high tea, or simply a snack before bedtime.

SNACKS AND SNACKING

The nineteenth century rural round appears to have involved a break for a drink every two hours or so. "Elevenses" were taken in the mid-morning, a habit which survives in the work place as the mid-morning coffee break. The structured system of "three square meals a day"—breakfast, followed by lunch/dinner, and dinner/tea—did not routinely include snacks, although drinks (especially coffee and tea) were taken between meals. In the late twentieth century, the breakdown of this pattern and the vastly increased availability of pre-packaged ready to eat items led to increased snacking, to the extent that meals were sometimes described as lying between the snacks, not the other way round. Market research into children's snacking habits recorded parental concern over this, especially pester power (children nagging adults to make impulse purchases of confectionery and salted snacks).[22] Midday eating habits for children also changed from the formal school dinner of the past to wider options—including pizzas, burgers, the possibility of visiting cafes or fast-food outlets, or a packed lunch brought from home; these were often observed to include savory snacks. Nutritionists have also expressed concern over the volume of snack foods, their targeting at children, and the phenomenon of grazing (the frequent consumption of snack foods and soft drinks between meals). One problem for researchers in this area is the difficulty in defining a snack, especially when more substantial foods including bread (sandwiches, burgers in buns) are involved.

THE DEATH OF THE MEAL

In the early 1980s, evidence indicated that the population of the United Kingdom still ate three meals a day plus snacks. Also, 70 to 80 percent of the population claimed to sit down to a family meal every day.[23] Since then, both researchers and journalists have prophesied the death of the meal, citing social change, especially in the role of women, as one reason for this, and claiming an increasing trend toward snacking. During the 1980s, the evidence for this was contradictory, and the concept (if not the actuality) of a proper meal remained central to the family food system, and even snacks of convenience food were taken together by family members. This pattern has shown signs of diminishing; in 1999, about half the adults in the United Kingdom claimed to sit down and eat with other members of the family every day, but 1 in 7 said they would rather eat in front of the television, and 1 in 10 that they only made the effort on special occasions, such as birthdays or anniversaries.[24]

The notion, if not the actuality, of a proper meal or cooked dinner is still the anchor that holds down the daily round of meals, culminating in a weekly pattern of Sunday dinner, and an annual one of Christmas dinner.

Demand for convenience food, especially for non-traditional and ethnic meals, is growing. Smaller households with one or two working adults appeared to have little time or inclination to cook from scratch during the week. A move away from regular mealtimes was discernible, together with a shift to a more varied diet. The historic pattern delivers the clichés of the cooked breakfast, meat and two veg, and the afternoon tea. These are still cited as examples of traditional meals. Yet any community with a size greater than a village will contain at least one takeaway hot food shop providing alternative meals—curry, Chinese food, pizza, kebabs, burgers, or the native tradition of fish and chips. All these things, of course, may also be home cooked depending on interests and ethnic origin. Cook-chill ready meals provide a third solution, which leaves family members able to choose portions for one, meat or vegetarian, traditional or otherwise, to be heated in microwave ovens and eaten at a time convenient for the individual. In practice, many people use a combination of these options, depending on taste and circumstance.

NOTES

1. Mary Douglas, "Deciphering a Meal," in *Food and Culture: A Reader*, ed. C. Counihan and P. van Esterik (New York: Routlege, 1997).

2. Michael Nicod, "Gastronomically Speaking: Food Studied as a Medium of Communication," in *Nutrition and Lifestyles*, ed. Michael Turner (London: Applied Science Publishers, 1980).

3. Nickie Charles and Marion Kerr, *Women, Food and Families* (New York: St. Martin's Press, Inc., 1988).

4. A. Murcott, "On the Social Significance of the 'Cooked Dinner' in South Wales," *Social Science Information*, pp. 677–96, quoted in Roy C. Wood, *The Sociology of the Meal* (Edinburgh: Edinburgh University Press, 1995), p. 55.

5. Charles and Kerr, *Women, Food and Families*, p. 80.

6. Wood, *The Sociology of the Meal*, p. 87.

7. Debbie Kemmer, Annie S. Anderson, and David W. Marshall, "The Marriage Menu: Life, Food, and Diet in Transition," in *The Nation's Diet: The Social Science of Food Choice*, ed. Anne Murcott (New York: Longman, 1998), p. 202.

8. Alan Warde, *Consumption, Food, and Taste: Culinary Antinomies and Commodity Culture* (London: Sage, 1997), p. 37.

9. Pat Caplan, Anne Keane, Anna Willetts, and Janice Williams, "Studying Food Choice in Its Social and Cultural Contexts: Approaches from a Social Anthropological Perspective," in *The Nation's Diet: The Social Science of Food Choice*, ed. Anne Murcott (New York: Longman, 1998), p. 175.

10. Warde, *Consumption, Food, and Taste*, p. 181.

11. Jamie Doward and Edward Gibbes, "Roasts Off Menu as We Eat on the Go," *Observer*, 27 July 2003.

12. Charles and Kerr, *Women, Food and Families*, p. 19.

13. C. Anne Wilson, *Luncheon, Nuncheon, and Other Meals: Eating with the Victorians* (Stroud, United Kingdom: Alan Sutton Publishing, Ltd., 1994).

14. B. Seebohm Rowntree, *Poverty: A Study of Town Life* (London: Macmillan and Co., 1901); Maud Pember-Reeves, *Round about a Pound a Week: 1913* (London: Virago Books, republished 1999).

15. Geoffrey C. Warren, ed., *The Foods We Eat* (London: Cassell, 1958).

16. "The Evening Meal," *Mintel Report*, April 2002, p. 5.

17. Ibid., pp. 29–34.

18. "Thai and Other Emerging Foods," *Mintel Report*, June 2003, p. 49.

19. Peter Atkins and Ian Bowler, *Food in Society* (New York: Arnold and Oxford University Press, 2001), p. 285.

20. "The Evening Meal," *Mintel Report*, 2002, p. 16.

21. "Seasonings," *Mintel Report*, July 2003, p. 9.

22. "Snacking on the Go," *Mintel Report*, April 2002, p. 6.

23. British Nutrition Foundation, "Eating in the Early 1980s," in *Eating in the Early 1980s. Attitudes and Behaviour: Main Findings* (London: BNF, 1985). Report on a survey carried out by MRB International Ltd. London for the British Nutrition Foundation.

24. Market Opinion and Research International (MORI), "Learning by Example: How Family Mealtimes Could Make 'Good Eating' Easier to Swallow," 10 February 1999, http://www.mori.com/polls.

5

Eating Out

In the 1980s, the nation's favorite meal out appeared to be prawn cocktail, steak, and chips followed by Black Forest gateau;[1] it is now sometimes claimed to be curry. These clichés have some truth in them but disguise the extraordinary complexity, dynamism, and the eclectic nature of eating out in contemporary Britain. By the 1990s, London was acknowledged to have one of the most vibrant and interesting eating-out cultures in the world, with numerous excellent restaurants, cafes, and pubs. London is a multicultural city with facilities that reflect its global importance. It sets the fashions for the rest of the country, so restaurants in other cities tend toward the eclectic style of London menus, rather than reflecting their locality. Most cities now have several good restaurants, and many pubs provide food of reasonable to excellent quality. Smaller towns may have one or more reasonable to good restaurants on the metropolitan pattern and several establishments serving Chinese or Indian food. The other side of this picture is one of a nation that can be sold the latest fad, and one that consumes fast food in enormous quantities.

As with all aspects of British food culture, the change over the last 50 years has been extraordinary. In mid–twentieth-century Britain, eating out had a dreadful image. Badly served, poor and unimaginative food, discourteous staff, and dining rooms with limited and inconvenient hours were some of the problems travelers and diners commented on. Some of this was due to British indifference to food and a national unwillingness to complain, and some was the effects of rationing and austerity working through.[2]

The reasons for the change are complex. On the consumer side, they include rising incomes generally, a greater proportion of disposable income, more foreign travel leading to greater curiosity about ethnic foods, and an interest in food as a leisure pursuit. In certain socioeconomic groups, time poverty is also a factor, leading to an increased demand for food prepared by someone else. On the industry side, the efforts of several informed and energetic individuals helped to alter the notion of cooking as a job for the relatively unskilled and less intelligent to one that is interesting and has the potential to make wealthy celebrities of a few. Cooking for a living acquired a higher-status image.

Any discussion of eating out in Britain involves problems of definition. Does eating out refer only to food taken in commercial establishments, or to meals taken in other people's homes as well? Is hot food purchased from a takeaway outlet but consumed at home a part of eating out? Does a meal eaten in a school, hospital, or work cafeteria count as eating out? Difficulties also arise when considering the places in which people pay to eat out. They exist in huge variety, but their distinguishing features are badly defined. Some establishments incorporate two elements in one (pubs with restaurants, ethnic restaurants offering takeaway food). Some have other primary functions (hotels provide accommodation and food, delicatessens essentially retail food but may have cafes attached). In addition, a combination of fashion and economics dictates that they are constantly evolving. The majority of businesses are small, run by individuals and families, although there are several large companies involved in chain hotels, pubs, fast-food franchising, and contract catering.[3]

Pubs, whose original function was to serve alcoholic drinks to, in all their variety, all comers at specified times, might be considered as one end of a spectrum, and hotels that provide menus of food suitable for all times of day to residents, with drinks as requested, as the other. In between is a huge variety of establishments: sandwich bars, coffee bars, tea shops, carveries, pizzerias, kebab houses, snack bars, fast-food outlets, motorway service stations, transport cafes (truck stops), train and station buffets, airport lounges, and restaurants in many forms. Although they are not, perhaps, technically part of eating out, takeaway shops providing hot food for consumption elsewhere (often taken home for eating) are also discussed here. Until recently, a substantial non-commercial or "institutional catering" sector, providing food in school or work cafeterias, messes for the armed forces, hospital catering, and university refectories existed. Such places do not automatically spring to mind when eating out is mentioned, but they are important. This has become more commercialized in the past decade as governments have chosen to subcontract catering activities formerly undertaken in-house.

Information on eating out in Britain is sparse. Sources include guides to eating out and places to stay, market research reports with all their limitations, the trade press, and a handful of studies on working in catering. These give an overall idea of the industry, but constant change, the lack of definition, and different collection methods make it difficult to compare statistics. A few memoirs have been published by hoteliers and chefs[4] together with one substantial discussion of postwar changes in food quality.[5] Recently, a major sociological study sought to investigate frequency of, and attitudes toward, eating out in urban England more deeply, comparing London with two provincial centers and providing much information on actual meals eaten out, how people felt about the overall experience, and the motivations for eating out.[6] A little quantitative information on consumer behavior is available from government sources: the National Food Survey (now the Expenditure and Food Survey) has included data on eating out since 1994, and the Family Expenditure Survey gives information on food eaten away from home and purchases of soft drinks, confectionery, and alcoholic drinks. In 2001–02, the average weekly expenditure of each household in the United Kingdom was £10.90 ($15.80), with another £8.90 ($12.00) being spent on alcoholic drinks away from home, £3.60 ($5.20) on takeaway meals for home consumption, £4.10 ($5.95) on other takeaway and snack food, £1.80 ($1.90) on food in cafeterias, and £1.30 on meals bought and eaten in the workplace.[7] Inevitably, these average figures disguise large differences between households, notably a higher amount spent on takeaway food by low-income groups. Market research also provides additional information.

SOME FIGURES

The rapid turnover of businesses and problems of definition make it difficult to establish figures relating to eating out. What is clear is that the catering industry is of huge economic importance to Britain. In 2002, there were about 25,950 restaurants, in the United Kingdom. They served 696 million meals a year, representing £4.7 billion ($6.8 billion) worth of food sales. In the same year, about 51,500 pubs served 1 billion meals, representing £3.3 billion ($4.8 billion) worth of sales. In addition, 19,342 contract catering outlets (in schools, hospitals, workplaces, etc.) served nearly 1.6 billion meals, representing sales of £3.7 billion ($5.4 billion).[8]

In 2002, just over 1,371,000 people were employed in catering: about 420,000 were employed in relatively lowly positions as kitchen porters and catering assistants, 265,000 as chefs, and 220,000 in waiting on tables. Thirty percent of all hospitality workers were working in the restaurant sector, 16 percent of hospitality workers in pubs, and 12 percent in contract catering.[9] The industry generally is notorious for low pay and poor conditions, especially long and antisocial working hours. At the top end, a handful of "celebrity chefs" can more or less dictate their terms, and some have almost developed their names as brands, using restaurants, books, televisions, and Web sites to provide trusted formulae and a reputation for good food.

Amount Spent on Eating Out

Eating out has taken a small but steadily increasing percentage of household expenditure. Over the years 1960 through 1993, the percentage of household expenditure on food fell from 31 to 18 percent, but within this, the proportion devoted to eating out rose from about 10 percent in 1960 to about 21 percent in 1993.[10] More money is spent on eating out in southeastern England than elsewhere in the United Kingdom, where both wealth and premium-priced restaurants are concentrated. Men spend more than women, and slightly more is spent at midday than in the evening. Professionals spend proportionately more on eating out, tend to use restaurants rather than takeaways, and also spend disproportionately more on wine.[11]

On the industry side, property is expensive, and the interiors of fashionable restaurants are expected to be stylish. The setup cost of a large restaurant for the upper end of the market in London was quoted as about £2 million ($2.9 million) in 2002.[12] To help recoup this, the profit margin on food costs in a restaurant is expected to be about 70 percent.[13] Value-added tax at 17.5 percent is levied by the government on food eaten out or purchased in takeaways (food purchased for preparation at home is zero-rated for this); substantial markups are also made on wine, water, and other extras. This makes eating out expensive. Some establishments include a service charge (tip) in the bill, but many do not. There are no hard and fast rules about tipping. In most restaurants it is customary to leave a small tip (10 percent of the bill is the normal rule), although debates sometimes break out in the press about whether this practice is archaic. Many staff rely on tips to raise the level of a small basic wage. A trend toward more casual, cheaper establishments, such as the idea of the "gastropub" (a pub that is run by a chef who is serious about good food), has become apparent recently.

Reasons for Eating Out: Necessity and Pleasure

For many, eating out is a necessity. More meals are eaten away from home at midday than in the evening, and many of these are taken at work (or at school by children). In one market research survey, 51 percent of respondents claimed to eat out at least once a week, and of these, 21 percent ate out "most days," but closer questioning revealed that only 3 percent of respondents actually did so in leisure time. Essentially, the eating out was a necessary part of their daily work routine.[14] In 2002, just over half of all British workers were reported to take a lunch break of about 30 minutes every day and most purchased lunch from a workplace restaurant or cafeteria, rather than outside the place of employment. Sandwiches were the most favored item, although jacket potatoes, soup, and savory pies were also popular choices.[15] Another group who eat out through necessity are travelers and tourists, a group which is extremely important to the U.K. restaurant economy, but is volatile, subject to fears about terrorism and public health scares.

While eating at work is of great importance both economically and in the daily lives of the population, it is not eating out in the sense that is popularly understood. For most people the phrase brings to mind the idea of eating for pleasure, as entertainment, a leisure pursuit, taking a meal in a restaurant or a pub, relaxing in the company of relatives or friends. Often, eating out is bound up with the idea of a special occasion. Inevitably service and food are important elements, although attitudes vary as to whether it should be "plain English" food or something more elaborate. Other factors that contribute to the enjoyment of the experience include the idea that it is a break from routine (especially for women, from routine food preparation); that it provides time to relax in a time-pressured society, an excuse to dress up, and is associated with a sense of occasion. Sharing a meal out—with a spouse, friends or relatives—is also important. Although eating in public appears to have become one method of displaying taste through consumption in contemporary British society, most people judge a meal on the overall experience, unless the food or service are particularly bad. The experience of having been a student in higher education seems to have a demonstrable link to the habit of eating out and to being prepared to try new foods.[16] Eating out also appears to play a part in strengthening social bonds, especially for urban populations whose lives are more likely to involve long commutes to work and less likely to have relatives living near by.[17]

LICENSING LAWS

Attitudes about alcohol have played a complex role in the development of places providing food and drink over the past two centuries. The sale of alcohol is regulated by licensing laws that state where, when, and to whom alcohol can be sold. An "on" license of the type held by pubs allows the retail sale of alcoholic drinks for consumption on or off the premises during specific hours. Other establishments may be licensed with the same conditions as those applying to the pub or have restricted licenses: for instance, a restaurant license that allows the sale of alcohol to people taking meals in premises habitually used for the supply of meals, or a residential license, for hotel guests. Licensing laws are being redrafted, and new legislation, which was due to be introduced in 2004, will give pubs and bars the flexibility to stay open 24 hours a day (they are currently limited to 11 A.M.–11 P.M., except on special occasions). "Going drinking" always implies the consumption of alcoholic drinks but has no implications for eating (although food might be taken at some point). Eating out, as well as taking food, usually implies consumption of some type of drink, but does not necessarily imply alcohol. It may mean water or coffee with a sandwich, wine with a restaurant meal, or beer with a pub meal.

EATING OUT: PLACES

The Restaurant

The restaurant, as a place that offers a choice off a menu prepared to order as a customer requests, is well understood in Britain. Apart from that, little about the concept is fixed. Distinctions may be stated in terms of specific cuisine (French, Italian, Indian, Mediterranean, modern British); particular type of food (pizzeria, kebab house, steakhouse); or the mode of operation (fast-food restaurant, carvery). They may be attached to hotels or pubs, stand alone, or be part of a large chain. Although the figure of 25,950 restaurants in Britain in 2002 is only about 650 higher than in 1996, the number of meals taken in them has increased substantially during that period, from 609 million to 696 million, as has the real value of food sales, from £4.1 billion ($6 billion) to £4.8 billion ($7 billion).[18] Most highly regarded restaurants are located in or within easy reach of London.

The notion of the restaurant is inherently French. Ideas about menu structure and dishes derived from haute cuisine sat uneasily alongside British food traditions when restaurants began to appear in Britain in the first half of the nineteenth century. Until well into the twentieth century, they were an essentially masculine environment, although it had become acceptable for women to dine out (in the company of men) sometime around the start of the twentieth century. The food available was of variable quality, although at its best was excellent. French influence was strong and chefs such as Escoffier (who worked at the Savoy Hotel in London at the close of the nineteenth century) were extremely influential. But the restaurant also absorbed nineteenth-century notions such as the chophouse, which served limited menus of plainly cooked food. The solid tradition of the roast dinner also became part of the restaurant experience. It still features prominently, especially on Sundays, and has become the staple of carvery-type operations, in which roast meat is carved from the joint at the customer's request. Steakhouses, too, echo a tradition of plainly cooked steaks and chops important in eating out in Britain over many years.

Restaurant in Lanes, Brighton. © TRIP/H. Rogers.

During the Second World War, restaurants still operated, although they, like everyone else, had to accommodate the stringencies of food rationing and prices were set by law. (Many National Restaurants were also established by the Ministry of Food to provide nutritious food at reasonable prices, as part of the general package of food control measures.) Some of the substitutions that chefs resorted to in restaurant cookery lasted beyond the limits of rationing—either through inertia or because they increased profitability once life returned to normal. This appears to have played a substantial part in the dire image that British restaurant food had in the 1950s and early 1960s. The general quality of food in restaurants and hotel dining rooms (the two categories overlapped) during the 1950s was extremely poor, but it was during this time that the foundations of the current interest in eating out were laid. Influential figures included Francis Coulson, at Sharrow Bay in the Lake District (said to be Britain's first country house hotel) and George Perry-Smith at the Hole in the Wall restaurant in Bath. They and a few contemporaries influenced a generation of restaurateurs with their personal styles, which depended on a deep interest in eating (as opposed to learning the business aspect via a college course). Another was an increasingly critical audience of consumers who found a voice in *The Good Food Guide* (first published in 1951) and the *Egon Ronay Guide* (first published in 1956, by Egon Ronay, a restaurateur of Hungarian origin working in Britain).

In the 1960s, a new approach to eating out began to evolve: it became more of a leisure pursuit. Several factors influenced this, notably the growth in ethnic restaurants and the development of bistros with a more casual atmosphere and frequently with owners who had no experience in running restaurants. Food in these places tended to be eclectic, mostly based on French country or Provençal recipes: garlic mushrooms, ratatouille, *moules marinère, salade Niçoise,* pâté, fondue, *boeuf a la bourguignonne,* plus a few items derived from elsewhere, such as chili con carne and eggs Florentine. Bistros of this type were influential in democratizing eating out during the 1960s and 1970s and still exist, although the menus are now more likely to include risottos, pasta, Thai curries, and reworked versions of pies and puddings.

Restaurants (and the chefs who ran them) began to really gain status in the 1970s. Consumer pressure from *The Good Food Guide*, the *Egon Ronay Guide,* and the Michelin (the first British *Red Guide* was published in 1974) all raised the profile of eating out. In 1977, four restaurants gained two Michelin stars each. The development of nouvelle cuisine from France (somewhat misunderstood in Britain, and often interpreted as cuisine *minceur*, a slimming version) led to increased media interest in restaurants and a new style of food presentation. Newspaper reviews, recipe books, and television did much to increase the profiles of individual chefs, including the French-born Roux brothers (Le Gavroche, Waterside Inn), Raymond Blanc (also of French origin, at Le Manoir aux Quat' Saisons, Swiss-born Anton Mossiman (The Dorchester Hotel), and Nico Ladenis (Chez Nico), among others. During the 1980s and 1990s, another generation of chefs emerged, many of whom had trained in these kitchens, although some emerged from the college system, and a few had no professional training but decided to run restaurants nevertheless. There are far too many of these individuals to list, but among them, Marco-Pierre White and Gordon Ramsay achieved notoriety both for exquisite, elaborate food and their attitudes toward life. Other factors that helped to fuel the restaurant boom were an increasingly knowledgeable body of consumers, a period of conspicuous consumption, and the activities of entrepreneurs such as Sir Terence Conran, founder of the Habitat chain of furniture shops, who moved his focus of interest away from food in the domestic arena and amassed a portfolio of London restaurant businesses. Inevitably, the high profile achieved by London restaurants affected the rest of the country, and several provincial restaurants have achieved similar status.

Food in the best restaurants is excellent in quality and expensive (wine also adds substantially to the cost). Atmosphere tends toward formality. The style of cooking can only be described as eclectic, with references to French, Italian, and other Mediterranean cookery, ideas derived from modern British (careful reworking of traditional British dishes) cooking and a style of presentation that owes much to the Japanese influence that underpinned the visual impact of nouvelle cuisine in the 1970s. The last decade has also seen a strong taste for "fusion food," combining ingredients and influences from all over the world, especially elements derived from the Pacific rim countries. Vegetarianism, once seen as an eccentricity, is now part of the culinary mainstream. Specialist vegetarian restaurants have existed since the 1960s, and most mainstream restaurants offer a vegetarian option on the menu.

Not everyone has the wherewithal or the desire to eat in expensive restaurants. There are numerous lesser establishments that also produce good, or at least competent, food. While there are plenty that use freshly prepared ingredients, many establishments rely on pre-prepared components, bought from large companies that specialize in supplying the catering trade, and heated on-site. At the less expensive end of the market, ethnic restaurants, chains, and fast-food restaurants compete with pubs, cafes, and other outlets to provide meals.

Ethnic Restaurants

Imported food and cuisines have long been an element of the British approach to food as migrants arrived throughout history, but the idea of a restaurant dedicated solely to the food of another country really blossomed in the latter half of the twentieth century. Before this, a few restaurants, especially in London, served French food; ice cream and other Italian food was served in cafes run by immigrants from that country; Chinese cafes existed in the dockland areas of London, Cardiff, and Liverpool; and the Jewish community of north London provided some traditional Jewish and middle European specialties, especially bakery items. An Indian restaurant, Veeraswamy's, opened in London in 1926.

The idea of the French restaurant still survives in some independent restaurants, bistros, and brasseries, and in two or three restaurant chains; a Belgian-inspired chain also operates in London. Although it is not British, French food is not what most people think of in the context of ethnic in Britain in the twenty-first century: more exotic alternatives, especially Chinese, Indian, and Thai food come to mind. In a recent study of eating out in London and two provincial towns, 8 percent of the sample had eaten their last main meal out in an Italian restaurant, 7 percent in a pizza house, 7 percent in an Indian restaurant, and 8 percent in some other ethnic restaurant (Greek, French, Turkish).[19] Ethnic restaurants were found to be more popular in London than in the provinces, partly a reflection of the greater diversity available in the capital. The success of these restaurants lies partly in the ability of those who run them to adapt their native cuisines into dishes that both suit the British palate and notions of a proper meal.

Ethnic restaurants began to spread during the 1960s. In this decade, the Italian community evolved fashionable trattorias serving dishes such as veal scaloppini, pasta alla carbonara, spaghetti Bolognese ("spag bol"), lasagna, calamari, and zabaglione. Italian restaurants on this general model gradually spread to most British cities, often absorbing elements of international cuisine such as chicken Kiev along the way. They became a less fashionable part of the culinary mainstream during the 1970s, and examples can still be found in many towns. Food derived from Italian traditions remains important, especially pasta and pizza, featuring both on the menus of independents and providing the mainstay of several chains. Pizzas, in particular, have become an innovative area, sometimes with toppings such as chicken tikka or barbecued steak, or elaborations of the base dough. In the 1990s, interest in Italian food at the expensive end of eating out moved toward simple, rustic dishes, but this has not penetrated far beyond the capital.

Chinese communities were established in Liverpool and London's East End by the late nineteenth century. In the 1950s, these grew rapidly as migrants arrived from Hong Kong. In the late 1950s, they began to open restaurants serving Chinese food based mostly on Cantonese cuisine rendered acceptable to British palates, with dishes such as sweet-and-sour pork, chow mein, and fried rice. A British option, such as steak and chips (fries), was frequently offered as well. By the mid-1970s, even quite small and remote towns boasted a Chinese restaurant, or at least a takeaway, from which a hot meal could be ordered and collected. Manchester and London developed Chinatown areas, in which restaurants played an important part. In the 1980s and 1990s, awareness both of other Chinese cuisines and of more authentic dishes grew, and restaurants, especially in London, specialized more. In 2002, there were about 5,410 Chinese restaurants in Britain, and it is sometimes claimed that Chinese food is more popular than either Italian or Indian food when eating out.[20]

An influx of migrant labor from the Indian subcontinent during the 1960s lies behind the current plethora of Indian restaurants. The migrants settled in industrial towns, especially Bradford, Birmingham, Leicester, Glasgow, Dundee, and, in London, the Southall and Brick Lane areas, all places that remain important centers for Indian food. Apart from basic cafes established to meet the needs of these communities, a particular style of restaurant developed, usually decorated with flock wallpaper and playing sitar music or Bollywood soundtracks, although a new generation of restaurants have more contemporary interiors. The food on offer is colloquially referred to as curry. Although this word is probably derived from Tamil, it is not used in India, and its current usage as a collective noun for dishes of perceived Indian origin is a product of Anglo-Indian culture. As with Chinese food, dishes show Anglicization, involving relatively large portions of meat in sauce, and less emphasis on side dishes and the smaller side dishes that make up a meal in Indian tradition. Menus normally include, among others, kormas (mild and creamy), vindaloos (containing large amounts of chili), and tandooris (spiced meat cooked in a tandoor, a clay oven that becomes extremely hot), as well as rice dishes, Indian breads, and small items such as pakoras (vegetable fritters) and samosas (deep-fried pastries). "Going for a curry" is often seen as an inexpensive night out with friends, or (notoriously, by groups of drunken youths) a good way to round off an evening's drinking.

In 2002, there were about 8,500 Indian restaurants in the United Kingdom (up from 3,000 in 1982), and the sector was worth about £2.4 billion ($3.5 billion).[21] The industry is dominated by people whose origins lie in a small district of Bangladesh Sylhet. In 2001, chicken *tikka masala* was described as "Britain's national dish" by a senior politician, but it seems that the nation's fascination with Indian food may be more apparent than real. In one consumer survey, it trailed behind Italian and French food as preferred type.[22]

Like the Chinese, Indian restaurants and takeaways have spread far beyond the original areas in which the migrants settled. Other developments include several high-class Indian restaurants, especially in London, some of which have found their way into the restaurant guides. As with other cuisines, awareness of different facets has grown, leading to restaurants specializing in the food of specific regions. Balti houses, which developed in Birmingham, offer *baltis*, a dish allegedly from an area called Baltistan but probably owing more to Karachi; they are curry sauces containing onions, tomatoes, and sweet peppers and some major ingredient such as chicken, served in *karhais*, traditional cooking dishes shaped like small woks. Sweet centers or *paan* houses are similar to cafes, serving *lassi* (yogurt-based drinks), snacks such as kebabs, and sweet dishes for second- and third-generation migrants who observe Muslim or Hindu dietary requirements. Some Indian restaurateurs are also beginning to develop chains.

There are numerous other ethnic minorities in Britain. Greco-Turkish Cypriots have established restaurants in most large towns. Most other minorities are confined to particular areas of London, where one can eat food from other Middle Eastern countries (especially Iran), North Africa, Spain, Portugal, Mexico, Japan, and in American-style diners, but none of these have become widespread in other cities. In the 1990s, Thai food established itself as a popular option, and shows signs of spreading in the way that Chinese and Indian food have done. In the three years prior to 2002, the number of Thai restaurants in Britain rose from 300 to 1,000.[23] Although there is a substantial population of Afro-Caribbean descent in several British cities, this has had little influence on eating-out culture beyond the boundaries of their communities.

Fast Food and Chains

Although chains can be found at all levels in British catering, they are principally associated with fast food. The idea of a chain cafe or restaurant has existed in Britain since the late nineteenth century, when Lyons opened their Tea Shops in London. During the 1960s and 1970s, several other chains flourished, including at least two steakhouses and several low-cost restaurant chains serving snacks. Fast-food restaurants also became a feature of city life and have remained so ever since. They are generally identified with North American culture. Burgers were provided by Wimpy and Burger King. McDonald's opened their first restaurant in Britain in 1974, and now have about 1,100 outlets in the United Kingdom. KFC (formerly Kentucky Fried Chicken) also established themselves. Fast food provides a more even, if less interesting, experience of eating out than ethnic restaurants and pubs, and the economic importance of the sector is huge: in September 2003, the number of fast-food outlets in Britain was almost 29,400; they were estimated to serve over 1.9 billion meals annually, with an estimated food sales figure of £6 billion ($8.7 billion).[24] Burger restaurants were affected in the late 1990s by the crisis in consumer confidence in beef provoked by bovine spongiform encephalopathy (BSE) and have tended to diversify their menus. Despite this, fast food has been one of the fastest growing sectors of the restaurant trade in the last five years.[25]

Travelers on major road routes provide a captive audience for motorway service stations and chain cafes serving variations on all-day breakfasts and burgers and chips. This is another sector in which the experience of eating out has been sacrificed to uniformity and utility. While these establishments fulfill a need, no one is ever going to pretend they provide a gastronomic highspot.

Pubs and Gastropubs

Bar meals in pubs, or meals taken in restaurants attached to pubs, have become an increasingly important element in eating out over the past three decades. Pubs appear to be more popular venues for eating out in the provinces than in London. Figures vary; according to one industry organization, there were about 57,400 pubs in the United Kingdom in 1996, down to about 51,500 in 2002. Despite the fall in pub numbers, the meal/restaurant aspect of pubs has been the fastest growing sector of the restaurant trade between 1997 and 2002;[26] in 2002, pubs served 1,070 million meals.[27] The original meaning of the word *bar* in the context of a pub refers to the counter across which drinks are served. Confusingly, establishments that closely resemble pubs but are called bars have begun to emerge in the past decade (see below).

Pub, a word universally understood in Britain, is an abbreviation of the term *public house*. The pub, or "boozer," has roots in three places in which

Beer in traditional glass.

food and drink was available in early modern Britain: the inn, which provided food and lodging for travelers in both towns and at strategic points along roads; urban taverns, which technically existed to retail wine, but many of which had developed a reputation for good food by the eighteenth century; and the alehouse, which sold beer and also served as a meeting place and social center for communities, especially rural ones. Social and economic change (especially the development of rail transport and hotels) removed much of the prestige of the inn, and taverns disappeared. Alehouses survived and flourished, absorbing some elements of the other two, and by the mid-nineteenth century, the public house as now understood had developed. Licensing restrictions were introduced in the 1870s under pressure from the Temperance Movement. They have been relaxed in recent years and pubs are now allowed to open between the hours of 11 A.M. and 11 P.M. In some cases, special dispensation is allowed: in London, pubs near major wholesale markets open in the early hours of the morning and serve both alcoholic drinks and breakfasts; and on special occasions, such as New Year's Eve, extensions are granted to allow all pubs to stay open late. Attitudes toward children in pubs have relaxed recently. Until the 1990s, their presence was frowned on, and their entry restricted by law to family rooms, away from the main bar area.

By the early twentieth century, the pub generally consisted of several rooms, used according to dress and status: a public bar (for the riff-raff), a lounge bar (for those who were dressed up), and a snug (often where the landlord's friends drank). The exact arrangement, furnishings, and fittings varied from the Georgian relics of a rural inn to the etched glass and mahogany splendor of an urban Victorian gin palace; village pubs remained more or less rustic, with locally made furniture, and often, locally produced beer. Examples of all of these styles can still be found. Attitudes about women in pubs varied over the years, but they were not considered places for respectable women to be seen in until the 1920s, and only then in the company of a male escort. Even now, pubs tend to be a masculine environment, and many women feel odd about visiting pubs alone (unless a local, a neighborhood pub in which she knows the staff or is likely to meet an acquaintance). The atmosphere of a particular pub can vary enormously throughout the day, from groups of gossiping office workers at lunchtime to raucous late-night revelers intent on a "pub crawl" (a tour of several different pubs).

Until the 1960s, pubs existed principally for the retailing and consumption of beer. In urban pubs, a packet of potato crisps (chips), a pickled egg, a sandwich, or sometimes a "ploughman's lunch" (bread, cheese, and pickle, a concept evolved in the 1930s with little reference to the diet of farm laborers) was as much as one could expect. A wider choice of food was more common in rural pubs; some establishments had considerable charm and verged on hotel status. During the 1960s, tightening of legislation relating to drinking and driving affected pubs, as did changes in attitudes toward food and leisure. The pub has always been a place for recreation, and food became part of that culture. Even in the early 1980s, pub food was dull: basket meals (chicken nuggets or breaded, deep-fried scampi and chips [fries]) were common; other staples were lasagna, moussaka, chili con carne, curry and steak pie, plus sandwiches or filled rolls.[28] A few served more imaginative food, and some none at all. Also by the early 1980s, most pubs were "tied houses" (owned by a specific brewery and obliged to sell their beer, and often decorated in a house style). Changes in the structure of the industry have led to more diversity of ownership, although worries about concentration are still expressed.

Food provides additional profit and has made pubs more attractive to women and families. This is especially important for isolated rural pubs as drunk-driving laws have made these less appealing to those for whom alcohol is the object. A trend toward food in pubs became strong in the 1980s, with some gaining substantial reputations, and Sunday pub lunches becoming popular. The quality of wine served in pubs also improved. The flippant term *gastropub* was coined around 1990 to indicate somewhere that preserved the original character of a pub, in which anyone could buy a pint of beer, while also offering good and imaginative food at reasonable prices. Sometimes there is little to distinguish a pub serving really good food from a restaurant (some have full restaurants attached), but the interiors and the service are likely to be more casual, and the range of the menu is usually wider so that diners can choose anything from an inexpensive snack to a full, and sometimes costly, meal. The menu is likely to be constructed from a range of modern British dishes, such as sausages and mash, steak pies, calf's liver and bacon, roasted cod, plus more eclectic items: grilled quail and saffron risotto, and warm brioche with black pudding and mango jelly were just two offerings noted in a recent guide.[29]

Pubs still display a remarkable range of architectural styles and interior fittings, although the variety was much reduced in the 1970s and 1980s by uniform decor imposed in tied houses. A pressure group, the Campaign for Real Ale (CAMRA), which began in the 1970s, fought to defend the British craft brewing tradition against growing uniformity. Although food was not technically part of their remit, the concept of a pub as a hospitable place was. In addition, an annual *Good Pub Guide* has been published since 1982, listing readers' reports on those with particularly good food. In the late 1990s, theme pubs began to appear, particularly so-called Irish pubs; these have been followed, in the London area, by the more outlandish notion of the Thai pub (specializing in Thai food).

Bars and Wine Bars

Apart from the specific meaning of the counter over which alcoholic drinks are served, the word *bar* was mostly used with reference to hotel bars until the 1970s. They were unlikely to serve food, except crisps and salted nuts. Then the concept of the wine bar evolved as a place with a license restricted to the sale of wine and a strong emphasis on food. Less masculine in atmosphere than pubs, they became popular places for women to eat and drink. The concept of a bar in the continental European sense, as a place in which one can buy soft drinks, coffee, or alcohol, or take a light meal, has only recently entered the British consciousness, and remains an urban phenomenon. It has developed largely through the influence of various chains that now have a presence in most large towns. Inevitably, given British ideas about drinking, there is an overlap with the idea of the pub, and a wide range of beers are served. Such bars are distinguished by lighter, more open, and contemporary interiors than those found in traditional pubs; hard surfaces, light-colored wood, and pale walls as opposed to carpets, tapestry, and leather upholstery and dark wood. They tend to be large and noisy and to attract a younger clientele.

Cafes, Coffee Bars, and Teashops

Cafes and teashops in some form are important places for drinks (mostly non-alcoholic) and light meals. They remain a distinct part of eating-out culture, as pleasant places to spend an hour or two with friends, but are seen as less special than restaurants, and less sociable than pubs.

In the late nineteenth century, places to take tea became common as chains such as Lyon's and the ABC (Aerated Bread Company) opened cafes, and in Glasgow, the Willow Tearooms, with interiors by Charles Rennie Mackintosh, became the place to be seen.[30] They provided places for women to meet. In Scotland, many Italian immigrant families established ice cream parlors that also sold coffee. Coffee bars serving espresso and cappuccino-type coffee became popular in the 1950s, important meeting places for the young.[31] Cafes have continued to be a part of urban life in Britain ever since, serving tea, coffee, and other soft drinks, cakes and light meals, and are popular with shoppers and travelers. Some also hold a license for alcoholic drinks, although this is not standard. During the late 1990s, several chain coffee shops selling cappuccino, espresso, chocolate drinks, and various permutations of flavored coffees expanded nationally, although their progress has been checked by high overheads.

The contemporary notion of the cafe covers a wide range. At one extreme, "greasy spoons" sell cheap and filling all-day breakfasts, pies, pasties, and chips (fries). At the other, elegant and relatively expensive establishments provide exquisite cakes and dainty sandwiches. In between there are cafes in art galleries, museums, department stores, delicatessens, train stations, airports, as well as on street corners and in settlements of all sizes; anywhere one might want to buy a cup of tea or a sandwich. The food served varies enormously in style and content. Sandwiches are an important item; soup is usually available, along with a few more substantial dishes. Cakes, scones, and other sweet things that go with tea are also important. Within this basic scheme, the style of cookery may reflect a traditional British approach, but is just as likely to include ciabatta bread round the sandwiches, cakes made to Italian recipes in the display cabinet, and soup based on continental European or Middle Eastern traditions.

Takeaway and Street Food

Takeaway food can be purchased either from shops that specialize in meals to be carried off the premises for consumption, or from restaurants (usually Chinese or Indian) that also provide cooked food to eat elsewhere. Takeaways in one form or another are of great importance in many people's lives, providing relatively inexpensive hot meals at short notice. Most settlements over the size of a large village have at least one takeaway establishment. Street food, of great importance in the nineteenth century, has diminished, the market eroded by takeaways and restricted by legislation relating to hygiene.

Ethnic Takeaways

Both the Chinese and the Indian communities have a substantial presence in the provision of takeaways. Shops that exist solely for this trade tend to be utilitarian with only a counter and a few chairs for customers. Their menus usually resemble those of Chinese or Indian restaurants (most of which also provide a takeaway service). Pizza is another common takeaway food, available in most towns. It bears little resemblance to the Neapolitan original, but may feature a wide range of toppings from the conventional tomato and cheese to ham and pineapple, sweet corn, or tandoori chicken. The other important ethnic takeaway item is the doner kebab, of Turkish origin; this is a mass of minced lamb packed onto a vertical spit revolving in front of a grill. Thin slices are carved off the meat as it cooks; they are served in pita bread with salad, yogurt and a tomato sauce. Beef burgers are also widely available, either from fast-food outlets, or from mobile stalls, which are a late-night feature of urban areas; these also sell doner kebabs. Attitudes toward takeaways are ambivalent; some people avoid them, claiming they are unhygienic or unhealthy. Others value them as a relatively cheap, swift source of precooked food, and use them as an element of socializing, ordering them to share with friends, or as a convenient meal when other factors (for instance, the presence of young children in the house) make it difficult to go out to eat. Many takeaways offer a delivery service.

Fish and Chips

"Fish and chips" is filleted fish dipped in batter and deep fried, plus chips—chunky french fries. The shops that sell this are often known as "the chip shop" or "the chippy." The combination developed sometime during the mid-nineteenth century and became an important ready-to-eat food, initially for the urban working class and later for many from other backgrounds too. Although it is regarded as quintessentially British, it owes much to immigrant communities: fish frying was a trade pursued by East End Jews, and the Italians, Chinese, and Greek Cypriots were all important in running fish-and-chip shops during the twentieth century. On the eve of the Second World War, there were estimated to be at least 30,000 fish fryers in Britain;[32] by the end of the twentieth century, the number was down to about 8,500.[33] The price of fish and chips has risen, as fish has become scarcer and more expensive, and there are now many competitors in the fast-food market, but in 1997, a market research survey found that more than 50 percent of their sample had consumed fish and chips within the previous month.[34]

Cod and haddock are the usual options, although some shops fry other fish as well, such as plaice and "rock salmon" (i.e., dogfish, a shark species). Various types of fat are used for frying, vegetable oil being favored in the south of England, and the Yorkshire area showing a distinct preference for beef dripping. Fish and chips are traditionally sprinkled with salt and vinegar and wrapped in newspaper (hygiene regulations now

Sprinkling vinegar on chips in a chip shop. © TRIP/H. Rogers.

demand layers of virgin greaseproof paper between the food and the newsprint) and carried off, either consumed with the fingers while walking down the street, or taken home. Some chip shops have cafes attached, in which the food can be eaten at a table, usually served with a pot of very strong tea and bread and butter or margarine. The best known of these is Harry Ramsden's, now a chain, but which began as a single small takeaway. Interiors are generally utilitarian, although the original Harry Ramsden's was noted for the opulence of its fittings.

Other foods available from the chippy include mushy peas (dried peas cooked to a purée), curry sauce (a runny sauce flavored with curry powder, usually eaten with chips alone), chicken portions, sausages, squid (popularized by cheap holidays to the Mediterranean), and sometimes pies. Scottish fish-and-chip shops also sell a selection of sausage-like puddings, especially mealie pudding made with oatmeal, and haggis. They also became notorious in the 1990s for deep-frying pizzas, Mars bars, and haggis, all dipped in batter before immersion in hot oil.

Eels, Pie, and Mash

Another great working-class food tradition is restricted to London. This is the eel, pie, and mash shop, which sells eels, cold, in a gelatinous mass (jellied eel) or hot, stewed and served with mashed potato and thin green parsley sauce ("liquor"). The pies are hot meat pies, filled with minced beef. In the 1940s, London had at least 130 eel, pie, and mash shops scattered throughout the city; only a handful remain, and most of those are in the East End, a formerly working-class area now much affected by social and economic change. Several of the shops are famous for their tiled and mirrored interiors and elaborate street fronts. The food could be eaten in, sitting at marble-topped tables, or bought as a takeaway from a window opening onto the street.[35]

Pie and Peas and Other Fast Foods

Pie and peas are a northern tradition, not strictly a takeaway, but usually a supper served at the close of a meeting or after an excursion. The pies are generally steak or steak and kidney, and are eaten with mushy peas.

Other native takeaway and street food traditions include shellfish stalls, still found in seaside resorts; these sell portions of cooked prawns or shrimps, cockles, whelks, and crab, often heavily vinegared. Pies, cooked tripe, black puddings, and other offal were a specialty of the cotton-processing towns of south Lancashire (in the northwest of England) but are waning in importance as the industrial communities that supported them change. Tripe restaurants were also a feature of Lancashire towns until relatively recently. Roast chestnuts are still sold in a few places in autumn. Ice cream is ubiquitous in tourist centers and seaside resorts, sold from street stalls and vans; it is often soft ice cream, piped from a machine into wafer cones and decorated with a chocolate flake bar.

Sandwiches

The sandwich, according to legend, was invented by an eighteenth-century nobleman, Lord Sandwich, who did not wish to leave the gaming table and requested his meat served between two slices of bread. Ever since, it has been an important part of British life, as a snack, a light meal, or a convenient traveling food. Until the 1970s, though, sandwiches were either consumed on the premises of a cafe or pub or made at home and carried to work or on a journey. Conventional sandwiches in the 1970s were made with sliced bread, spread with butter, and filled with ingredients such as sliced beef, ham, or cheese, egg mayonnaise, or tinned salmon and cucumber. At this point, sandwich bars began to appear in the business districts of many cities, and several large food retailers also entered the market with prepacked sandwiches, notably Marks and Spencer.

Since then the sandwich market has continued to expand. Changes in packaging technology such as sealed plastic packs helped to improve the shelflife of prepacked sandwiches. Growing affluence, a desire for convenience, and shorter lunch breaks appear to underlie the growth in prepacked sandwiches, and consumer interest is maintained by constant innovation. Sandwiches now are made from baguettes, ciabatta, foccaccia, rolls of various types, and wraps (flour tortillas, or something similar). Popular fillings include grilled bacon, lettuce, and tomato; prawns and mayonnaise (a bestseller); tandoori chicken; duck in hoisin sauce; crayfish tails and rocket; as well as more conventional options. They are available chilled from almost all food stores, many chain stores such as Boots (principally a pharmacy and drugstore), and some newsagents, as well as from specialist shops and chains. Often, delicatessens offer a made-to-order sandwich service as well. Some companies sell other snacks, including the traditional options of sausage rolls and pasties, and the non-traditional ones of sushi and spiced noodles.

Institutions and Schools

A substantial amount of eating out is still accounted for by meals in institutions, including work canteens (cafeterias), hospitals, army messes, and university refectories. These are usually inexpensive, because although recovery of costs is considered important, meals are often subsidized and profit is not the primary motive. Meals in institutions are generally undistinguished, seen as an exercise in refueling rather than eating for pleasure. The cooked dinner model remains important in institutional catering, although in the last 15 years, menus have begun to reflect changes in eating habits with pasta, pizza, vegetarian meals, and, in some locations, halal food (prepared according to Muslim dietary laws) provided.

One sector of institutional provision experienced by almost all the inhabitants of the United Kingdom is the school meal. School meals have been important in British life for more than 50 years, contributing to ideas about the form of meals, and as a means of socializing children and learning table manners. Until the 1980s, they were defined partly by nutritional guidelines, and partly by the notion of a proper dinner; meat and two veg, followed by some type of pudding (usually hot) with custard were the standard offering, with no choices. Meals were (and remain) free to the poorest pupils. Opinions on the quality of school meals, produced on a large scale within a tight budget, were mixed but generally indifferent or negative. Removal of the nutritional guidelines, the introduction of a cafeteria system in many schools, and more recently, the use of contract caterers and industry sponsorship, has changed provision substantially. In 2002, roast dinners remained a popular choice, but pizza, burgers, and pasta were all more popular with 8-to-16-year-olds, as was curry.[36] Popular puddings included cakes, buns, ice cream, and yogurt, although the traditional option of sponge pudding was also in the top five choices.

Entertaining in Other People's Homes

Eating out in other people's houses with family or friends is an important part of British social life for some socioeconomic groups, but there is little information on the subject. That which is available suggests that domestic entertaining as now understood has its origins in the middle-class dinner party of the early-to-mid–twentieth century. It forms part of a network of mutual reciprocal hospitality, most important among the educated, affluent middle classes. The standard form is a highly structured meal of three or more courses, although inevitably there is much variability within this.[37]

NOTES

1. Roy C. Wood, *The Sociology of the Meal: Food and Social Theory* (Edinburgh: Edinburgh University Press, 1995), p. 87.

2. Christopher Driver, *The British at Table, 1940–1980* (London: Chatto and Windus, 1983).

3. Alan Warde and Lydia Martens, *Eating Out: Social Differentiation, Consumption, and Pleasure* (Cambridge, U.K.: Cambridge University Press, 2000).

4. Nicolas Freeling, *The Kitchen and the Cook* (London: Big Cat Press, 2002), and Kit Chapman, *An Innkeeper's Diary, September 1996–September 1997* (London: Orion, 1999).

5. Driver, *The British at Table.*

6. Warde and Martens, *Eating Out.*

7. Bev Botting (ed.), *Family Spending: A Report on the 2001–2002 Expenditure and Food Survey* (London: HMSO, 2003).

8. "Industry Reports: General, Hospitality Industry FAQ," 2 October 2003, Web site of *Caterer and Hotelkeeper* Magazine, http://www.caterer-online.com.

9. "Industry Reports: General, Employment in Hospitality by Occupation," 29 September 2003, http://www.caterer-online.com.

10. Warde and Martens, *Eating Out,* p. 34.

11. Alan Warde, *Consumption, Food, and Taste: Culinary Antinomies and Commodity Culture* (London: Sage, 1997), p. 117.

12. Joanna Blythman, "Are You Being Served?" *The Guardian Weekend Magazine,* 20 July 2002, pp. 24–28.

13. Ibid.

14. Warde and Martens, *Eating Out,* p. 36.

15. "Industry Reports: Time for Lunch?" 16 August 2002, http://www.caterer-online.com.

16. Warde and Martens, *Eating Out,* p. 90.

17. Warde and Martens, *Eating Out,* p. 217.

18. "Industry Reports: Restaurants," 23 September 2003, http://www.caterer-online.com.

19. Warde and Martens, *Eating Out,* p. 77.

20. Restaurant Association, quoted in Robert Mendick, "Sweet and Sour Is the New Chicken Tikka Masala," *Independent on Sunday,* 4 August 2002.

21. "Indian Innovations," 1 August 2002, http://www.caterer-online.com.

22. Ibid.

23. Ibid.

24. Ibid.

25. "Themed Restaurants," *Mintel Report*, March 2003, p. 10.

26. Ibid.

27. "Industry Reports: Pub Trends 1996–2002," 9 September 2003, http://www.caterer-online.com.

28. Alisdair Aird, *The Good Pub Guide* (London: Ebury Press, 2001), p. 6.

29. "The Guide to Gastropubs," *The Guardian*, 8 November 2003.

30. Perilla Kinchin, *Tea and Taste: The Glasgow Tea Rooms, 1875–1975* (London: Cockade Publishing, 1991).

31. Marguerite Patten, *Marguerite Patten's Century of British Cooking* (London: Grub Street, 1991).

32. John K. Walton, *Fish and Chips and the British Working Class, 1870–1940* (New York: Leicester University Press, 1992).

33. "History," National Federation of Fish Friers, http://www.federation offish-friers.co.uk.

34. MORI, "Fish and Chips," http://www.mori.com/polls/1997/fish.shtml.

35. Chris Clun, *Eels, Pie, and Mash* (London: Museum of London, 1995).

36. "Sodexho School Meals Survey," 8 October 2002, http://www.caterer-online.com.

37. Warde and Martens, *Eating Out*, pp. 38–50.

6

Special Occasions

Special occasions fall into two basic categories: calendar occasions and family events. Calendar occasions include Christmas and Easter, New Year, Burns Night, Shrove Tuesday, Halloween, and Guy Fawkes Night. Christianity now plays a token part in most people's lives, and Christmas and Easter have been obscured by consumerism, celebrated with large amounts of food. Britain is also a multicultural society, which has given a diversity of festivals. Communities from other religious backgrounds observe occasions such as Passover, Eid-el-Fitr, and Diwali with ritual fasts, feasts, and specific foods, and visits to specific areas of various British cities at the right time can transport one temporarily to another country. Family events are still celebrated with vigor, but are less obvious at the community level. The most important celebrations include high-status foods such as fruitcake, large pieces of meat (beef, turkey), alcohol, and sweet things.

A NOTE ABOUT RICH FRUITCAKE

Rich fruitcake, or plum cake, is an important celebration food, used at Christmas, Easter, weddings, christenings, birthdays, and other occasions. Many families have a recipe that they regard as distinctive, although the net effect is generally similar. The cake should have a rich flavor and a moist texture, and they usually are matured for several weeks before eating. The older name of plum cake reflects the importance that "plums"

Child mixing Christmas cake. © TRIP/H. Rogers.

(dried fruit in general) were given in the late medieval and early modern kitchen, and have retained, symbolically, down to the present day. Other examples of celebratory foods that use them include Christmas pudding, mince pies, black buns, and hot cross buns. Originally, making a cake involved considerable labor in terms of sifting flour, pounding sugar, and cleaning dried fruit. This is now done by packers and processors of dry goods. It has removed the hard work, but some residual magic lingers around the idea of a rich fruitcake. The decoration is often elaborate, and classes in icing and sugarcraft became popular in the 1980s.

CHRISTMAS

Christmas is a two-day public holiday, Christmas Day (December 25) and Boxing Day (December 26; the name may derive from it being the day when servants received their Christmas boxes, or gifts). It is a season for lavish displays and luxury foods. Festivities start before the 25th, as a pre-Christmas lunch or dinner in a restaurant with workmates has recently become a custom. Parties for friends and family extend celebrations up to New Year. In contemporary England and Wales, most emphasis is on Christmas Day, with a ritual menu of roast turkey. Boxing Day is for visiting friends or relatives, going walking, or hunting. Meals on this day may be leftovers, or items such as ham and stand pies (raised pies with fillings of pork or game). Christmas in Scotland is a lower-key celebration: the major festive emphasis there is on New Year's Eve. Twelfth Night (Epiphany, January 6), very important until the mid-nineteenth century, is now scarcely remembered.

Throughout the whole season, mince pies are an important food, offered with coffee or a glass of sherry or mulled wine, at almost any gathering between late November and early January. They are small double-crust pies filled with mince or mincemeat of currants, raisins, sultanas, candied peel, sugar, spices, apples and suet minced together. Originally, the sweet mixture was made up in large quantities and stored. Meat such as beef, mutton, or tripe was added to the mixture (fish or egg versions are also recorded), but this is now rare. The shape of mince pies is now round, but in the past, they were made in decorative shapes such as fleur-de-lis or crescents.

Mincemeat and Mince Pies

Mincemeat of finely chopped dried fruit, sugar, and other ingredients has been a feature of midwinter food in Britain since at least the sixteenth century. It is often made with beef suet, the last remnants of a custom of mixing beef or other meat with the mixture. Butter or a vegetarian alternative can be used if preferred. The mixture keeps well.

- 8 oz currants
- 8 oz raisins
- 8 oz sultanas
- 4 oz candied peel
- 8 oz apples, peeled and cored
- 4 oz suet
- 8 oz Demerara sugar (coarse brown sugar)
- grated rind and juice of 1 lemon
- 1 tsp mixed spice
- brandy or rum to mix

Pass the fruit and suet through a mincing machine (an old-fashioned hand-cranked machine produces good results) or chop finely. Stir in the sugar and spice, and add 3 or 4 tbsp of brandy. Mix well. Cover and leave to stand for a couple of days, then put in jars and store in a cool dry place till required.

Make into small double-crust pies, using either puff pastry or shortcrust pastry. The latter is made by rubbing 4 oz of butter or other pastry fat into 8 oz of flour with the tips of the fingers until the mixture resembles fine breadcrumbs. Add a little iced water, about 4 tbsp, just enough to make a dough. Rest in a cool place for about 30 minutes, then roll thinly and cut in rounds to line the base of patty tins. Put a teaspoonful of mincemeat in each one and cut pastry circles for the lids. Press together and bake in a moderately hot oven for about 20 minutes. Eat warm or cold.

The typical Christmas Day menu is imposed by tradition. Christmas dinner (usually taken in the middle of the day) is highly structured: roast turkey with stuffing (often chestnut), gravy, bread sauce, sausages, bacon rashers (in neat little rolls), roast and boiled potatoes, brussels sprouts, and other vegetables as desired. A minority favor alternatives to turkey, such as goose, game, or a large joint of beef. Vegetarian dishes also make an appearance, recipes for these usually being given in magazines in December. A light appetizer, such as smoked salmon, may be served. The primary importance of poultry at this time of the year derives partly from seasonality in rearing domestic fowl—spring hatched turkeys and geese being in prime condition at Christmas—and from the former importance of large birds in festive menus.

Family Christmas dinner. © TRIP/H. Rogers.

The main course is followed by Christmas pudding, a rich steamed plum pudding, made in a basin shaped like a truncated cone (on Christmas cards it is often shown as a sphere, as it would have appeared in the nineteenth century when cooked in a cloth). Traditionally, it contains a silver coin, or charms which denote the future for the finder, and is flambéed with brandy. Few alternatives are offered; a trifle is one possibility, or perhaps a Christmas pudding ice cream, containing dried fruit and nuts. Plum pudding, first recorded in the eighteenth century, developed from seventeenth-century bag puddings of suet and breadcrumbs or flour with dried fruit and sugar and replaced an earlier dish, plum pottage, of beef or mutton in broth with dried fruit, spices, wine, and bread. The Scots have their own version, clootie dumpling (the "cloot" is the cloth which it is boiled in). It is plainer than Christmas pudding. The cloth is scalded and floured before the mixture is put in, forming a "skin" on the dumpling, much enjoyed by many. Both left-over Christmas pudding and clootie dumpling can be reheated by frying.

Christmas Pudding

Also known as plum pudding. Traditionally, a silver coin is hidden in the mixture to bring luck to the finder. Serve with either custard, cream, a sweet rum-flavored white sauce, or rum or brandy butter—sugar, butter, spices, and rum or brandy beaten together.

- 8 oz stoneless raisins
- 4 oz sultanas
- 4 oz currants
- 2 oz candied peel, chopped
- a few almonds, blanched and chopped
- 8 oz suet
- 4 oz brown breadcrumbs
- 1 1/2 oz flour
- 2 oz soft light brown sugar
- 1 tsp salt
- 1 tsp grated nutmeg
- 3 eggs, beaten
- 5 fl oz milk or stout (Guinness)

Sieve the flour, salt, and nutmeg together into a large basin. Add all the other dry ingredients and stir well. Beat the eggs and mix with the milk or beer and stir into the mixture. Leave to stand for several hours, stirring periodically.

When ready to cook, put a large pan or steamer on to boil. Grease a pudding basin and fill to the top. Cover with greaseproof paper, making a generous pleat in the middle (the pudding will expand slightly during cooking). Cover with a pudding cloth, tying it on with string. Lower the basin into boiling water (this should come about two-thirds of the way up the side of the basin) and boil for 5 hours, replenishing the water as necessary with boiling water from a kettle. Alternatively, steam the pudding for 7 1/2 hours.

When cooked, take off the cloth, wipe the basin, and re-cover with a dry, clean cloth. Store in a cool dry place. The pudding will keep for several weeks.

To serve: boil for another 4 hours, or steam for 6 hours. Turn out onto a hot dish and put a sprig of holly in the center. Just before serving, pour a little warmed brandy or rum around it, and set it alight. Bring to the table while still flaming.

The 25th also brings Christmas cake at teatime, a rich fruitcake iced and decorated with appropriate motifs. In the seventeenth and eighteenth centuries, the idea of cake was less associated with Christmas Day itself, and more with Twelfth Night. During this period, it, not the pudding, contained the lucky charm, or a dried bean, which identified the finder as "King of the Bean" for the night, apparently the origin of the charms now found in the pudding.[1]

Christmas Cake

Also known as rich fruitcake, and still occasionally called by the older name of plum cake. Used at christenings, weddings, Christmas, and for Easter simnel cakes.

- 10 oz butter
- 10 oz caster sugar
- 6 large eggs
- 12 oz flour
- 1 tsp ground cinnamon
- 1 tsp mixed spice
- a good pinch salt
- 4 oz mixed candied peel, chopped
- 4 oz blanched almonds, chopped
- 1 lb currants
- 1 lb seedless raisins
- 8 oz sultanas
- 4 oz glacé cherries, halved
- 2 tbsp brandy or rum

- a cake tin about 8 inches in diameter, lined with a double thickness of greased paper

Sieve the flour, salt, and spices together. Put the butter and sugar in a large bowl and beat until light and fluffy. (It helps if the butter is well softened, but it must only be soft, not starting to oil.) Beat the eggs in separately, making sure that each one is thoroughly blended in before adding the next. If they are added too quickly, the mixture will curdle. To help prevent this, add a tablespoon from the flour mixture after beating in each egg. Stir in the dry ingredients and the spirit. Add a little milk if the mixture seems stiff. Turn into the prepared tin. Bake in a slow oven at 300°F for about 1 1/2 hours, then reduce the heat to 275°F and bake for another 4–5 hours.

Cooking times for rich cakes vary according to ovens and the exact dimensions of the tin. When the cake is fully cooked, it should be coming away from the sides of the tin a little, and a fine skewer inserted into the center of the cake will come out clean. A rich fruitcake, carefully wrapped and stored in an airtight tin, will keep for several months. Some people sprinkle a little brandy over the base of the cake periodically. When wanted for use, cover the cake with a layer of marzipan or almond paste, and then ice it with royal icing and decorate as desired.

Other foods associated with Christmas generally are nuts in their shells (almonds, hazelnuts, Brazil nuts, and walnuts); dried fruit, especially dates; candied fruit; sweets and chocolates generally; and oranges. Tangerines (small, aromatic, easy peeling orange varieties) are traditionally associated with the Christmas season. Certain cheeses are also important, especially Blue Stilton, which is sold in vast quantities at this time. Wensleydale cheese was formerly kept for Christmas, a tradition which has now lapsed, but many northerners consider that a piece goes well with fruitcake and maintain the habit of serving the two together. Alcohol is also an important part of Christmas celebrations, often drunk in large quantities. Even families who do not routinely drink at home will relax this rule on Christmas Day.[2]

NEW YEAR

New Year is most important in Scotland, where Christmas was banned in the early modern period as being idolatrous. Emphasis transferred to December 31, now the principal midwinter festival for the Scots. Although it has changed in recent years the habit of "first footing" has not entirely died out: this is to visit neighbors and friends after midnight on New Year's Day (i.e., in the early hours of the morning). Symbolic items, such as coal, to represent warmth, are supposed to be carried; in practice, a bottle of whiskey is what counts. Food plays a secondary role, although both shortbread and black bun are traditional to the season. The former is a mixture of flour, butter, and sugar in the proportions 6 to 4 to 2, respectively, mixed into a coherent mass and baked very slowly to develop a buttery flavor and pale color. The latter is a mixture of raisins, currants, almonds, candied peel, and spices, wrapped in short pastry to make a flat cake, then baked gently.

Elsewhere, New Year celebrations are a matter of personal taste; some celebrate it, some do not. The form can be anything from an elaborate meal to a "piss up" (drinking session). Pubs are granted extended licenses so that they can remain open until the early hours of the morning; the emphasis here is always on drinking, although food may be provided. Restaurants offer special dinners with champagne at midnight.

BURNS NIGHT

Burns Night dinners are held in many parts of the United Kingdom around January 25 in celebration of the life and work of Scottish poet Robert Burns. The food consists of haggis, neeps, and tatties (turnips and potatoes, boiled and mashed), washed down with whiskey.

SHROVE TUESDAY, LENT, AND MOTHER'S DAY

Shrove Tuesday is the day immediately before Lent, a time for using up fat and other rich ingredients. The British method for this is to make pancakes. An egg, flour, and milk batter mixed to the consistency of pouring cream is fried on both sides to make large, thin pancakes. They are eaten with sugar and lemon juice, although syrups of various kinds, ice cream, and savory fillings have found their way into the repertoire recently.

Observation of Lent itself ceased in the seventeenth century, but people still talk about giving up something for Lent, chocolate being a frequent choice. Mid-Lent Sunday is known as Mothering Sunday, or, now, Mother's Day. This was originally a day when people visited the mother church of a parish. It became a day when servants were allowed to visit their families and to bake a special, rich cake to take with them—a simnel. In the mid-twentieth century, Mothering Sunday was conflated with the idea of Mother's Day, imported from North America. It is now a day for remembering one's mother and possibly taking her out to lunch or dinner. Simnels have transferred their association to Easter Sunday, although a special bun—light, white, iced, and decorated with comfits, is made by the bakers of Bristol for this weekend; it is known as a mothering bun.

EASTER

Good Friday and Easter Sunday are important as far as food is concerned. Good Friday is celebrated with hot cross buns, light, spiced buns marked with a cross on the top. The cross can be cut into the dough, made with strips of candied peel, or, commercially, by piping a flour paste over the top. Hot cross buns are produced in industrial quantities during the season (some supermarkets sell them all year round). They are eaten warm or cut in half, toasted, and buttered. In some areas, especially the south and southwest, a large spiced biscuit known as an Easter cake is also associated with Easter.

Hot Cross Buns

Lightly spiced and fruited buns made of yeast dough, distinguished by a cross on top. Traditionally only produced in this form for Good Friday.

- 1 3/4 lb flour
- 1 oz yeast
- 4 oz soft light brown sugar
- 10 fl oz milk or milk and water
- 1/4 tsp salt
- 1 1/2 tsp cinnamon

Hot cross buns.

- 1 1/2 tsp grated nutmeg
- 4 oz currants
- 1 oz candied peel, chopped
- 4 oz butter
- 2 eggs

For glazing the buns:

- 2 tbsp milk
- 2 tbsp of caster sugar

Put 1/2 lb of the flour into a bowl. Cream the yeast with a pinch of sugar. Heat the milk to tepid and stir in the yeast. Mix with the flour in the bowl and set in a warm place for 20 minutes to set the sponge.

Sieve the remainder of the flour with the spices and salt. Stir in the sugar, currants, and peel. Melt the butter and beat the eggs. When the yeast mixture is frothy, stir in all the dry ingredients. Add the butter and the beaten eggs, beating well with the hand. Cover and put in a warm place to rise for about an hour.

When almost doubled in size, flour the hands, divide the dough into 16, and shape each portion into round buns. Place on a well-greased and floured baking tin, allowing room for the buns to spread. Cut a cross in the top of each one and prove in a warm place for about 20 minutes.

Bake in a very hot oven, 475°F, for 10–15 minutes, or until golden brown.

Just before they are ready to come out of the oven, boil the milk and sugar together until it is bubbly and syrupy, and brush the buns with this glaze while they are still hot. Cool on a wire rack.

Easter Day also has special foods. Easter eggs are sold by all confectioners in numerous sizes, styles, and prices, from tiny sugar ones to gigantic chocolate versions. The simnel cake is now considered an Easter specialty. The modern version is a variant on the theme of rich fruitcake. Before baking, the mixture is divided in half. The first portion is used to cover the base of the tin, a thick layer of marzipan is laid over it, and the other half spread over this. After baking, the cake is decorated with a layer of marzipan on top. It is not iced, although decorations (such as spring flowers) appropriate to the season may be added; or part of the marzipan formed into balls and placed on top. There are usually 11 of these, said to represent the apostles without Judas. This form is a relatively recent development, no more than a century or so old.[3]

Easter Day is not, on the whole, celebrated with special meals, although lamb is sometimes suggested as a suitable meat. Historically, veal with sorrel sauce was one meat eaten on this day, but the habit seems to have died out.

HALLOWEEN AND GUY FAWKES NIGHT

Halloween, the 31st of October, and All Souls, the 1st of November, gradually faded from the festive calendar in the early modern period. They were never entirely forgotten. Remnants of festive food traditions linger, some now observed on Guy Fawkes Night (November 5). This has its roots in the Catholic-Protestant arguments of the early seventeenth century. Also known as Bonfire Night, it commemorates an event in 1605 when a Catholic plot to blow up the king and Parliament was uncovered and the traitors executed. It is celebrated with fireworks and bonfires, which traditionally are topped with an effigy—the "guy."

In the last decade, Halloween has been influenced by the North American tradition of trick or treat, bringing orange and black confectionery and pumpkins. In British tradition, a food specially associated with Halloween was soul cake, yet another spiced bread bun, but these had disappeared by the twentieth century. Apples are also associated with this time of the year; bobbing for apples, trying to catch apples floating in water with one's teeth, and toffee apples (apples dipped in molten sugar) are both traditional. Toffee is also the name given to a confection of sugar and butter boiled to hard crack, associated with both Halloween and Guy Fawkes Night. In the mid-twentieth century, bonfire toffee was sold loose, broken from large trays with a special hammer, but modern hygiene practices discourage this. In northern England, parkin, a soft, sticky type of gingerbread made with flour, oatmeal, and golden syrup is made for November 5, and thin gingerbread dough is cut into parkin pigs with currant eyes. Baked potatoes and sausages are often cooked as party food.

MINOR FESTIVALS

Other calendar festivals have lost importance because of social change. The meals and fruitcakes that once celebrated communal efforts of rural labor, such as sheepshearing and harvest home, have become rarer, as has the tradition of wassailing trees in cider orchards around Christmas time, with bowls of hot spiced cider. The rural communities who kept these alive are almost extinct. One festival that has grown in importance is St. Valentine's Day. This is now heavily commercialized by chocolate companies, and restaurants offer special meals.

FAIRS AND REVELS

Most towns in Britain had a day or a week during the year that was dedicated to a fair, either a saint's day or marketing a commodity, such as the Nottingham Goose Fair. Those that have survived are now pleasure fairs. Foods associated with fairs generally are candyfloss (cotton candy), toffee apples, ice cream, and hot dogs. Most fairs had specialties, usually a cake, biscuit, or gingerbread. Some of these survive as recipes or items made more generally; brandysnaps, crisp ginger-flavored rolled wafers, are the best known. In Lancashire, a county that has several distinctive food traditions, one dish associated with fairs is black peas, pigeon peas boiled and served with vinegar.

On a larger scale, the Scots, Welsh, and Irish celebrate their respective patron saint's days with traditional and characteristic food and drink. St. Patrick's Day has also become more obvious on mainland Britain recently, partly because of the activities of Irish pub chains. The English, however, pay little attention to St. George's Day.

FESTIVALS FROM OTHER COUNTRIES AND RELIGIONS

Various ethnic communities have introduced their own festivals. These include Diwali, the Hindu festival of lights celebrated with sweetmeats in November (Leicester); Chinese New Year, in February (London and Manchester); the mela (an East Indian fair, Bradford); and the West Indian carnival in Notting Hill (London, late summer). Muslim communities in Britain observe the fasts and festivals of their religious year, though these tend to be less obvious, as are the festivals and fasts of the Jewish communities.

FAMILY EVENTS

The three major life events—birth, marriage, and death—are still celebrated with vigor, and special foods are associated with them all.[4]

Weddings and the Wedding Cake

Weddings are the most visible of the three events, estimated to cost between £5,000 and £15,000 ($7,250 and $21,750), depending on size and style. The cake is an important ceremonial food, and this alone may cost several hundred pounds (in U.S. terms, approaching $1,000). Tradition-

ally, the reception is paid for by the bride's father, and the food can be provided either by the bride's mother or by a caterer, at the bride's home, in a
hired club or hall, or at a hotel. A meal, the "wedding breakfast," is served
after the ceremony and before the departure of the bride and groom.
There is no formalized menu, and the meal is usually composed with the
disparate tastes of different generations and social backgrounds in mind,
with influences from women's magazines and specialist wedding journals.

Meals tend to take one of two forms: an event with waiter service and
hot food of the cooked dinner type, or cold collation of luxury foods from
which guests help themselves. Roast beef, turkey, or chicken, ham, or
salmon are likely to form the centerpieces of either meal, followed by
creamy desserts. At large weddings, two meals may be served: a formal one
for a relatively small number of guests in the afternoon, followed by a
much larger informal party for more people in the evening. In England,
the party ends with the departure of the bride and groom. Irish and Scottish weddings lay more emphasis on dancing, and the party is expected to
continue all night.

Apart from sparkling wine, there are no prescribed drinks for the occasion: wines and other drinks are a matter of personal choice. This was not
always so in the past, when a posset, a rich concoction of spiced, sweetened
wine or ale beaten with eggs and cream, similar to eggnog, was considered
an essential part of the proceedings. It was generally served just before the
bride and groom retired to the bedchamber. A pale shadow of it survived
into the twentieth century in the Orkney Islands. Although such drinks
have disappeared from British practice, the idea of heavy drinking around a
wedding has not. One ritual that has become more apparent since the Second World War is the stag night, traditionally the evening before the wedding, when the bridegroom and his (male) friends indulge in heavy drinking
and a certain amount of practical joking. In recent years, a similar custom,
the hen night, has evolved for the bride and her friends.

Most ritual importance is given to the wedding cake. Rich fruitcake is
the basis, baked by the bride's mother or bought from a professional baker.
Small weddings might be celebrated with one cake, but most have at least
two or three, and in recent years, sometimes four or five cakes in diminishing sizes. Square or round are the most common shapes. Until the
1980s, the standard presentation was to cover each cake with marzipan
and then with royal icing. This is confectioner's sugar, egg white, and
lemon juice beaten together for a long time; it becomes very white and
sets hard. Surface decoration is added later with elaborate piping. It is
hard to escape the conclusion that the cake and the bride, in a lacy white

Traditional English wedding cake.

dress, resemble each other. The cakes are piled up in tiers separated by columns, and the whole is displayed throughout the meal, either as the centerpiece of a buffet table or on a separate table of its own.

After speeches and a toast of champagne or other sparkling wine, the cake is cut: a photograph of the couple cutting (or posing as if cutting) the cake is part of the proceedings; they hold the knife handle together, and usually make a ritual incision in the bottom tier. The cake is then whisked away and cut into small portions that are distributed among the guests. One is not obliged to eat all or any of it, and many wrap it in a napkin to take home. Portions are kept for friends or family who could not be present (in the mid-twentieth century, it was normal to send these through the post in special little boxes, although this custom seems to have waned). The top tier of the cake may be kept uncut for use at the christening of the first child. At Scottish weddings, cakes are decorated with favors, detachable ornaments, which are distributed among the female guests. Simpler, smaller versions of the wedding cake, appropriately decorated, are made for significant wedding anniversaries.

In the 1980s, the presentation of cakes began to change. The cake itself was still rich fruitcake in about 80 percent of cases (sponge cake, chocolate cake, and even carrot cake were occasionally chosen instead), but the decoration changed. A new form of icing, soft sugar paste that could be rolled out and cut like cloth was introduced from Australia and rapidly became popular in place of royal icing; flowers made of sugar paste were also used as decoration. Instead of columns, the tiers of cake were supported one above the other on stands, or piled directly on top of each other (a presentation known as "American"). Colored icing became allowable, usually ivory or pastel pink, blue, or lilac, although strong colors such as red or gold were occasionally used. Other shapes, from simple hexagons to an "open book" shape became more popular. Changes in family structure were also reflected, for instance, in a cake for a couple each with children from previous marriages, surmounted by a sugar paste model of themselves together on a settee with their new combined family around them.[5]

The history of the wedding cake is complex. In a seventeenth-century recipe, yeast-leavened dough was divided into two; one portion was kneaded with dried fruit, sugar, and perfumes such as musk, ambergris, and rosewater; the other was rolled out and used to enclose the mixture, giving an oval cake (a bit like a giant version of the modern Scottish black bun). Also important was the marchpane, an iced disc of marzipan decorated with comfits, fruit paste, and a gilded rosemary branch. In the eighteenth century, the cake became richer and lost the yeast leavening and outer crust, but gained a topping of iced marzipan. By the nineteenth century, the cake was darker with more dried fruit but without the perfumes, encrusted with marzipan and icing, decorated with molded sugar paste birds and cupids. Records hint at regional variants, such as the northern English pastry cake with currants, which was broken over the bride's head as she entered her new house. Onlookers scrambled for pieces as it was believed that if one slept with it under the pillow it foretold one's future spouse. In Scotland, a shortbread, known as the bride's bun, was shattered over the girl's head. By the late-nineteenth century, everyone aspired to rich fruitcake. Royal weddings provided models of cakes for the public to copy. White with gilding or silvering became the only color allowable; height was added by a vase of flowers on top. With minor variations, such cakes remained the norm except during wartime rationing when cardboard imitations were used.

Christenings

These are generally low-key events for immediate family. Celebrations range from "wetting the baby's head" (a drinking session for the father and his friends immediately after the birth) to a decorous tea party for parents and older relatives, usually on the day of the christening. Food is generally buffet style, with cold meats, salmon, or finger food, followed by cake and champagne. If the top tier of the wedding cake is not available, a fruitcake is iced and decorated with some motif appropriate to the day, usually a baby in a crib. A special cake has been associated with christenings since at least the mid-seventeenth century, when the gathering of female friends was known as a "gossiping" (from "god's sib," sibling in god). Cake and cheese were kept specially for the occasion. Hot spiced ales or possets were also served. The new mother might expect to receive special nourishing foods such as caudles, and the rest of the party celebrated with strong drink. Wealthy families laid in stocks of comfits and other sweetmeats to distribute to visitors (as continental Europeans still do), but this practice has died out in Britain.

Funerals

A funeral service is generally followed by some type of gathering involving eating and drinking. For much of the twentieth century, the height of respectability was to be "buried with a ham," that is, to have the relatively expensive and high-status item of a whole cold ham on the table at the funeral tea. By the end of the century, this had evolved into an afternoon tea type presentation, with items such as sandwiches, pies, and sausage rolls. Sherry or wine is generally offered to drink. The meal is rarely formal, as it is generally impossible to predict the number of guests, or how much time they will have to spare for a gathering arranged at short notice. In Ireland, a wake is often held. These were formerly quite widespread in the British Isles, but have disappeared on the mainland, partly because they were regarded as occasions when merrymaking got out of hand. In the eighteenth and nineteenth centuries, special funeral biscuits, wrapped in paper with black edges, carrying a verse appropriate to the occasion, were distributed to the mourners, together with wine or brandy.

Birthdays

Most families celebrate birthdays. A traditional birthday tea for children consists of small sandwiches, sausage rolls, potato crisps, and cakes, plus jelly and a birthday cake (often fruitcake) with the number of lit candles appropriate to the birthday on top. Recently, foods such as pizza have been incorporated into the scheme. A cake is still important, although it is more likely to be sponge or chocolate, and they are usually made in novelty shapes such as dogs, trains, or cartoon characters. The individual whose birthday is being celebrated blows the candles out and makes a wish. Teenagers and adults celebrate birthdays with special foods and drink according to taste. Birthdays become less important with age, and adults tend to concentrate on significant ones, such as those marking decades. Novelty cakes are often a feature of these as well.

Families celebrate other events as individual tastes and inherited customs dictate. Engagements, graduations, and anniversaries all provide the excuse for parties, but there are no traditional forms for these to follow.

ROYAL AND NATIONAL EVENTS

Attitudes about the rulers of countries comprising the United Kingdom have varied enormously over the centuries and across regions, but sometimes significant events in the life cycle of members of the royal family become public celebrations. Queen Victoria's diamond jubilee (60th anniversary of her coronation) was an occasion for public rejoicing. In the twentieth century, tins of chocolate or commemorative mugs were given to schoolchildren to commemorate coronations. Since the Second World War, important days have included the coronation of Queen Elizabeth II, and her 25th and 50th jubilees. A typical way of showing patriotic spirit for such an event is a street party, with tables set up in the middle of a residential street and everyone contributing to the food. Celebrations held on other extraordinary days have included the 50th anniversary of VE (Victory in Europe) day, and the millennium, but these have been mostly dictated by feelings in proportion to the significance of the event for the individual. There are no overt celebrations of a day of national importance equivalent to Independence Day in the United States or Bastille Day in France.

Coronation Chicken

A cold dish of chicken in a lightly curried rich sauce was devised for the coronation of Elizabeth II, and recipes of this type have been known as coronation chicken ever since. Popular for summer buffets, and sometimes used as sandwich fillings.

- 1 chicken, cooked and cooled
- 1 tbsp oil
- 1 small onion, chopped

- 1 level tbsp curry powder
- 5 fl oz chicken stock
- juice of 1/2 a lemon
- 2 tbsp mango chutney (chop any large pieces of fruit in it finely)
- 1/2 pint mayonnaise
- salt
- flaked almonds

Heat the oil, add the onion, and fry very gently until soft but not colored. Stir in the curry powder and continue to cook gently for a few minutes. Stir in the stock, lemon juice, and chutney. Simmer for 5 minutes, then strain the sauce into a bowl. Allow to cool and stir in the mayonnaise. Taste, and correct the seasoning. Remove the meat from the chicken, cut in bite-sized pieces, and arrange on a serving dish. Spoon the sauce over and decorate with flaked almonds. Serve with rice and salads.

NOTES

1. Bridget Ann Henisch, *Cakes and Characters: An English Christmas Tradition* (London: Prospect Books, 1984).

2. Nickie Charles and Marion Kerr, *Women, Food, and Families* (New York: Manchester University Press, 1988), p. 29.

3. Alan Davidson, *The Oxford Companion to Food* (New York: Oxford University Press, 1999), p. 724.

4. Laura Mason (ed.), *Food and the Rites of Passage* (Totnes, U.K.: Prospect Books, 2002).

5. Simon R. Charsley, *Wedding Cakes and Cultural History* (New York: Routledge, 1992), p. 142.

7

Regional Specialties

For most of the twentieth century, regionality in British food was generally ignored except in relation to a few special items. Industrialization, imports, and the growth of cities in the nineteenth century almost annihilated the idea. Purchasing boards for agricultural produce in the mid-twentieth century, bulk buying, and centralized distribution of supermarket chains reduced it even further. It was often considered unimportant, mostly invoked in relation to a handful of archaic recipes and practices. In fact, people often had a strong idea of what "their" food was, but the strength of national food culture tended to obscure differences. Conscious ideas about distinctiveness tended to focus on items such as family recipes for rich fruitcakes, which actually show relatively few variations. More subtle differences, for example, between cuts of meat, intricacies in the way meat and vegetables were combined in dishes, or the techniques of making and shaping pies, would pass with little comment.

Standardization in ingredients, and in the adoption of gas and electricity as cooking fuels also reduced reliance on traditional fuels and methods in, for instance, the highlands and islands of Scotland, where the gentle heat from peat gave many slow-cooked dishes and griddle breads. Those who worked with food sometimes remarked that tastes varied between areas, but evidently did not consider any attempt at codification worthwhile. Little attempt was made to elucidate the subtleties from one place to another. However, in the 1970s, the idea of local food became a marketing tool often developed by tourist organizations. This led to local publications that tended to be self-conscious in their references to the past, and to unquestioningly incorporate new developments, whether they used local traditions and ingredients or not.

Region was most often invoked in relation to dairy products. Cheeses retained regional names—Cheddar and Chesire, for example. In practice, these (with the exception of Stilton, whose manufacture was limited by law to a small area) indicated recipes, not a reliance on the subtleties of milk from specific cattle in specific landscapes. The cheeses could be made anywhere in the country, and in the case of Cheddar, were frequently made round the other side of the world. The growth of artisan cheese making in the 1980s revived interest in regional manufacture of well-known varieties, renewed interest in some that had vanished, and stimulated new recipes. One item that remained very much a product of the southwest of England is clotted cream.

Some bakery traditions showed strong regional links, with numerous recipes for breads, cakes, biscuits, and pastries that had regional names or close links to particular places. These include items such as small bread rolls, which have several regional variants, differing slightly in additions of fat, sugar, or dried fruit, in shape, and in baking method, and several cakes, actually made from pastry and filled with dried fruit, some of which retained regional names (for instance, Eccles cakes, which took their name from a suburb of Manchester). In practice, most had lost direct links to the communities they took their names from, although Banbury cakes still retained a strong link with that town, and Goosnargh cakes, a shortbread-type confection, remained a local specialty in Lancashire. Larger fruited loaves also have some regional links, such as saffron cake (Cornwall), bara brith (Wales), and spice loaf (Yorkshire).

Other traditions included a southern English one for lardy cakes, bread dough kneaded with lard, sugar, and dried fruit, and the northern English and Scottish use of oats. This could be seen in local forms of flat oatbread in northern England, a more general use of hard oatcakes in Scotland, and a use of oatmeal in some parkin recipes (northern forms of gingerbread). Welsh baking included use of the planc, an iron hotplate, for making small cakes and pancakes; Scottish baking also relied heavily on the girdle, a small, round iron plate heated over a fire or stove. These countries also included a number of slow-cooked meat dishes in their repertoires.

Regional tastes in fresh produce such as meat and the methods for cutting it were possibly quite distinct, but the knowledge was part of the skills of buyers and butchers. It was rarely remarked on by the consumer unless they happened to move to another part of the country and found them-

Planc.

selves unable to purchase a specific cut. Britain has several different breeds of cattle, sheep, and pig, usually named for the area in which they were developed. Some of these retain strong regional affiliations even now, for instance, the Herdwick sheep, which are largely restricted to the Lake District of northwest England.

Meat products show some regional distinctions. Cornish pasties (pastry turnovers filled with beef, potato, onion, and turnip) are widely available, although the Cornish would no doubt claim they make the best. Some sausage recipes, such as Cumberland sausage (a coarse-cut fresh pork sausage presented in one big coil), which has strong links with the northwest; hog's puddings (pale sausage-like items of cereal, pork, and seasonings), which are associated with the southwest; and mealie puddings (similar, but based on oatmeal and beef suet), which are linked with Scotland. Haggis (made from the pluck—liver, lungs, and heart—of a sheep, mixed with oatmeal and seasonings, stuffed into the cleaned paunch and simmered) is still closely identified with Scotland, and cawl, a soup-like stew of beef, bacon, and vegetables is important in Wales. Stuffed chine, a section of the backbone of a pig with the meat attached on either side, cured, slashed, and stuffed with large amounts of chopped parsley, is a regional specialty of Lincolnshire. Although several local cures for ham and bacon were recognized in the nineteenth century, they had tended to spread beyond their places of origin to become methods rather than locally distinctive items by the twentieth century. A number of local fish cures had also been known but are now much reduced: a few herring cures, such as kippers and bloaters, are still used in places, and Arbroath Smokies, small smoked haddock, are still produced near Aberdeen. Shellfish in the form of cockles are a traditional food of south Wales, cooked with bacon, made into pies, or added to scrambled eggs, and laverbread is also used in this region.

Cornish pasties, sausage rolls, and pork pie. © TRIP/R. Bamber.

The southeasternmost county of Kent was noted for orchards of apples, plums, and cherries; cobnuts (hazelnuts), grown for dessert, are also produced on a very limited scale. Apples and pears and plums were also grown in the west Midlands and in East Anglia, and some of the counties immediately north of London also grew apples, plums and cherries. Berries tended to be grown near large population centers; those from Hampshire on the south coast were well known, partly because they reached London early in the season. Vestiges of this pattern still remain, but orchards are labor-intensive, do not attract subsidies, and many have been grubbed up. Early rhubarb is grown in Yorkshire. Cider is produced across much of southern England but is particularly important in the west Midlands (as is perry, fermented pear juice) and southwest. Beer is brewed over the whole of the United Kingdom, but a few breweries have strong regional affiliations and use traditional methods.

Steamed haggis ready for eating. © Art Directors/
TRIP/Helene Rogers.

More recently, diversification in agriculture, concern with the welfare
of rural communities, and a formal legislation protecting local foods at the
European level has led to an increased interest in the idea of regional
food.[1] Since the early 1990s, there seems to have been a growing awareness of locally produced food, to the extent that supermarkets have begun
using it as a marketing tool, but it is unclear how deep this interest is.

NOTE

1. Laura Mason, with Catherine Brown, *Traditional Foods of Britain: An Inventory* (Totnes, United Kingdom: Prospect Books, 1999).

8

Diet and Health

The British appear to have two basic approaches to diet and health. The routine one is essentially permissive, along the lines of "if you feel okay, your diet's okay" and "a little of what you fancy does you good." The other is to focus intently on, for example, a pathogen in a foodstuff such as beef, or a group of possibly harmful ingredients such as food colorings, and consider them as sinister threats to health in a "food scare." Neither attitude reflects the major concerns of nutritionists, which currently center on obesity and cardiovascular disease. Hypertension, stroke, diabetes, and dental cavities, all of which also have high incidence in the U.K. population, are also linked to diet. These are sometimes called "diseases of affluence" because they are linked with wealthy societies; but there is evidence that the poorest are most likely to suffer from them.

Issues relating to diet, health, and nutrition in the United Kingdom are often clouded by the origin of the information. It is not always clear whether it comes from a public interest body, the food industry, or a pressure group; or whether it is relatively impartial, rooted in scientific research, or information presented selectively through advertising copy. At the government level, most is published in reports and policy documents. The Web site of the Food Standards Agency (a government-funded but independent body) provides summaries of information both from government and independent sources. The Web site for the Public Health Institute of Scotland also provides much information on the particular problems of that country, and links to other useful sites. The views of food manufacturers and retailers can be accessed through the industry-funded British Nutrition Foundation. Research into the social aspects of poor diet and dietary change is carried out by many institutions, including organizations such as the Joseph Rowntree Foundation and pressure groups such as The Food Commission and the Child Poverty Action Group.

THE CHANGING DIET

Underlying the apparent confusion between popular and expert points of view is the fact that diets have changed greatly throughout the twentieth century. Nutrition began to develop as a science in the late nineteenth century. At that time, problems relating to diet in Britain included rickets (vitamin-D deficiency), iron deficiency anemia, and simple lack of food. In the early twentieth century, emphasis was laid on foods such as milk, a simple way of boosting the nutritional value of poor diets, and on meat because of its protein content. Problems of inadequate diet continued into the 1930s.

Second World War rationing is often invoked as an example of circumstances and government intervention colluding to improve the nation's health. Emergency measures were introduced in 1939. Their explicit aim was to boost home-grown food supplies and distribute them, and the limited supplies of imported food, as equitably as possible. The perception that this was done to ensure optimum nutritional health for the whole population has recently been questioned; economics, as much as nutrition, seems to have been a driving force.[1] Essential foods were rationed through a coupon system, with some luxuries available on a points scheme. Milk production was increased, margarine fortified with vitamins A and D, and bread was made from flour with a higher extraction rate, closer to wholemeal than white, and fortified with calcium. The nation was encouraged to "Dig for Victory," growing vegetables to boost vitamin-C intakes. Extra vitamins were targeted at specific groups such as infants and pregnant women, and factory cafeteria and school meal provisions were expanded. A program of nutrition education taught the public how to make the best of unfamiliar ingredients such as dried egg.[2] People who can recall wartime food remark that it was monotonous, but adequate. For those who had suffered the extremes of urban poverty in the early twentieth century, it was a higher quality diet than they were accustomed to. It is often claimed that the British population generally was better nourished during the Second World War than at any time in the 150 years before, although the evidence is not clear cut.[3]

When rationing ended in 1954, consumption of brown bread fell dramatically, and that of sugar, confectionery, meat, and dairy products rose. In the 1950s and 1960s, the attitude toward diet was generally permissive along the lines of "moderation in all things," as long as requirements for essential nutrients such as protein, vitamins, and minerals were fulfilled, although ideas about slimming and weight loss became more apparent (the notion of slimness as a desirable state goes back to the 1920s and before). The idea of "three square meals a day," one of which should be a properly cooked meal was central. Growing affluence and the increasing range of processed and pre-prepared foods available meant the proportion of saturated fat in the diet was creeping up. Increasingly sedentary lifestyles meant less overall requirements for energy. Intensification of farming led to changes, notably cheaper chicken and higher production of milk and dairy products. Food processors and manufacturers introduced new foods that tended to be high in fat and salt or sugar, such as potato crisps (chips), other salted snacks, confectionery, fast foods such as fried chicken and burgers, and heat-and-serve convenience foods.

1980s ONWARD

The early 1980s were a turning point in nutritional thinking. Worries had been expressed about rates of cardiovascular disease, hypertension, stroke, diabetes, and colon cancer in the 1970s; diet was considered a factor in these diseases. Fat, especially saturated fat, intake associated with meat and dairy products and manufactured foods became an issue. In 1983, a report from the National Advisory Committee on Nutrition Education made recommendations on the proportions of carbohydrate, fat, and protein in the diet. It proposed that, in the overall diet of the nation, protein should provide about 11 percent of total daily energy (the same as before); the percentage of energy derived from fat should be reduced, to about 34 percent; that derived from carbohydrate should be increased, to about 50 percent. It also allowed for 5 percent of energy to be derived from alcohol. Also recommended were a decrease in protein derived from animal sources (and thus a decrease in saturated fat) and an increase in complex starches and vegetable protein, plus a higher intake of dietary fiber generally. Salt intake should also be reduced if possible. The report met much opposition from the food industry, and was found confusing by the public, but sparked a debate over food and health that has been maintained.[4] Subsequently, the recommendations were widely accepted and have been echoed in many other reports and policy statements. Improving diet is now an intrinsic part of health policy. In 1999, the Government White Paper *Our Healthier Nation* set targets to reduce death rates from cancers, coronary heart disease, and stroke in the under-75 age group and commented on the need to improve diet, in particular to increase fruit and vegetable consumption.[5] In addition, an increase in the consumption of fatty fish (high in essential fatty acids) is advised.

The apparent changes in dietary advice given by nutritionists in response to the changing circumstances of society often leads to complaints that "they"—the experts—change their minds, engendering mistrust from the public. However, ideas about healthy diet evolve in response both to scientific research and the circumstances of society, and information relating to issues can date quickly. Issues relating to obesity, weight loss, and fat also become conflated with societal pressure, especially on women, to remain slim.

Except during rationing, the United Kingdom has never had an overt food policy. From the late 1950s until the end of the 1990s, the government ministry responsible for food was also responsible for agriculture. Critics pointed out that having a ministry that represented the consumer while having strong links with farming and food processing was undesirable, and not in the interest of the nation's health. The committees that advised on food standards in the latter half of the twentieth century were also often criticized for a lack of independence and for financial links to the food industry. Balance of power increasingly moved toward food manufacturers, and then, in the 1980s, to retailers. In 2001, consumer aspects went to the new Food Standards Agency while the Department for Environment, Food and Rural Affairs took over agricultural interests, with more emphasis on the environment due to concerns about the impact of industrial farming on the landscape. The Food Standards Agency now carries out a Diet and Nutrition Survey, which provides information to complement that derived from the Expenditure and Food Survey.

DIET AND HEALTH IN THE TWENTY-FIRST CENTURY

The current position with regard to diet and health in the United Kingdom is that few individuals suffer from lack of food (starvation), or from lack of basic nutrients, although some groups show cause for concern with certain essential nutrients such as iron and vitamin D. However, health professionals consider that the proportions of macronutrients (protein, carbohydrate, and fat) in the overall diet of the nation do not provide optimum health. Particular concern is expressed over the total energy (calorie) content, the proportion of energy derived from fat, and, within that, the proportions of saturated and unsaturated fat. A higher than desirable fat intake, containing a relatively high proportion of saturated fat, is thought to contribute to the incidence of cardiovascular disease, of which the United Kingdom has one of the highest rates in the world. This has been an increasing focus of concern for three decades, addressed by both nutritionists and campaigners for public health and against corporate power, including one high-profile case against McDonald's in the 1990s.[6]

Across the regions, the Scots are recognized to eat especially high levels of salt, sugar, and fat, while the Expenditure and Food Survey shows that those in the southeast of England spend the most money on fruit and vegetables.[7] It also varies according to socioeconomic group. Income is inevitably a factor in how much people spend on food, both overall and on specific items. The number of people living in poverty (defined by the number of households with earnings below half the U.K. average) is about 14.1 million.[8] Links between poverty, poor diet, and disease are complex, derived from large-scale population studies and linked to several other factors. Diet, along with exercise and smoking, is a changeable factor (unlike, for instance, genetic inheritance), and health policies have focused on this. Diet also varies according to ethnic group. Dietary change for low-income households is complicated by lack of money, innate conservatism, and a desire to keep up with perceived norms. One study showed that low-income families shop little, often tend to resist change, eat cheaper versions of mainstream meals, and avoid experiments with new foods. Although children were often allowed more of their favorite foods than their more affluent peers, these were not necessarily the healthiest choices. Knowledge of food issues tended to be fragmentary, and advice on healthy eating not considered feasible.[9] Sometimes direct experience of illness is what persuades people to make changes in their diets.[10]

Relative perceptions of risk to health from diet vary between health professionals, the media, and the public. Health professionals perceive poor diet and food-borne illness from bacteria or viruses as the highest risks (borne out by epidemiological evidence). The media concentrate on scares and stories with sensational and sinister implications. The public, often not in receipt of full explanations, but nervous of the increasingly industrialized food supply and cynical of advertising, tend to be confused and continue to make choices on the basis of personal likes and dislikes, fashion, and convenience. In addition, advice on food is often presented in negative terms ("cut down on fats, sugar, and alcohol"), although emphasis has changed recently to the positive ("eat more fruit and vegetables").

"Eat Five a Day"

The importance of fruit and vegetables as sources of vitamins and minerals has long been recognized. They are valued for their contributions of other substances, such as antioxidants and dietary fiber, now believed to play an important role in protecting the body against cancer. In 1998, the Committee on Medical Aspects of Food Policy and Nutrition concluded that higher vegetable consumption would reduce the risk of colon cancer, gastric cancer, and possibly breast cancer, as well as helping to reduce risk of coronary heart disease and stroke. Encouraging the population to eat more fruit and vegetables is now a Department of Health priority. Average consumption of fruit and vegetables is less than three portions a day, tending to be lower among children, young men, and people on low incomes. The "Eat Five a Day" campaign, aimed at raising awareness and encouraging everyone to eat five portions, preferably fresh, from a varied selection of fruit and vegetables (excluding potatoes).[11] More targeted action is via the National School Fruit Scheme, to give all four-to-six-year-old children in state schools one free piece of fruit (an apple, banana, pear, or a satsuma) every school day, and the idea of vouchers exchangeable for fruit and vegetables for parents on low incomes with small children has also been considered.

Obesity

Currently, the most prominent concern with diet and health is the rising incidence of obesity in the British population. In the United Kingdom, obesity is defined as having a body mass index score of over 30. In February 2004, 25 percent of men and 20 percent of women aged between 19 and 64 years were considered obese (an increase from 8% and 12%, respectively, in 1987).[12] The incidence of obesity increased with age and was highest among the 50–64 year group. A physical activity diary showed that only 35 percent of men and 22 percent of women did enough activity to meet current recommendations of 30 minutes on five or more days of the week. Levels of obesity are also rising among children, and over the past 10 years, have doubled among 6-year-olds and tripled among 15-year-olds. Obesity generally is of concern because of its implications as a factor in other diseases, such as cardiovascular disease and diabetes, which are already prevalent in the U.K. population, and childhood obesity because it has implications for overall longevity and health. In the past, individuals have been expected to take responsibility for their weight, and nutrition education is still viewed as a strong component in helping the population in general lose weight. Recently suggestions have included controls on food and drink advertisements (generally for high-fat, high-sugar items) for children's television and stricter nutritional standards for school meals.

Cardiovascular Disease

In 2001, cardiovascular disease caused 40 percent of deaths in the United Kingdom, some 245,000 people. Of these, 120,000 were classified as coronary heart disease, and this is the most common cause of premature death in the United Kingdom. The death rates from coronary heart disease vary according to locality and socioeconomic group. They are highest in Scotland and lowest in the southeast of England, and higher among those in manual occupations than those in non-manual ones. Certain ethnic groups are also more at risk, notably South Asians (Indians, Bangladeshis, Pakistanis, and Sri Lankans). The rate for those of Caribbean and West African descent is much lower than average.[13] Death rates for coronary heart disease have been falling in the United Kingdom since the 1970s, but not as fast as for some countries, and the rate remains among one of the highest in the world. The National Diet and Nutrition Survey found 48 percent of all adults had blood cholesterol levels above the optimal level, increasing with age.[14]

Diabetes

About 1.4 million people in the United Kingdom have been diagnosed with diabetes.[15] Of these, some 18,000 people under 18 have type I diabetes (insulin dependent). The majority of the remainder have type II, in which weight and activity levels are a factor in development. Incidence of type II diabetes is higher in the Caribbean and West African population than among other groups in the United Kingdom. Weight control and diet are also important in the management of diabetes, and a high fruit and vegetable intake, plus complex carbohydrates and more modest fat levels, with an emphasis on unsaturated fats is recommended.

Malnourishment

Although the general diet of the United Kingdom provides more than adequate nutrition, when it is broken down by age, gender, social class, and ethnicity, it seems that a few groups have lower than desirable intakes of certain nutrients. The principal areas of concern relate to low-iron intake in the diet of teenage girls, and low vitamin-D levels among some ethnic groups, particularly South Asians. The latter may in part relate to the difference in sunlight levels between South Asia and Britain, and traditional culture, which demands that women, especially, expose as little skin as possible outside the home, cutting down on the amount of vitamin D synthesized by the body.

Alcohol

Moderate consumption of alcohol is generally regarded by health specialists as beneficial, but heavy drinking as something to be avoided. Advice on alcohol consumption is generally framed in terms of units equivalent to 10 mL of pure alcohol. In terms of actual drinks, one unit translates to half a U.K. pint of ordinary strength beer or cider, a small (125 mL glass) of wine, or a pub measure of spirits. Men are recommended to drink no more than three to four units a day, and women no more than two to three, with pregnant women restricting themselves to one to two units a week, although disquiet is expressed about binge drinking, intermittent excessive alcohol consumption among young adults.

Special Diets

Substantial minorities observe special diets. These include religious requirements including kosher, halal, and Hindu diets, all of which are perfectly adequate given sufficient access to food overall. Other groups pursue special diets through personal choice, notably vegetarians. Their numbers have risen since the 1980s, and in 2001, an estimated 4 percent of the population was estimated to be vegetarian, with a further 33 percent saying they only ate meat occasionally.[16]

Food-Borne Illness

The link between poor food handling and illness has been observed for centuries, but the reasons were unknown until the late nineteenth century. Pasteurization of milk was a major step forward, helping to eliminate tuberculosis. Microbiology became increasingly important in the late twentieth century, as more food is pre-prepared and held in a partially or fully cooked state; intensive farming systems and industrial processing have also given rise to concerns about pathogens ranging from salmonella in eggs to bovine spongiform encephalopathy (BSE) in beef. Responses have ranged from public health measures, such as tightening legislation relating to food safety, to individual choice in pursuit of a vegetarian or an organically grown diet. Pesticides, irradiation, and genetic modification have been (or are) all the subject of intense debate and suspicion.

Basic standards are enforced at a local level by Environmental Health Officers and Trading Standards Officers. Over and above this, supermarket retailers create their own, more stringent standards, which they police themselves. However, this does not mean uniformity of product, as multiple retailers are divided into tiers aiming at different market sectors, and thus have different ideas about the choices and qualities of product to offer. The word *quality* has no concrete definition in relation to food, but points such as price and safety are more easily quantified, and these tend to be the focus of British consumer concern. The rise in concern over food hygiene issues, for instance, has made it almost impossible to purchase unpasteurized milk, a direct consequence of government policy relating to health concerns. Consumer reaction has affected both irradiation and genetically modified (GM) foods, with multiple retailers refusing to handle these because they feel there would be consumer reaction against them.

Major Pathogens

In 2002, there were 81,562 cases of food poisoning notified to the health authorities, although the actual number was probably much higher, as many cases are never officially diagnosed and recorded.[17] The majority of cases of food-borne illness are probably related to five species of bacteria: *E. Coli* O157, salmonella, *Listeria monocytogenes*, campylobacter, and *Clostridium perfringens*.[18] *E. Coli* O157 was first reported as a cause of food poisoning in the early 1980s, and has grown in importance. The worst outbreak to date was in 1996 when 17 elderly people died and another 496 fell seriously ill in Lanarkshire, Scotland. It was traced to poor handling of meat products. The main reservoir of infection is cattle (about 5% of cows are thought to be carriers in England and Wales), although sheep and goats can also be carriers. The infection can be picked up through contaminated food or from direct animal contact. Salmonella became a focus for public concern in 1989, when a government minister made an overt statement about levels of infection in chicken and egg production. Listeria has also been the subject of food scares, usually in association with soft cheese. Although it receives less attention from the media, *Campylobacter* is the most commonly identified cause of food poisoning.

OTHER FOOD ISSUES

Beef and Bovine Spongiform Encephalopathy

BSE (or "Mad Cow Disease") was first diagnosed in the 1980s and confirmed in cattle in 1986.[19] Despite much research, no one is certain where the disease came from, but it is theorized that it spread through the use of meat and bonemeal that was added to cattle feed to increase its protein content. BSE is one of a group of prion diseases, another of which, scrapie, affects sheep and goats and has been observed in the British flock for over 250 years. No link has been shown between scrapie and human illness. A prion disease that does affect humans is Creutzfeldt-Jakob Disease (CJD), mostly occurring in the 40–80 age group. In 1996, a new strain, predominantly affecting younger people, was discovered; it became known as variant CJD, or vCJD. Because the protein involved is similar to that found in BSE-infected cattle, a possible link between the two was suggested. Researchers eventually concluded that human exposure to the BSE agent was the most likely cause of vCJD. Up until June 2003, 135 cases of definite and probable vCJD had been diagnosed in the United Kingdom. The epidemic of BSE in cattle in the United Kingdom has declined to the point where the number of new cases had fallen to its lowest point since 1988 (when records were first kept).

Several controls on beef production were introduced as preventative measures. These include banning cattle from over the age of 30 months for sale as food (a measure shortly due for review); removal of specified risk material (including brain and spinal cord); a ban on the use of meat and bonemeal in feed for all farm animals in 1996 (it had been banned for use in feed for ruminants, such as cattle, in 1988); and banning the production of mechanically recovered meat (meat stripped from bone at high pressure, which had been used in low-cost burgers, sausages, pies, and mince) from the backbones of cattle. The use of ruminant bones (which includes cattle) for mechanically recovered meat is now banned throughout the European Union (EU).

The issues surrounding BSE and vCJD are complex. The incubation period for both diseases is long and the infective agent still not fully understood. BSE is a disease linked with industrial methods of food production, which appears to have been spread by the imperative to utilize every scrap as economically as possible, including adding meat and bonemeal to animal feed. In turn, it seems the necessity for a protein-rich feed for high-yielding dairy cattle spread BSE through the British dairy herd. Dedicated grass-fed beef herds have a very low incidence of BSE. The principal use of beef from elderly dairy cattle and their offspring in cheap meat products, especially as mechanically recovered meat, is one way in which infective material may have entered food for human consumption.

Genetically Modified Foodstuffs

GM foods have been the subject of a lively and ongoing debate in the United Kingdom and the EU generally. They are regarded with extreme suspicion. This is partly based on an emotional reaction to a method that is often quoted as producing unnatural "frankenfoods," and partly worries over lack of knowledge about their effects on human health and the wider environment, especially in cross-pollination with conventional crops. A more politicized debate revolves around disquiet over issues relating to gene patenting and control by multinational companies, and the potential for adverse effects on third-world farmers. These include worries over potential loss of biodiversity and the employment of "terminator technology" (genetic use restriction technology—meaning that plants produce sterile seed, forcing farmers to buy annually from biotech companies). In the EU, the only food ingredients approved for food use are from GM soya, maize, and oilseed rape, but very little is used. By 2001, a few foods sold in the United Kingdom contained GM ingredients but some major food retailers, for instance, Marks and Spencer, declared themselves "GM free." However, GM soya and maize is imported to the EU for animal food, and GM maize has recently been approved as a crop for the United Kingdom.

Organic Food

The arguments over GM food are, to some extent, an extension of a longer running debate on conventional versus organic food production. The use of pesticides and herbicides on crops becomes an issue on occasion, often as part of a wider expression of disquiet about intensive farming methods and the environment. The conventional view is that there is no threat to human health as long as they are used carefully, but an increasingly large number of consumers choose to buy organically grown food. The most widely recognized organic standard is that of the Soil Association. A report on organically produced food commissioned by the Food Standards Agency concluded that it provided more choice but that current scientific evidence does not show organic food to be any safer or more nutritious than conventionally produced food. Despite this, and despite the sometimes higher costs of organic food, the market for it seems set to grow.

Food Miles and Fair Trade

The debate about intensively produced and organic food, and control of the market by multiple retailers, is often linked to other trade and environmental issues. The idea of food miles addresses the transport of perishables, mostly out-of-season fruit and vegetables, between the places of production (often in the southern hemisphere) and the point of sale. The issues relate to the use of petroleum products to move what are essentially luxury foods over long distances, often by air freight, and the impact this has on the environment, especially relating to transport issues. The idea of fair trade—paying third-world producers a fair price for tropical crops such as cocoa, coffee, and bananas, instead of the present fraction of the retail price these goods command—has also received more prominence recently.

Hormones

The use of hormones as growth promoters in animals is banned in the EU, and antibiotic growth promoters are to be phased out by 2006 because of concerns over antibiotic resistance. Recombinant bovine somatotropin is also banned in milk production in the EU because of its effects on animal health.

Food Additives

This phrase covers a large and disparate group of chemicals, from colors to stabilizers, often added to manufactured foods for cosmetic purposes. EU legislation requires most of these to be labeled by name or E-number, a system that identifies each one with a unique number prefixed by the letter E. From time to time, they become a focus of public concern. Azo dyes (synthetic coloring agents) were a particular concern in the 1980s, when some researchers linked them to hyperactivity in children.

Intolerance and Allergies

A small proportion of the population develops serious allergies to specific foodstuffs. In recent years, nut allergies have become increasingly common in children. Food intolerance has also become a subject of discussion, but the incidence is much less clear cut. One form, gluten intolerance, which manifests itself as celiac disease, is well recognized.

Eating Disorders

Anorexia nervosa and bulimia nervosa have received much attention in the press. They mostly affect adolescent girls and, increasingly, adolescent boys. That women have a problematic relationship with food, having one role as providers and nurturers, but another in which slimness is equated with attractiveness, is widely explored in feminist literature.

Infant Feeding

Department of Health recommendations are that babies should receive nothing but breast milk for the first six months of life, followed by breast milk and substitutes, plus small quantities of appropriate solid foods. New mothers often find this difficult to fulfill, as breastfeeding in public places is often frowned on, and provision of adequate private space provided in cafes, restaurants, and other establishments is patchy.

Children and Food in Schools

Cooked midday dinners and milk were provided in schools by law through the middle decades of the twentieth century. The foundations of the legislation go back to the early twentieth century, but only extended to the majority of children during the Second World War. By law, junior schools were required to provide a third of a U.K. pint of milk a day from the Second World War until the 1980s, when this was reduced to only those children under the age of seven. School dinners were also provided at a small charge, or free to the neediest children. From 1944 until 1980, they were made to a specified minimum nutritional standard, providing one-third of the recommended daily intake of calories.[20] Apart from the nutritional value, school meals were regarded as being educationally valuable in socializing children and teaching them table manners.

In 1980, legislation freed Local Education Authorities from the obligation to meet nutritional standards and provide for all children (provision of free meals for those in receipt of certain welfare benefits continued). School meals had been the subject of criticism, but health professionals considered that removal of guidelines made things worse, allowing the introduction of snack foods high in fat, salt, and sugar, and more fizzy drinks. In 2001, adolescents questioned about their eating habits showed a very low consumption of fruit and vegetables.[21] In 2003, pizza, followed by cake or a bun or ice cream, was found to be a favorite school meal among children; burgers, pasta, roast dinner, and curry were other top choices. Parents rated fruit, "healthy meals," roast dinners, salads, jacket potatoes, and fruit juices higher than children.[22] Regulations on national minimum nutritional standards were reintroduced in 2001 in England and Wales, and are currently being evaluated. School milk has also been reintroduced on a limited scale for younger children and those whose parents claim welfare benefits.

Other schemes relating to food in schools include pilot projects for healthier breakfast clubs, tuck shops, lunch boxes, cookery clubs, and the development of whole school food approaches, bringing together all nutrition-related activities both within and outside the formal curriculum. Cookery is no longer a subject in the core curriculum for formal education in secondary schools. Many school leavers have little or no formal cookery training, and their knowledge of food-related issues depends on the interests of individual teachers and schools.

Recently, a campaign has started to promote and strengthen the status of practical food education in schools. Known as the Cooking Bus, this involves mobile classrooms fitted as kitchens, aimed at providing some cookery, food hygiene, and healthy eating education for the next generation.[23]

NOTES

1. Derek J. Oddy, *From Plain Fare to Fusion Food: British Diet from the 1890s to the 1990s* (Rochester, N.Y.: Boydell and Brewer, 2003).

2. See John Burnett, *Plenty and Want: A Social History of Diet in England from 1815 to the Present Day* (New York: Methuen, 1983); J. C. Drummond and Anne Wilbraham, *The Englishman's Food: Five Centuries of English Diet* (London: Pimlico, 1991).

3. Oddy, *From Plain Fare to Fusion Food*, pp. 113–68.

4. Caroline Walker, with Geoffrey Cannon, *The Food Scandal: What's Wrong with the British Diet and How to Put It Right* (London: Century Publishing, 1984); Felicity Lawrence, *Not on the Label: What Really Goes into the Food on Your Plate* (New York: Penguin, 2004).

5. "Saving Lives: Our Healthier Nation," 1999, Department of Health Web site, http://www.ohn.gov.uk.

6. John Vidal, *McLibel: Burger Culture on Trial* (London: Macmillan, 1997).

7. "Food, Diet, and Nutrition as a Public Health Issue," Public Health Institute of Scotland, http://www.phis.org.uk.

8. "Evidence: Poverty," http://www.phis.org.uk.

9. Barbara Dobson, Alan Beardsworth, Teresa Keil, and Robert Walker, "Eating on a Low Income," *Social Policy Research* 66 (November 1994), http://www.jrf.org.uk.

10. Nickie Charles and Marion Kerr, *Women, Food, and Families* (New York: Manchester University Press, 1988), pp. 117–18.

11. "Health and Social Care Topics: 5 a Day," Department of Health, http://www.dh.gov.uk.

12. "Adult Obesity Rising," News Archive, Food Standards Agency, http://www.foodstandards.gov.uk.

13. "Mortality," British Heart Foundation, http://www.heartstats.org.

14. "National Diet and Nutrition Survey (Volume 4) Shows Rise in Number of Obese and Overweight Adults," Food Standards Agency, http://www.food standards.gov.uk.

15. "Fact Sheet No. 2—Diabetes: The Figures," 2000, Web site of Diabetes UK, http://www.diabetes.org.uk.

16. "Summary of Realeat Polls," Web site of the Vegetarian Society, http://www.vegsoc.org.

17. "Food Poisoning," Foodlink, http://foodlink.org.uk.

18. Food Standards Agency, "A Bug's Life," http://www.foodstandards.gov.uk.

19. "What is BSE?," http://www.foodstandards.gov.uk.

20. Elizabeth Dowler and Shelia Turner, with Barbara Dobson, *Poverty Bites: Food, Health, and Families* (London: Child Poverty Action Group, 2001), pp. 30–33.

21. MORI, "Poll Finds Children's Diets Seriously Short on Fruit and Veg," 6 November 2001, http://www.mori.com.

22. "Food and Drink," *Mintel Report, 2003.*

23. "About the Cooking Bus," http://www.foodstandards.gov.uk.

Glossary

aubergine   Eggplant

bannock   (Scottish) a small baked roll of bread, now usually made with wheat flour but often from barley in the past

biscuit   Cookie, cracker

carry-out   (Scotland) food to go

chips   French fries

cider   Always a fermented drink in Britain

coriander, green   Cilantro

corn   In English indicates grain in general—wheat, oats, rye, barley, and maize

cornflour   Corn starch

courgette   Zucchini

crisps   Potato chips

crumpet   Small, thick yeast-leavened pancake, eaten toasted and spread with butter

demerara sugar   A coarse-crystal, pale brown sugar used for baking, in some desserts, and in sweetening coffee

dripping   Fat rendered from cooking meat, usually beef or pork

garam masala   Spicing mixtures used for Indian dishes

garum   A sauce made by fermenting fish, used as a condiment by the Romans

girdle   (North English/Scottish) a heated iron plate for baking small breads and cakes

golden syrup (colloquially, "syrup")   A trade name for a viscous pale gold by-product of sugar refining, used in some baking. It is lighter in color and flavor than molasses, but with similar applications.

grilling   Broiling

haggis   (Scottish) a sheep's stomach, cleaned, filled with a mixture of oatmeal, offal, and seasonings

ice lolly   Popsicle

icing   Frosting

icing sugar   Confectioner's sugar

jam   Jelly

laver bread, laver   *Porphyra umbiliculis*, a species of seaweed used in south Wales and north Devon as a vegetable

leechdoms   An early medieval word indicating a remedy or medicine

mixed spice   A proprietary mix, usually containing cloves, cinnamon, and allspice often called for in British sweet baked items

muffin   Small, round yeast-leavened bread, partially baked on a griddle. They are toasted, split in half, and spread with butter for eating

muscavado sugar   A small-crystal semirefined sugar, dark brown in color with a pronounced flavor, used in baking

offal   Variety meats, organ meats

orache   Wild or cultivated plants of the genus *Artiplex*

pikelet   Similar to a crumpet, but thinner

pint   Liquid measure, now 20 fluid ounces; was 16 fluid ounces until 1878

planc   (Welsh) a heated iron plate used for small breads and pancakes

pottage   Semiliquid dishes of grain, pulses, and vegetables, with meat when available

prawns   Shrimp

pudding   A collective name for sweet dishes considered suitable for the dessert course; also, several classes of cereal-based foods common in British cookery, some savory, some sweet

scones   Small baking-powder–raised confections of flour with a little fat and sugar, similar to an American soft biscuit

shrimp   *Cragnon cragnon*, a small crustacean found on sandy coasts

sodium bicarbonate (bicarbonate of soda)   Baking soda

spring onions   Scallions

sweets, sweeties   Candies

takeaway   (England/Wales) food to go

teacake   A small, flat bread roll with a little dried fruit kneaded into the dough, often toasted and eaten with butter

tin (for cooking loaves or cakes)   Pan

treacle   Black treacle is similar to molasses. The word is also sometimes applied to golden syrup.

wholemeal   Wholewheat

Bibliography/Resource Guide

GENERAL BACKGROUND

Atkins, Peter, and Ian Bowler. *Food in Society*. New York: Arnold and Oxford University Press, 2001.

Burnett, John. *Plenty and Want: A Social History of Diet in England from 1815 to the Present Day*. New York: Methuen, 1983.

Burnett, John. *Liquid Pleasures: A Social History of Drinks in Modern Britain*. New York: Routledge, 1999.

Davidson, Alan. *The Oxford Companion to Food*. New York: Oxford University Press, 1999.

Drummond, J. C., and Anne Wilbraham. *The Englishman's Food: Five Centuries of English Diet*. London: Pimlico, 1991.

Food Standards Agency. "Fifty Years of Food." http://www.foodstandards.gov.uk.

Oddy, Derek J. *From Plain Fare to Fusion Food: British Diet from the 1890s to the 1980s*. Rochester, N.Y.: Boydell and Brewer, 2003.

Patten, Marguerite. *Marguerite Patten's Century of British Cooking*. London: Grub Street, 1991.

Shephard, Sue. *Pickled, Potted, and Canned*. London: Headline Books, 2000.

Spencer, Colin. *British Food: An Extraordinary Thousand Years of History*. London: Grub Street, 2002.

Government Departments

Department for Environment, Food, and Rural Affairs. http://www.defra.gov.uk.
Department of Health. http://dh.gov.uk.

Food and Drink Federation. http://fdf.org.uk. Web site representing food manu-
facturers, including information for public and press.
Food Standards Agency. http://www.foodstandards.gov.uk.
Foodline Web. http://www.foodlineweb.co.uk. Acts as a portal to much informa-
tion about the food industry and business.
National Statistics. http://statistics.gov.uk.

Public Broadcasting about Food

British Broadcasting Corporation (BBC). http://www.bbc.co.uk/food.

HISTORICAL OVERVIEW

Black, Maggie. *Food and Cooking in Medieval Britain*. English Heritage series. Lon-
don: Historic Buildings and Monuments Commission for England, 1985.
Black, Maggie. *Food and Cooking in 19th Century Britain*. English Heritage series.
London: Historic Buildings and Monuments Commission for England,
1985.
Brears, Peter. *Food and Cooking in 16th Century Britain*. English Heritage series.
London: Historic Buildings and Monuments Commission for England,
1985.
Brears, Peter. *Food and Cooking in 17th Century Britain*. English Heritage series.
London: Historic Buildings and Monuments Commission for England,
1985.
Davidson, Alan, with Helen Saberi. *The Wilder Shores of Gastronomy: 20 Years of
the Best Food Writing from the Journal Petits Propos Culinaires*. Berkeley: Ten
Speed Press, 2002.
Day, Ivan, ed. *Eat, Drink, and Be Merry: The British at Table 1600–2000*. London:
Philip Wilson, 2000.
Edwards, John. *The Roman Cookery of Apicius*. London: Rider, 1984.
Hagen, Ann. *A Handbook of Anglo-Saxon Food: Processing and Consumption*.
Hockwold-cum-Wilton, United Kingdom: Anglo-Saxon Books, 1992 (re-
vised 1998).
Hagen, Ann. *A Second Handbook of Anglo-Saxon Food and Drink: Production and
Distribution*. Hockwold-cum-Wilton, United Kingdom: Anglo-Saxon
Books, 1995.
Hardyment, Christina. *Home Comfort: A History of Domestic Arrangements*. New
York: Viking Penguin, 1992.
Hieatt, Constance B., ed. *An Ordinance of Pottage*. London: Prospect Books,
1988.

Hieatt, Constance B., and Sharon Butler, eds. *Curye on Inglysch: English Culinary Manuscripts of the Fourteenth Century (Including the Forme of Cury)*. New York: Oxford University Press for the Early English Text Society, 1985.

Lehmann, Gilly. *The British Housewife: Cookery Books, Cooking, and Society in Eighteenth-Century Britain*. Totnes, United Kingdom: Prospect Books, 2003.

Mennell, Stephen. *All Manners of Food: Eating and Taste in England and France from the Middle Ages to the Present*. New York: Basil Blackwell, 1985.

Paston Williams, Sara. *The Art of Dining: A History of Cooking and Eating*. London: The National Trust, 1993.

Pember-Reeves, Maud. *Round about a Pound a Week*. London: Virago, [1913] 1999.

Renfrew, Jane. *Food and Cooking in Prehistoric Britain*. English Heritage series. London: Historic Buildings and Monuments Commission for England, 1985.

Renfrew, Jane. *Food and Cooking in Roman Britain*. English Heritage series. London: Historic Buildings and Monuments Commission for England, 1985.

Rogers, Ben. *Beef and Liberty: Roast Beef, John Bull, and the English Nation*. London: Chatto and Windus, 2002.

Rowntree, B. Seebohm. *Poverty: A Study of Town Life*. London: Macmillan and Co., 1901.

Scully, Terence. *The Art of Cookery in the Middle Ages*. Rochester, N.Y.: Boydell and Brewer, 1995.

Stead, Jennifer. *Food and Cooking in 18th Century Britain*. English Heritage series. London: Historic Buildings and Monuments Commission for England, 1985.

Strong, Roy. *Feast: A History of Grand Eating*. London: Jonathan Cape, 2002.

Warren, Geoffrey C., ed. *The Foods We Eat*. London: Cassell, 1958.

Wilson, C. Anne. *Food and Drink in Britain from the Stone Age to Recent Times*. London: Constable and Co. Ltd., 1991.

Additional Resources

The British Museum. http://thebritishmuseum.ac.uk.

English Heritage. http://www.english-heritage.org.uk.

http://www.historicfood.com

The Museum of London. http://museumoflondon.org.uk.

Prospect Books. http://www.prospectbooks.co.uk. Additional information on food history books can be found at http://www.foodbooks.com.

Skara Brae settlement. http://www.orkneydigs.org.uk.

Vindolanda Roman Fort. http://vindolanda.csad.ox.ac.uk.

INGREDIENTS

Botting, Bev, ed. *Family Spending: A Report on the 2001–2002 Expenditure and Food Survey*. London: HMSO, 2003.

DEFRA: National Food Survey 2000. London: 2001.

Geissler, Catherine, and Derek J. Oddy, eds. *Food, Diet, and Economic Change: Past and Present*. New York: Leicester University Press and St. Martin's Press, 1993.

Oddy, Derek J., and Derek S. Miller. *The Making of the Modern British Diet*. Totowa, N.J.: Rowman and Littlefield, 1976.

Slater, J. M., ed. "Fifty Years of the National Food Survey: 1940–1990." The proceedings of a symposium held in London in 1991. London: HMSO, 1991.

Additional Resource

http://www.statistics.gov.uk (for results from the National Food Survey).

Specialist Cheesemakers Association. http://www.specialistcheesmakers.co.uk.

TYPICAL MEALS

Beardsworth, Alan, and Teresa Keil. *Sociology on the Menu: An Invitation to the Study of Food and Society*. New York: Routledge, 1997.

Charles, Nickie, and Marion Kerr. *Women, Food, and Families*. New York: Manchester University Press, 1988.

Davidson, Caroline. *A Woman's Work Is Never Done: A History of Housework in the British Isles 1650–1950*. London: Chatto and Windus, 1982.

"The Evening Meal." *Mintel Report*, 2002.

Hardyment, Christina. *From Mangle to Microwave: The Mechanization of Household Work*. Cambridge, Mass.: Basil Blackwell, 1988.

Hardyment, Christina. *A Slice of Life: The British Way of Eating since 1945*. New York: Penguin, 1995.

Lawrence, Felicity. *Not on the Label: What Really Goes into the Food on Your Plate*. New York: Penguin, 2004.

Mennell, Stephen, Anne Murcott, and Anneke H. van Otterloo. *The Sociology of Food: Eating, Diet, and Culture*. London: Sage, 1992.

Murcott, Anne, ed. *The Nation's Diet: The Social Science of Food Choice*. New York: Longman, 1998.

Turner, Michael, ed. *Nutrition and Lifestyles*. London: Applied Science Publishers, 1980.

Warde, Alan. *Consumption, Food, and Taste: Culinary Antinomies and Commodity Culture*. London: Sage, 1997.

Wilson, C. Anne. *Luncheon, Nuncheon, and Other Meals: Eating with the Victorians*. Stroud, United Kingdom: Alan Sutton Publishing Ltd., 1994.

Wood, Roy C. *The Sociology of the Meal*. Edinburgh: Edinburgh University Press, 1995.

Additional Resources

The Co-operative Society. http://www.co-op.co.uk (for current information) and http://www.archive.co-op.ac.uk (for history).
Corporate Watch. http://www.corporatewatch.org.uk. Pressure group, including information on supermarkets.

EATING OUT

Barr, Andrew. *Drink: A Social History*. London: Pimlico, 1998.
Driver, Christopher. *The British at Table 1940–1980*. London: Chatto and Windus, 1983.
Ehrman, Edwina, Hazel Forsyth, Lucy Peltz, and Cathy Ross. *London Eats Out: 500 Years of Capital Dining*. London: Philip Wilson, 1999.
Freeling, Nicolas. *The Kitchen and the Cook*. London: Big Cat Press, 2002.
Haydon, Peter. *Beer and Britannia: An Inebriated History of Britain*. Stroud, United Kingdom: Alan Sutton Publishing Ltd., 2001.
Hopkinson, Simon, and Lindsey Bareham. *The Prawn Cocktail Years*. London: Macmillan and Co., 1997.
Parkinson, Andrew, with Jonathon Green. *Cutting It Fine: Inside the Restaurant Business*. London: Jonathan Cape, 2001.
Walton, John K. *Fish and Chips and the British Working Class 1870–1940*. New York: Leicester University Press, 1992.
Warde, Alan, and Lydia Martens. *Eating Out: Social Differentiation, Consumption, and Pleasure*. Cambridge, United Kingdom: Cambridge University Press, 2000.

Additional Resources

Fish and chips. http://www.federationoffishfriers.co.uk.
Food and Drink Federation. http://www.fdf.org.uk.
The Good Pub Guide. http://www.goodguides.com.
Indian food. http://www.redhotcurry.com.
Industry statistics. http://www.caterer-online.com.

SPECIAL OCCASIONS

Charsley, Simon R. *Wedding Cakes and Cultural History*. New York: Routledge, 1992.

Henisch, Bridget Ann. *Cakes and Characters: An English Christmas Tradition*. London: Prospect Books, 1984.

Mason, Laura, ed. *Food and the Rites of Passage*. Totnes, United Kingdom: Prospect Books, 2002.

REGIONAL SPECIALTIES

Mason, Laura, with Catherine Brown. *Traditional Foods of Britain: An Inventory*. Totnes, United Kingdom: Prospect Books, 1999.

DIET AND HEALTH

Dowler, Elizabeth, and Sheila Turner, with Barbara Dobson. *Poverty Bites: Food, Health, and Poor Families*. London: Child Poverty Action Group, 2001.

Oddy, Derek J., and Derek Miller. *Diet and Health in Modern Britain*. Beckenham, U.K.: Croom Helm, 1985.

Salmon, Jenny. *Dietary Reference Values: A Guide*. London: HMSO, 1991.

Spencer, C. *The Heretic's Feast: A History of Vegetarianism*. London: Fourth Estate, 1994.

Walker, Caroline, and Geoffrey Cannon. *The Food Scandal: What's Wrong with the British Diet and How to Put It Right*. London: Century Publishing, 1985.

Additional Resources

British Nutrition Foundation. http://www.nutrition.org.uk. Industry-funded organization supplying information on food and health.

Diet and Nutrition Survey. http://www.statistics.gov.uk.

The Food Commission. http://www.foodcomm.org.uk. Pressure group campaigning for a healthier diet.

McLibel Trial. http://www.mcspotlight.org.case.

Our Healthier Nation. http://www.ohn.gov.uk. Government paper on public health, including policy related to cancer, coronary heart disease, and stroke.

Public Health Institute of Scotland: http://www.phis.org.uk.

Soil Association. http://www.soilassociation.org.uk. For information on organic food.

Vegetarian Society. http://www.vegsoc.org.

Index

About the Author

LAURA MASON is an independent scholar who lives in York, England. She writes on aspects of British food culture for various publications.